THE NEW
CRAFT
BEER
WORLD

MARK DREDGE

THE NEW
CRAFT
BEER
WORLD

CELEBRATING OVER 400
DELICIOUS BEERS

DOG 'n' BONE

Published in 2021 by Dog 'n' Bone Books
An imprint of Ryland Peters & Small Ltd
20–21 Jockey's Fields   341 E 116th St
London WC1R 4BW   New York, NY 10029

www.rylandpeters.com

10 9 8 7 6 5 4 3 2 1

A CIP catalog record for this book is available from the
Library of Congress and the British Library.

ISBN: 978-1-911026-79-2

Printed in China

Editor: Caroline West
Designer: Geoff Borin
Illustrators: flavor wheels on pages 17 and 39 by Andrew
Henderson with text by Mark Dredge; other illustrations by
Anna Galkina.

Art director: Sally Powell
Production manager: Gordana Simakovic
Publishing manager: Penny Craig
Publisher: Cindy Richards

CONTENTS

INTRODUCTION

Beer continues to excite and surprise me—and sometimes challenge me, too. My love for beer started with the taste and the continual search for something new in my glass. I wanted to try everything. I wanted to know what every single beer tasted like and I was forever searching for the next beer—for the *best* beer. After a decade of writing about beer I'm still looking for the best and while the excitement of opening something new hasn't disappeared, I now also feel more balanced by context and the social situations and stories of beer, and that's where my love of beer is today—a beer glass has become a consistent lens through which I can learn about the world, a lens that opens to reveal experiences, cultures, customs, and characters.

Beer has forever been evolving and progressing, changing with technology and trends. That's been true for hundreds of years, but never have those changes happened more rapidly—and perhaps unexpectedly—than right now: there are more breweries, more beers, and more styles; more people drinking beer in more places; new processes, ingredients, and different taste expectations. And that makes my job as a beer writer always varied and interesting, but it does mean that illustrated books like this come to reflect a moment in time.

I wrote my first book, *Craft Beer World*, in the summer of 2012. I wanted it to be a book that looked for the most interesting and innovative world beers. I wanted to find unexpected breweries in unexpected places. I wanted to include the curious local styles, and I wanted the classics of the world of beer to sit alongside the best new beers. But those new beers didn't stay new for long and the constant progression of the industry meant that the book was getting increasingly out of date and less relevant to drinkers, with many well-known breweries and beer styles not represented. It was time to write a new book.

This is a complete rewrite of *Craft Beer World* (only 20 or so beers feature in both books), though a handful of the early pages may look similar because I like what I wrote before and there was no need for a full revision. Hopefully, you'll see that I've learned a lot more about beer in the intervening years, that I've drunk more broadly, and that I still have the same love for excellent-tasting beers and the stories behind them. You might notice that alongside the excitement for the new brews, I've discovered a deeper enjoyment and respect for the classic beers, or classic examples of styles, because I think that the

continual presence of these classics gives us a foundation of knowledge which we need in order to understand the world of beer; without the classics we're potentially just looking at fads and fashions.

I'm still on my never-ending search for great beers, and this book is a celebration of the best brewers and beers in the world—and it is fully global, featuring beers from over 50 countries. Beer is a drink with a rapidly progressing present and a future that makes us wonder what we'll be drinking next week, month, or year. Beer is also a drink with history, traditions, and classics. It's that intersection of innovation and tradition which makes it an especially fascinating drink for me.

My aim with this book is to give a snapshot of craft beer as we progress through the early 2020s, pouring you a worldwide mix of classics, classic-interpretations, modern evolutions of traditional styles, and completely new brews following the contemporary trends. Some may excite, some may surprise, some may challenge, but they are all interesting in their own way.

CRAFT BEER TODAY

Craft beer and small-scale brewing has truly become a global phenomenon and there are very few places in the world where you *can't* find a local craft beer now. Writing this book allowed me to look all around the world to see what brewers are making, no matter whether I was looking in Vancouver, Miami, Manchester, Oslo, Athens, St. Petersburg, Seoul, Sydney, Cape Town, Buenos Aires, or Bogota, the trends were the same.

The significant global craft beer trends in the early 2020s have, arguably, been popularized and impacted by social media; by the visual impact of beers on image-sharing platforms like Instagram and in beer-rating apps like Untappd. What's most interesting to me is that so many of these new beers don't taste or look like traditional beer. By that I mean that I often can't taste the malts in them (or they are so strong that they're almost cartoonishly sweet), while some are so fruity that it's sometimes hard to believe the aromas actually came from hops, with shopping baskets of flavorsome adjuncts being added to them and many looking like smoothies (you want tropical, berries, or chocolate?). Far from being a negative thing, this is drawing in more and more drinkers. But it has significantly changed what we drink.

A decade ago, a list of the world's highest-rated or best beers was quite predictable: some Trappist Quadrupels, some bourbon barrel-aged Stouts, some bitter Double IPAs, and probably a classic Belgian Gueuze or two. Today there are still the barrel-aged Imperial Stouts, only they've gotten stronger, sweeter, and fuller-bodied, often containing additional ingredients like chocolate, vanilla, coconut, and lactose (milk sugar). Alongside the sugary Stouts, Sour Beer has developed from a niche nerdy brew into something far fruitier and sweet, brewed with large volumes of fruit to be thick, sweet and sour, and strong, like actual smoothies. And the big styles that are now trending everywhere are Hazy IPAs and Double IPAs. These are beers that look and smell emphatically like glasses of tropical fruit juice. Whether we're looking at Stouts, Sours, or Hazy IPAs, we find that they all share several traits: full textures, smooth bodies, intense flavors, high strength, and a side-step from traditional beer characteristics.

Go to almost any taproom, anywhere in the world, and the beer choice has become greater than ever before, but that breadth belies a lack of actual variety, because the tap lists are universally saturated with IPAs and Sours. There are more beers and breweries than ever before in history, but we've arguably got less style variety than we've ever had. And everywhere you look brewers are moving in the same mass direction. It's like watching a load of six-year-olds play soccer, all chasing the ball until someone boots it in another direction, then everyone going after it again. There's excitement in that movement but there's also an instability to it, and no one quite knows for sure where we're going to end up.

Yet one of the consequences of several years of wild experimentation is a refocusing on classic beer styles and beers that have a more permanent appeal. The revolution is to go back to the basics and reconsider them, refresh them, and revive interest in them. There are now more great lagers being brewed

LEFT A colorful tasting flight in South Africa, with a beautiful view of mountains in the background.

by small breweries; the pulpy popularity of juicy IPAs has seen brewers revert to the kinds of bright, bitter West Coast IPAs that probably got them into brewing in the first place; there are more brewers making wild and spontaneously fermented ales which are aged for years before they can be drunk. And local tastes are becoming increasingly important: local ingredients, local influence, seasonal variation. As one side of craft beer goes bonkers for newness, so the other side settles down and relaxes back with a renewed focus on traditions. The constant forward momentum alongside the foundation of history is what ensures that beer remains a diverse and remarkable drink.

My concerns for craft beer right now are not that there's too much newness, or that some older styles have been forgotten (because they'll be back again, for sure), it's that not every beer that's brewed is excellent. Many aren't of a high quality, or they suffer from brewing faults, especially with the more progressive styles. If a brewer wants to make a classic Pilsner or Porter, then there are recipes, but there aren't many recipes for these triple-fruited brews which are sweet with adjuncts. Sometimes these beers are approximations and best-guesses, and often brewed to match a certain appearance as much as an intense flavor profile. Also, because many of these beers are only brewed once, there's rarely the chance to perfect that recipe. And that troubles me, as the

ABOVE *The Craft Beer Market restaurant in False Creek Olympic Village, Vancouver, Canada.*

lack of consistent brewing and refinement of recipes gives too much variation in quality. The enormous worldwide growth of the industry is incredible to see, but just because it's new or from a small brewery doesn't automatically make it good or better than the beer from a big national brewery. It's very easy to make a beer with lots of flavor in the same way that it's very easy to make a chili which is so spicy it's inedible...

The current state of craft beer is one that is often looking for what's new. That makes the writing of a book like this a challenge because what was new yesterday is out of date tomorrow—and I'm writing this months or years before you're reading it. At the same time, the return to a focus on classic styles, and on making beers more local and seasonal, is seeing the industry evolve in numerous different directions. This makes craft beer more exciting than ever before. I don't know what's next, but I'm looking forward to drinking it and seeing how this great industry is able to change beer-drinking around the globe, whether that's with a crisp Pilsner, a classic Pale Ale, or a super-strong Stout with several pounds of chocolate whipped into it.

THE INGREDIENTS OF BEER

Beer-making is as old as civilization. Sure, it's been refined and improved over the millennia, made in larger volumes, in more places, and with more variety, but the essence of combining water, grain, hops, and yeast to make beer is remarkably similar to the earliest brews.

Beer's surface simplicity belies the complexities of brewing: the limitless possible processes and the variety of ingredient combinations; how different grains can be mixed together to create flavor, texture, color, and sweetness; how the timing of adding hops can maximize the desired characteristics, affecting bitterness, flavor, and aroma; the importance of manipulating billions of living yeast cells to ensure a good fermentation and flavor; the ways that a couple of degrees in temperature can change a beer entirely; and how using ingredients beyond the traditional four can give beer completely new characteristics. Here we look a little closer at the main ingredients of beer and how they combine to create the great beer varieties we know today.

Water

Water is fundamentally important to brewing great beer. When you think about the brewing process, the beer we end up drinking is essentially a glass of water that has been infused with the flavors of grain and hops—in a way, it's like producing a broth or stock from bones, vegetables, and fresh herbs, only brewers take it a little further and convert its essence—the sugars in the liquid—into alcohol.

Consider water as the foundation of beer, with the malt being the base structure and the hops and yeast the decorations. Each beer needs a good foundation and that foundation will vary depending on the beer being made. Water's mineral composition varies

LEFT *This panel, dated 1874, on the facade of an old brewhouse shows how the basics of making beer have not changed over the centuries.*

ABOVE *An ancient well in the Kronenbourg brewery, Strasbourg, France.*

ABOVE *A handful of barley in the malthouse.*

depending on where you are—even just pouring a glass from the faucet or tap in different cities around the world will give you subtle differences.

You've probably heard of soft water and hard water, the difference being their mineral content. Rainwater is naturally soft, and it absorbs minerals from the ground, so, depending on where your water is coming from and what the water has flowed through, the mineral content will vary. This means, for example, that a city in the mountains will have a different local water from a city by the sea.

Different waters in the brewhouse will have an impact on several elements of the beer's overall balance and composition, with an oversimplification being that softer waters give a softer, cleaner, gentler malt flavor, while a harder water profile will sharpen the flavor of hops and dark malt, perhaps also leaving a dryness on the palate.

Historically, brewers could only make beer with the water source local to them, often drawn from a well. From this we can see how certain important beer styles became linked to a place, and in turn linked to the water of that place. For example, Pilsen, in the

Czech Republic, had very soft water, which helped the brewers there make soft-textured Pilsner; the hard waters of London balanced the dark malts of a Porter; and the mineral-rich waters of Burton-on-Trent, in the English Midlands, enhanced the dry bitterness of India Pale Ale. Back then, brewers couldn't easily change the water, but now they can.

Today, every brewer can control their brewing water, sometimes just by adding different minerals, and at other times by first using a water treatment like reverse osmosis. All beers have a specific water composition, which is adjusted to suit the style of beer. This control is essential to brewing great beer. Water might not be an exciting ingredient, but it's a vital one, and there's a lot more to it than just using what comes out of the faucet or tap.

Malt and grain

The base of any great beer is built on grain—it's the structure of a beer, and its heart. Malted barley is the most common brewing grain and it gives beer several important qualities and characteristics: color, which

LEFT *The brewhouse at the Orval Brewery, Belgium.*

can range from pale yellow to black; texture and body, which could be tonic-dry or syrup-thick; flavors that range from bread and toast to caramel to chocolate and coffee—basically anything you might find in your local bakery; and the alcohol content, which is derived from the grain's sugars, where an average brew will ferment around 70 percent of the malt sugars into alcohol, leaving the rest as body and flavor.

Barley is the best brewing grain for a couple of simple reasons. On a chemical level, it contains enzymes which, during the brewing process, are able to turn its own unfermentable starches into fermentable sugars. It also has a husk, which helps during the separation of wort and spent grain (if that doesn't make sense now, then it should do in a few pages' time—see page 22).

The broad spectrum of flavor and color in beer mostly comes from the **malting process**. Malting makes barley into something usable in the brewhouse. In the natural world, barley grows and its kernels fall to the ground, hopefully landing in a puddle of water and growing into a new plant, forever repeating this life cycle. When barley kernels are harvested, they are effectively put into a dry hibernated state until they get to the malthouse (historically breweries had their own maltings, but now only a few do this themselves), where the first stage of the malting process is to steep the grain in water. This awakens the barley, so that it comes back to life and begins to grow. After a day or two, the barley is taken out of the water and it germinates, with rootlets sprouting from the grain. After a few

more days, the maltster needs to stop the grain growing, which they do by kilning it. This reduces the moisture content considerably to leave a dry and crunchy malt kernel, and it's here that the kilning temperature and duration will influence the characteristics of the grain in a way that's similar to cooking toast: it's pale and bready to begin with, then caramelized and sweet, then black and burned. You might also see crystal malt, which goes through a stewing process that converts the starches into sugars, so when it's kilned those sugars crystallize, giving a sweeter, caramelized flavor to the final beer.

There are dozens of types of malt, each with a different color, sweetness, and character. Most beers use a combination of different malts to build the beer's structure. There will always be a large percentage of a base grain used and this will provide most of the fermentable sugars, which will become the alcohol—even in a strong Stout, something like 90 percent of the grain bill will be the sugar-rich pale malt, with the dark grains giving color and flavor.

Barley is not the only brewing grain. Other common grains include wheat, which has a higher protein content than barley and leaves more haze and more body in a beer, but not necessarily a strong flavor; oats give a full, smooth texture; rye adds a nutty, spicy flavor; rice, corn, or maize—often referred to as adjuncts—will lighten the body and flavor of a beer and give a crisper finish; while other grains like spelt and buckwheat can also be used to give their own flavors or different characteristics.

In addition to the grain's natural sugars, brewers can add actual **sugar** to their beers to give more fermentables to the yeast. These sugars will typically contribute to the alcohol content but, because they are completely fermentable, they won't leave much body or flavor in the beer, therefore leaving it dry. It's long been common for Belgian strong ales like Dubbel and Tripel to use sugar for this reason. Brewers can use simple table sugar and dextrose, which will give alcohol but little flavor; muscovado and dark candi sugar, which will give both color and a caramelized flavor; or honey and maple syrup, which will add sweetness, potential alcohol content, and some flavor.

Common Malts

Here are some of the most common malts you'll see in beer today:

Pilsner malt
Very pale base grain, light biscuit taste

Pale ale malt
Lightly toasty, cereal-like base grain

Wheat malt
Very pale, light bready taste, gives fullness, foam, and haze

Munich malt
Toasty, bread crusts, adds reddish color

Caramalt
Toffee, chewy, sweet, raisin

Crystal malt
Caramel sweetness, bulks bodies in beer

Chocolate malt
Dark and bitter, big roast, low sweetness

Roasted barley
Black, acrid, sharply bitter, stains beer black

Oats
Creamy, smooth texture, can add haziness

Grain Bills in Common Beer Styles

Here is how you might expect the above malts to be combined to create the base recipe structure for popular contemporary beer styles, though every recipe will vary:

Pilsner: 100% Pilsner malt

Dunkel: 75% Munich malt, 25% Pilsner malt

Hefeweizen/Witbier: 50% Pilsner malt, 50% wheat malt

Saison: 70% Pilsner malt, 20% wheat, 5% oats, 5% spelt or specialty malt

Dubbel: 80% Pilsner malt, 10% dark candi sugar, 8% wheat, 2% chocolate

Tripel: 90% Pilsner malt, 10% dextrose/candi sugar

American Pale Ale: 90% Pale ale malt, 5% wheat malt, 5% Munich malt

West Coast IPA: 100% Pale ale malt

Hazy DIPA: 80% Pale ale malt, 10% oats, 7% wheat, 3% dextrose

Red IPA: 80% Pale ale malt, 10% Munich malt, 5% crystal malt, 5% Caramalt

Best Bitter: 90% Pale ale malt, 5% Caramalt, 4% crystal malt, 1% chocolate malt

Porter: 85% Pale ale malt, 5% Caramalt, 5% brown malt, 5% chocolate malt

Imperial Stout: 85% Pale ale malt, 5% Caramalt, 5% chocolate malt, 5% roasted barley

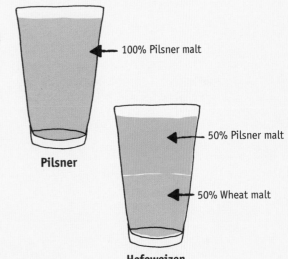

100% Pilsner malt

Pilsner

50% Pilsner malt

50% Wheat malt

Hefeweizen

5% Munich malt

5% Wheat malt

90% Pale ale malt

American Pale Ale

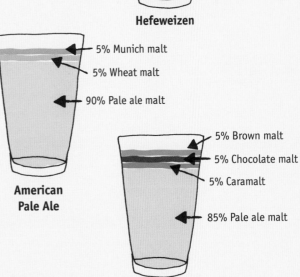

5% Brown malt

5% Chocolate malt

5% Caramalt

85% Pale ale malt

Porter

To begin the **brewing process**, the grain is milled and mixed with warm water in the mash tun. There are two typical methods for mashing the grain in modern breweries. The first is an **infusion mash**, where the water is heated to the desired temperature (around 153°F/67°C), mixed with the grain, then held at that temperature for an hour. The other is the **step mash**, where the temperature of the mash is gradually increased in step increments—this has the benefit of holding at specific temperatures to try to maximize the enzymes activated in the grain (brewing is a complicated science...). There's also an old European mash process called **decoction**. Many Central European brewers, especially in Germany and the Czech Republic, still use this, and some modern brewers do, too. It involves mashing in and removing a portion of the grain and water, boiling that portion separately, then putting the decocted mash back into the mash tun. This raises the overall temperature and will also produce some sweeter flavors and more body. Some beers use a double or even triple decoction.

Hops

Hops have become the defining ingredient in craft beer. It's these perennial, varietal flowers that give beer its bitterness, much of its flavor, and most of its aroma. This aroma could be anything that you might find in the fruit and vegetable aisle of the grocery store: juicy tropical fruits, sweet citrus flesh, tangy citrus pith, stone fruits such as peaches and apricots, berries, grapes, gooseberries, hard green herbs, floral herbs, peppery spices, even onion, garlic, and—not typical in most grocery stores—pine and marijuana.

Hop flowers are harvested once a year in each hemisphere—they are picked in September in the north and March in the south. Once picked, they are dried and can then be baled as flowers or processed into smaller pellets—most breweries use hop pellets, which are a more efficient product with a better possible extraction of flavors. Hops can also have their bitter acids and aromatic oils extracted to be used as a liquid (I'll explain the acids and oils separately), while the desire for maximum fruity aromas has given us Cryo hops, which have been frozen with liquid nitrogen and processed to capture as many of the pure aromatic oils as possible.

Hops have been used in beer for at least a thousand years, but it wasn't until around the 16th century that they became the almost exclusive bittering and flavoring ingredient. One main reason that hops got this job was because they're naturally antibacterial, keeping out any bacteria that could do harm to the beer or the drinker, while also preserving the liquid for longer.

In brewing, we can think of hops in the same way as seasoning, herbs, and spices in the kitchen. Some dishes just want salt and pepper in the same way that some beers, like Light Lager, Witbiers, or Sours, just want a light or neutral bitterness to balance and complete the flavor. Some dishes want herbal, grassy, spicy, and zesty flavors, like using hard green herbs, fragrant spices like ground coriander, aniseed vegetables such as fennel, and a squeeze or zest of lemon—these are the food equivalents of the hops in styles like Pilsner, Saison, or Belgian Tripels. Then there are the dishes that combine handfuls of strong chili peppers, aromatic spices like star anise and cinnamon, soft herbs such as Thai basil and cilantro (fresh coriander), and squeezes of lime juice. These are your IPAs and DIPAs.

Hops are typically added to the brew kettle during a one-hour rolling boil, and often there are three separate additions: the first will give bitterness, while later additions give more flavor and then aroma. It's common in the most aromatic of beer styles, like IPAs, to add hops after the boil has finished, and then again as a "dry-hop," which happens toward the end of fermentation and into its maturation (this is on the "cold side" of brewing instead of the "hot side" in the boiling kettle). In simple terms: the later the **hops are added**, the more you'll smell them.

Any hop varieties can be added at any time and in any combination throughout the brewing process, but some hops are seen as better for giving bitterness, while others are more desired for their aroma profiles.

Understanding the composition of hops and the brewing process helps us to see how these flowers give beer both bitterness and aroma, and why those characteristics differ by variety.

Hops contain **acids and oils**; the acids will give bitterness and the oils give flavors and aromas. Each hop variety has a different composition of acids and oils, which means they will produce different potential

RIGHT *Hops on the bine, soon to be picked.*

ABOVE *Adding dry hops at the Orval brewery.*

characteristics as well as varied volumes of bitterness and aroma.

The hops are added to the brewing kettle where the wort is boiled for an hour or so. Hops added as the wort reaches boiling point will therefore be boiled for an hour. During that time the acids will isomerize (becoming water soluble), giving out their bitterness and boiling away all the aromatic oils, which are volatile. Hops added later in the boil will not have as much chance to add bitterness to the beer, but will contribute aromas—think of it as being like adding fresh basil to a ragu. If you cook the basil in the sauce for an hour, it will add flavor, but use it as a garnish when you serve up the ragu and you'll get all of those great aniseed, spicy aromatics. Dry-hopping works in a similar way and is used to bring out the aroma. It's like adding mint to a pitcher of water, where all the natural oils in the mint give the water a new flavor and aroma. We look more into specific hop flavors over the following pages.

America is now the world's leading hop-growing nation, accounting for something like 40 percent of global hop production, with most of it grown in the Pacific Northwest. Germany grows around 36 percent of the world's hops, mostly in the Hallertau region, north of Munich. Third comes the Czech Republic, with less than 5 percent of all the hops. Then come China (bet you didn't expect that—they grow for their domestic production and, as the largest beer market in the world, they need a lot of hops), Poland, Slovenia, England, Australia, New Zealand, France, and Spain. And do you know the top three hops in the world in terms of acreage in 2020? It's German Herkules, Czech Saaz, and American Citra—the last only introduced to the market commercially in the early 2000s.

There are now more than 200 commercially available hop varieties in the world, and more are appearing every year as a result of successes in global hop-breeding programs. Many of the more popular contemporary hops have come from breeding programs where the aim is to get either a strong acid constituent for bitterness or a bold, flavorsome oil potential with lots of tropical and citrusy aromas, all with good agronomics for the farmers. Each new variety brings different flavor profiles, some with characteristics like chocolate, oak, coconut, berries, and more. See the Hop Aroma & Flavor wheel opposite or on my website, www.beerdredge.com, for an example of these hop aromas.

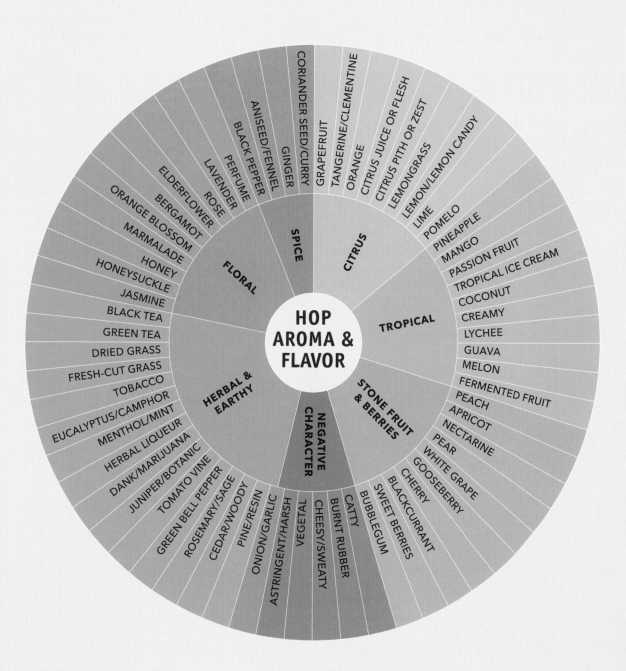

Yeast and fermentation

Yeast metabolizes sugars and creates alcohol and carbon dioxide, plus some aromatic by-products. More prosaically, yeast eats sugar, digests it, pees alcohol, burps bubbles, and sweats different smells. That doesn't make it sound delicious, I know, but it's pretty much what happens to turn sweet, malty, and non-alcoholic wort into a glassful of dry, fizzy beer.

Yeast is a living microorganism and a great variable in the brewing process; if the yeast isn't happy or healthy, then it won't produce a good beer. Before the end of the 1800s, every beer would have most likely been what we now call "mixed fermentation," meaning it contained a variety of different yeast strains and probably some bacteria. From the mid-1880s onward brewers were able to isolate single strains of yeast and brew with just those—the scientific discovery of pure yeast, which happened in Carlsberg brewery's laboratory, was one of the most significant events in beer's history as it helped brewers make more consistent beer with less chance of spoilage.

There are many strains of yeast, each of which is often linked to a particular classic style (and derived from a classic brew). So, for example, a brewer might use an American ale yeast in a Pale Ale, Vermont yeast in a Hazy IPA, a Bavarian lager yeast in a Dunkel, or a Belgian Saison yeast in their Saison, with these yeast strains contributing to the expected characteristics of those beer types.

Step back from the style-specific strains and look at beer's family tree, and you'll see that it can be split into three: ale yeast, lager yeast, and wild yeast (and bacteria). Ale, lager, and wild are different species of yeast. It's sort of like gorillas, chimpanzees, and bonobos—all are similar-ish, and have some distant relations and breeding history, but each is now a different species that lives and behaves differently.

Ale yeast—scientifically known as *Saccharomyces cerevisiae*—typically prefers ambient to warm conditions, fermenting in the range of 59–77°F (15–25°C). This temperature pushes the yeast to work to metabolize the malt sugars in 3–5 days and will naturally produce a variety of different aroma compounds—known as esters and phenols—although they won't always be prominent. Ale styles like Hefeweizen, Witbier, Saison, and most other Belgian ales will often ferment at the warm end of the range and that warmth helps to produce the strong aromas common in those styles. The yeast used in Hazy IPAs often produces a large amount of esters which contributes to the fruity aromas in the beer—esters are an often-overlooked part of the flavor profile of most beers. Common ester aromas are sweet and fruity, like banana, pear, stone fruit, rose, and vanilla.

Lager yeast—scientifically known as *Saccharomyces pastorianus*—prefers cooler temperatures and will work well in the range of 46–54°F (8–12°C), where it'll take 4–10 days to ferment the sugars, typically producing fewer esters. *S. pastorianus* is a hybrid of *S. cerevisiae* and another *Saccharomyces* yeast, and, while it isn't known where or how they hybridized, *S. pastorianus* got its cold tolerance from the non-*S. cerevisiae* strain. This ability to thrive in a colder environment, along with the Bavarian process of storing—or lagering—beer in cold cellars for an extended amount of time, created a perfect combination of circumstances to produce what we now call lager. Crucially, this maturation time allowed any potentially negative characteristics given out by the yeast during fermentation to be reabsorbed, leaving a better-tasting beer.

Historically, ale yeast was referred to as top-fermenting and lager yeast as bottom-fermenting, named because of how the yeast was collected by brewers either to be reused or removed from the fermentation vessel. Ale yeast was cropped off the top of the open-topped fermenter (because all fermenters were once open-topped), whereas lager yeast was removed from the bottom of the fermentation vessel

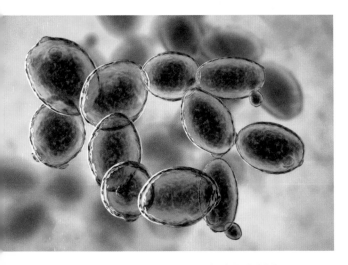

LEFT Saccharomyces cerevisiae *yeast cells.*

ABOVE *Wooden barrels filled with maturing beer at a Lambic brewery.*

Fruit, spices, barrels, and other ingredients

Beyond the four core ingredients of beer, brewers are able to add whatever else they want to their tanks. Fruit is common and increasingly so with more fruited IPAs and Sour Beers being brewed—citrus and tropical fruits are most popular in IPAs, while berries and stone fruits are the common choice for Sour Beers. Fruits can be added in various forms and can be fresh or frozen, peel or pith, puréed or pulped, or even extract or syrup; sometimes these fruits will be added to give fermentable sugars (meaning the yeast converts the fruit sugars into more alcohol), while at other times they will be added to give as much fruity flavor as possible.

Chocolate, cacao, coffee, coconut, honey, and vanilla are also often used in beers. Spices, like ground coriander, ginger, chili, and pepper, and hard herbs are popular. Then there's everything else—if you can think of it, then it's probably been used in a beer.

Barrel-aging continues to be popular. This process of putting a beer into a barrel to mature draws out new flavors from the wood and pushes them into the beer, while microflora might also contribute new complexities or acidity, depending on the barrel and the type of beer being brewed. The barrel, the amount of char inside it, and whether that wood previously held a different drink—like wine or whiskey—will all impact the finished beer. The two most common kinds of barrel-aged beer are dark, strong ales matured in old whiskey barrels to pick up caramel, spice, and vanilla flavors, and beers matured in old wine barrels—these may or may not give acidity to the finished beer, which could be a variety of styles and strengths.

BELOW *Vanilla (left), and rosemary (right).*

after the beer was drawn off and moved into a storage barrel. Today, the distinction of top and bottom is less valid as almost all yeast has been trained to be cropped from the bottom of the tank—a modern evolution that suits the enclosed cylindroconical vessels used by most brewers.

Wild yeast is the third family and it can produce a more rustic or "wild" collection of flavors and aromas, sometimes also producing acidity if combined with bacteria like *Lactobacillus* or *Pediococcus* (wild yeast doesn't necessarily make a beer sour on its own, whereas a mixed fermentation of yeast and bacteria will usually create acidity). The primary wild yeast is *Brettanomyces* and there are numerous strains that produce varying characteristics, sometimes being more earthy, funky, and barnyard-like, while others can be fruity like pineapple. Typically, they can ferment more of the malt sugars and work over a longer period of time, producing an overall drier—and often more complex—beer (if allowed to work for longer, that is; some brewers use this yeast in non-aged beer like IPA). For Spontaneously Fermented beers, the natural wild yeast in the environment of the brewery will begin the fermentation, with yeast resident in old wooden barrels additionally influencing fermentation. Those Wild Beers that aren't spontaneously fermented will have a cultured and cultivated strain of *Brettanomyces* added.

WORLD OF HOPS

Alongside the different hop varieties and their specific acid and oil composition, the location where the hops are grown also contributes to their qualities, with the soil and weather having an impact—in the same the way that winemakers talk about the terroir of a grape.

Hop-growing regions

North America

Grown: Washington, Oregon, Idaho

Qualities: Citrus pith and juice, tropical fruits, stone fruit, melon, resinous pine, hard herbs, allium, creamy coconut, sweet berries

Main varieties: Citra, Mosaic, Simcoe, Cascade, Centennial, Amarillo, Talus, Ekuanot, Alacca

Beer styles: Golden Ale, Pale Ale, IPA, Double IPA

Great Britain

Grown: Kent, Herefordshire, Worcestershire

Qualities: Herbals, woody, spicy, minty, floral, orchard fruit, stone fruit, light tropical fruit

Main varieties: Goldings, Fuggle, Target, Bramling Cross, Olicana, Jester, Endeavour, Bullion

Beer styles: Best Bitter, English Pale and Golden Ale, Belgian Blonde, Saison, Mild, Stout, Porter

Central Europe

Grown: Germany (Hallertauer), Czech Republic (Žatec), Poland (Lublin), Slovenia (Žalec)

Qualities: Grassy, herbal, pepper, floral, stone fruits, botanic, lemon peel

Main varieties: Hersbrucker, Tettnanger, Perle, Spalt, Hüll Melon, Saphir, Saaz, Kazbek, Marynka, Lublin, Styrian Golding

Beer styles: Pilsner, Pale Lagers, Dark Lager, Belgian Ales, some Pale Ales

South Pacific

Grown: South Australia and Tasmania, Nelson region of New Zealand

Qualities: Juicy tropical fruit, lychee, tangy citrus, mango, passion fruit, gooseberry, grapes

Main varieties: Galaxy, Ella, Vic Secret, Topaz, Enigma, Nelson Sauvin, Motueka, Riwaka

Beer styles: Pale Ale, IPA, Double IPA, Pacific Pale Ale, Modern Pilsner

THE BREWING PROCESS

Brewing begins by combining milled grain with hot water in the mash tun. The grains steep or mash for an hour before the liquid—now known as wort—is separated from the spent grain, often in a vessel called a lauter tun. The spent grain will usually be sent to feed livestock while the sweet wort moves into the kettle and is boiled for an hour, which is when the hops are added, often as three separate additions—the first for bitterness, the later ones for flavor and aroma. Next, the hopped wort is cleared of the hop particles (they disintegrate but don't dissolve in the kettle), usually in a whirlpool, then it's cooled down, and the liquid moves into a fermenter, where the yeast is added, and fermentation begins.

The actual brewing process takes 4–8 hours. Fermentation typically takes 3–10 days, depending on the beer style, and most beers are then matured until they are ready—each beer type will be different, ranging from a few days to a few years, though 2–6 weeks is common for most craft beers, and they are most often held at close to 32°F (0°C). When the beer is ready, brewers can (but don't always) centrifuge or filter it to remove the hazy yeast, then it can be packaged and drunk.

LEFT *The Kühlschiff or coolship at the Schafferhof brewery in Germany. See pages 192 and 194 for more about the role coolships play in brewing certain kinds of beer.*

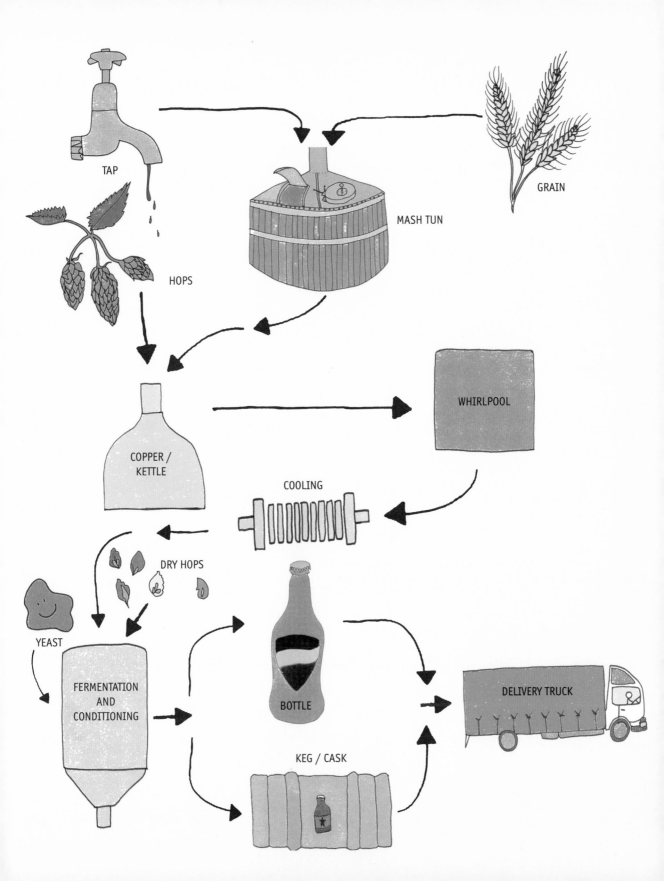

TAP

GRAIN

MASH TUN

HOPS

WHIRLPOOL

COPPER / KETTLE

COOLING

DRY HOPS

YEAST

FERMENTATION AND CONDITIONING

BOTTLE

DELIVERY TRUCK

KEG / CASK

WHEN BEER GOES BAD

Not every beer is good. Some just won't be to your taste, whereas others are technically faulty. There are a number of factors that can contribute to the detection (or not) of actual faults in beer. Firstly, some people are "taste-blind" to certain flavors, so they might not be able to taste some of these faults; secondly, the quantities present in a beer can vary—at low levels some of these characteristics might be pleasant, while at high levels they may be revolting; and thirdly, it's all dependent on the beer style, where, for example, a banana-like aroma is great in a Hefeweizen, but bad in a Pale Ale.

Butter, buttered popcorn, butterscotch, fatty mouthfeel

What? Diacetyl

Why? A natural by-product of fermentation. If it's in your beer, it could mean the beer was hurried out of the brewery or the brewers didn't make time for a diacetyl rest. It can also mean infected yeast, a by-product of a lactic fermentation, or a result of beer that's sat in a dirty beer line for a while.

Appropriate? Only in trace amounts in some Lagers and British ales. It can totally unbalance hoppy beers. Some drinkers are strongly averse to diacetyl, while some like it, and others are taste-blind to it.

Apple skin and juice, cider, paint in high volumes

What? Acetaldehyde

Why? A natural by-product of fermentation. If present it's because the beer is "green," usually due to haste in the brewery, or the yeast is of poor quality. If it becomes cidery, then it's got to an extreme level.

Appropriate? No, although some Light Lagers have this present.

Sweetcorn, stewed vegetables, cabbage, tomatoes

What? Dimethyl sulfide (DMS)

Why? Comes from pale malt if it hasn't had a vigorous enough boil in the kettle. Could also appear if fermentation has been slow.

Appropriate? Only in very small amounts in some Pale Lagers, where it can add a pleasant malt-sweet aroma, but it should never become overstewed or cabbage-like.

Bananas, pear drops, apples, stone fruit, strawberry, honey, pineapple

What? Esters, including isoamyl acetate (bananas and pear drops), ethyl caprylate and caproate (apples and aniseed), ethyl acetate (solvent), and phenylethyl acetate (honey, roses)

Why? Fruity aromas that are a by-product of fermentation.

Appropriate? Yes, but appropriateness is down to the detectable level and the style of beer. Expect banana in Hefeweizens and maybe in Witbier or other Belgian ales, but it's often a fault in other styles. Can be more evident in strong beers. The recent trend for very fruity IPAs has seen brewers using yeasts that naturally produce more of these fruity esters to enhance the general fruitiness of a beer. Lagers have a subtle ester profile, but it's often a key quality of the beer.

Clove, smoky, Islay whisky, band-aids, disinfectant, vanilla, drying tannins

What? Phenols

Why? Aromas that develop with fermentation or may be a result of bad temperature control in the brewery. It could come from bacterial infection (you might taste this in some Sour Beer) or from high chlorine levels in brewing water.

Appropriate? Where esters are often okay in beer, phenols are not so good, although in some styles you can expect a small amount of phenols from the yeast— Hefeweizen, Witbier, and some Strong Belgian Ales, for example—which can positively add to the character of the beer. Some drinkers are strongly averse to phenolic flavors.

Paper, cardboard, stale, sherry, caramel

What? Oxidized

Why? Oxygen is not good for beer and will turn it stale. It can totally change a beer and make it thin and papery. In very hoppy pale beers, oxidation can taste like an unwelcome caramel flavor.

Appropriate? Never in fresh beer, but can be an integral part of aged beers like Barley Wine, Old Lambic, or Strong Belgian Dark Ales, and contribute to their character.

Eggs or burning matches

What? Sulfur, of which there are two main kinds: hydrogen sulfide is eggy, while sulfur dioxide is like a struck match.

Why? Could be from the yeast or from water with a high sulfur content. It could also be a sign of infection or of a young beer. It's a volatile aroma, so while you may smell it to begin with, it could dissipate as you drink.

Appropriate? Only in small amounts in some British ales and some lager styles, especially unfiltered lagers—lager naturally produces more sulfur and this can be pleasant and add a sweet fruitiness (Augustiner Hell classically has a little fresh sulfur in the aroma). No one wants a beer that smells like eggs, though.

"Skunky," rotting vegetables, garlic, marijuana

What? Light-struck

Why? UV rays can break down hop molecules, causing a sulfurous reaction and producing some of the same stinky chemicals as a skunk.

Appropriate? Never. Avoid beer in clear or green bottles as they can't block out the UV light. Keep beer out of direct sunlight as it can be light-struck very quickly (even in a glass in the beer garden). The aroma tends to be volatile, so may disappear after a few minutes.

Soy sauce, burned tires, Marmite

What? Autolyzed yeast

Why? Yeast that has died and ruptured its beer-spoiling guts into your beer.

Appropriate? In some aged beers it's acceptable in small volumes as it can add complexity.

Sour milk, vinegar, lemon juice

What? Your beer is sour.

Why? It could be a number of things, but often it's due to a bacterial infection in the beer (the same kind of bacteria that makes yogurt tangy). This could come from the brewery or could be a result of a slow-selling beer in dirty lines.

Appropriate? If the beer is meant to be sour, then it's fine. If not, it's a problem.

Cheesy, sweaty socks

What? Isovaleric acid

Why? Could be a bacterial infection or a sign of using old, oxidized hops.

Appropriate? No. Beer that smells like sweaty socks is rarely going to be delicious.

BEER GLOSSARY

Beer has its own language full of scientific and brewing terms, plus trendy words, slang, and abbreviations. Here's a beer glossary to tell you all you need to know about what you're drinking.

ABV Alcohol-by-volume. This is the percentage of ethanol per 3½ ounces (100ml) of liquid. In beer it can range from less than 1.0% to more than 15.0% ABV.

Ale A large family of beers brewed with a *Saccharomyces cerevisiae* yeast. Many of the most popular beer styles are ales: Pale Ale and IPA, Stout and Porter, British ales, Witbier and Hefeweizen, Saison, and most Belgian beers, like Tripel and Quadrupel.

Alpha acid This is where hops' bitterness comes from. The alpha acid in a hop variety can range from less than 3 percent to more than 20 percent. The alpha acids need to be isomerized to contribute their maximum bitterness and this happens as the hops are being boiled in the brewing kettle. A high alpha hop is like a chili with a high Scoville score.

Attenuation A measure of the percentage of sugars that the yeast converts during fermentation. A highly attenuated beer will be dry, whereas an under-attenuated beer will have a sticky residual sweetness. It's common for most beers to attenuate in the 70 percent range, but particularly strong beers will be lower than that (and therefore sweeter), while some Belgian-style ales, especially sour ales, can attenuate further—it's possible for some beers to finish with zero residual sweetness, making them the same "sweetness" as water.

Balance My favorite characteristic of great beer, this is where the flavors of malt, hops, and fermentation come together in harmony. There's a reason why so many drinkers enjoy pale, simple lagers and that's because they are always perfectly balanced. This doesn't mean that balance is synonymous with boring, however. The best beers—whether Sour, DIPA, or Barley Wine—need to work together to be enjoyed.

Beer A fermented drink made from grain. The best drink in the world.

Body Light, thin, heavy, full, rich: this is the weight of the beer in the mouth. It comes from a combination of the grain base and whether the beer is filtered or not, and is dependent on the residual sugar in the beer.

Bottle-conditioned beer Beer that undergoes an additional fermentation in the bottle. A priming sugar and yeast are added to the bottle when it's filled with flat beer, and this starts a slow, gradual conditioning process that produces carbon dioxide. As that carbon dioxide can't escape the bottle, it's absorbed into the beer, making it fizzy. Be careful to store these bottles upright and pour them without the sediment, unless you want to drink the yeast. Strong bottle-conditioned beers can be good candidates for aging over an extended period.

Clean Clean means an absence of unwanted flavors and a clarity of good flavors. My favorite analogy here is of looking at a photo of a beautiful landscape. If that photo is perfectly in focus, then you can see everything clearly, but if it's a bit blurry, then it's not so enjoyable to look at. A clean beer is perfectly in focus.

Collaboration brews Beers made by two or more different companies. These beers are often creative, one-off specials.

Color From very blonde to opaque black. Most of us will just say yellow, gold, red, brown, or black, but beer color can be measured on two different scales: Standard Reference Method (SRM) and European Brewery Convention (EBC). A Pale Lager will be as low as 1 SRM or 2 EBC (yellow). American IPA ranges from 6–14 SRM or 12–28 EBC (gold to amber). The darkest stout will be 70 SRM or 138 EBC (black). The majority of beers get their color solely from the grain used, but some heavily fruited beers might take on a red to purple color from the fruits added.

DDH Double Dry-Hopped, with two additions of dry hops. A lot of IPAs and DIPAs are DDH'd.

Degrees Plato A way of measuring the alcohol content in beer. This is drinker-facing in Central Europe and brewer-facing around the rest of the world. In countries such as the Czech Republic you'll see beer listed as 10° or 12° on the tap or menu. This refers to the number of dissolved solids (basically malt sugars) in wort, where 10°P means 10g of sugar in 3.5 ounces (100ml) of wort, and where the higher the percentage of sugars, the higher the expected alcohol content. What you need to know when ordering is that a 10° beer will be around 4.0% ABV, 12° is about 5.0% ABV, and 16° is around 6.0% ABV.

Dry-hopping Adding hops to beer during or after fermentation to give extra aroma and flavor. Brewers can—and do—dry-hop any style of beer. The hops are often added while the beer is still in the warmer fermentation temperatures and before it's cooled to near freezing.

Esters These come out of beer as aromas that are created during the higher temperatures of fermentation when alcohol and organic acids react with each other. They are often fruity aromas but can be potently harsh and veer toward nail polish remover. Expect banana, pear, apple, rose, honey, stone fruit, and light alcohol/solvent. Sometimes these are brewing faults and other times they are desirable—it depends on the beer style and the volume at which they are present (they are in every single beer, but in many of them they are low or below the flavor threshold). Esters are part of the essential characteristics of most Belgian ales, all German Hefeweizens, some British ales, and modern Hazy IPAs.

Finish A word we've borrowed from wine to indicate how the flavor ends in the mouth and then hangs around. It could be short or long, dry, bitter, sweet, or sharp.

Gravity Original gravity (OG) and finished gravity (FG). Gravity is the weight of the wort relative to the weight of the water and it's the brewer's measure of sugars in the beer—it's an alternative measure of Degrees Plato. OG is the sweetness out of the mash tun and FG is after it's finished fermenting. The OG is a guide to what level of alcohol can be expected in the finished beer and the FG will tell you how sweet or dry the finished beer is, depending on how it has been Attenuated. 1.000 means no sugar. A Pale Ale or Pale Lager with an OG of 1.050 and an FG of 1.012 will give a beer of around 5.0% ABV and a balanced sweetness. An FG of 1.005 will be very dry, while 1.030 will be very sweet.

Hoppy A general term used to describe a beer with a dominant hop character. I use it primarily to talk about the aroma, where a "very hoppy" beer is one that has an abundant and fresh hop aroma.

IBU International Bittering Units. Also known as EBU (European Bittering Units) or just BU. This is the measure of bitterness in a beer and represents the parts per million of dissolved isoalpha acids in the beer. Each beer style will have an appropriate IBU level. A Light American Lager might be 10 IBU, Pilsner will be between 25–40 IBU, IPAs will range from 40–70 (though the Hazy IPA trend has lowered the bitterness levels for that sub-style), Stout might be around 50 IBU, while Imperial Stouts and Barley Wines can get to 100 IBU. This used to be a more common measure and one communicated to drinkers, but it's now less prevalent. IBU is also only a useful measure if you understand the sweetness; a 50 IBU Pilsner will be very bitter, while a 50 IBU Imperial Stout will taste very sweet––bitterness is always relative to sweetness (a pot of black coffee served in two mugs will taste different if one of those mugs has a spoonful of sugar in it).

IPA The style that continues to define and drive craft beer. It's become its own family of beer, one that is a showcase for hops. If we see IPA on a beer, then we know to expect aromatic hops, but we will also look for a qualifying prefix such as Session, Double, Hazy, Sour, or Black.

Lager A family of beer brewed with *Saccharomyces pastorianus*. These are fermented at cooler temperatures than ales and typically undergo an extended cold lagering time of a few weeks or months. The name comes from the process of lagering, or storing, beer in a cold place for it to mature. Lager is not just cold, fizzy, yellow beer—there's a huge variety of different styles.

Malty Typically used to describe a prominent flavor of malt, often toasty or biscuity, but it could also go toward a darker, more roasted flavor.

Mouthfeel How the beer feels in the mouth: prickly, delicate, creamy, sharp, dry, smooth, tannic, fizzy, flat, light, heavy, rich.

Nitrogen/Nitro If you see a gas beer described as Nitro, this means it's had nitrogen added to it. Nitrogen has smaller bubbles than carbon dioxide and they don't pop in the same way, so you get a full, creamy, and smooth mouthfeel. It's most often seen with Stouts, though some brewpubs will push nitrogen into a wide variety of styles.

Pastry Stout Like many of the other beers in this edition, Pastry Stout wasn't in the beer lexicon when I wrote *Craft Beer World* back in 2012. Pastry (not just linked to Stout) refers to a rich and sweet beer that's loaded with adjuncts like chocolate, vanilla, nuts, lactose (milk sugar), and other flavorings to deliberately make it sweet, decadent, and dessert-like.

Session Beer The idea of the "session" is a British way of drinking where you go out and drink lots of pints, often of the same beer, over a long period of time. The beers typically drunk are low in alcohol (4.0% ABV or less), facilitating a day of drinking. The session idea was appropriated by American craft beer and applied to any beer of moderate strength, with the word "session" becoming a by-word for lower strength, but not necessarily for drinking lots of the same beer. Ironically, many Session Beers have an ABV of 4.5% and over and are inherently unsessionable because of their strength and the volume of hoppiness.

Sour Beer A family of beers that all have a sour taste. They could be Fast Sours, like Berliner Weisse or Gose, made in a couple of weeks and often soured by bacteria, or they could be Slow Sours, spontaneously fermented or brewed with wild yeast and bacteria, then allowed to evolve over months or years to develop complexity. Most are acidic, like lemon or yogurt, while some are acetic, like vinegar. "Sour" has become the cool and established way to describe acidic beers, though describing classic styles like Lambic and Gueuze in this way is scorned by the traditional brewers who use the word "sour" to mean bad (as in: "This beer has gone sour!").

Spontaneous fermentation Beer that ferments with natural wild yeast and bacteria found resident in the atmosphere and brewing environment (wooden barrels, old vessels, old farmhouse breweries), instead of a cultured pitch of yeast being added. It's the traditional way of brewing Lambic and has become more popular with world brewers.

Trappist brewery An appellation for beers brewed by Trappist monks. There are some rules: it has to be a monastery that follows the Order of Cistercians of the Strict Observance; the beer must be produced, or overseen, by the monks; brewing should not be intended for profit, and any money made should go toward funding the monasteries and local communities. Some Trappists are very large, while others are very small. Most are in Belgium but there are also Trappists in the Netherlands, Austria, Italy, Spain, France, England, and the USA. As Trappist is an appellation and not a style of beer, monasteries can make any beer they want—the Spencer Trappist beers from St. Joseph's Abbey in Massachusetts make IPAs, for example.

Unfiltered Beer that hasn't had the yeast filtered out of it. These beers are generally hazy and have more flavor and texture than their filtered equivalents (though I'd argue that sometimes the crisp character of a filtered lager can be better than the unfiltered version). It's now common to see hazy and cloudy beer as standard—it's even become an integral part of some styles, like the Hazy IPA, where the haze is a mix of grain proteins and hop polyphenols, plus some residual yeast.

Wild yeast and bacteria If these get into a brew unintentionally, they can turn the beer sour. However, some brewers deliberately add wild yeast and bacteria to get funky aromas and a sour taste. A good beer made with wild yeast (like Lambic, Gueuze, and Wild Ales) will be sharp, without a vinegary quality, and clean-tasting. *Brettanomyces* is a common wild yeast and *Lactobacillus* and *Pediococcus* are common bacteria.

Yeast These living microorganisms are responsible for producing the alcohol in beer. There are several species of brewing yeast and many different strains, with each working slightly differently and producing a variety of characteristics. The beer styles with the most obvious yeast character are Belgian ales (Witbier, Tripel, Saison, etc.) and German Wheat Beer.

BEER AND FOOD

Want to know the perfect beer to go with your dinner? Planning on opening a beer and need something great to serve it with? Here, I've made some suggestions for how to bring beer and food together in the best ways possible.

A sweet Stout or Wheat Beer and chili con carne

The first and main consideration for bringing beer and food together is the **intensity**. Session IPA and Double IPA have comparable taste profiles, but the stronger beer typically comes with way more impact, flavor, and body. You wouldn't put a Session IPA with a citrus cheesecake, for example, and you wouldn't necessarily want a Double IPA with a Vietnamese salad. Likewise, a Dunkel lager will be great with a roast chicken or cauliflower, yet washed out with a banoffee pie, whereas a Doppelbock would be perfect with the dessert but would overpower the chicken or cauliflower.

Then it's important to consider the **mouthfeel and texture** of a beer, which will work in different ways with different foods. Is it full-bodied and smooth? Is it light and briskly carbonated? A full-textured beer like Imperial Stout is rich and luscious, while that prickly Saison is crisply refreshing, providing an invigorating effervescence.

Watch out for **chili heat**. Capsaicin is the active ingredient in chili that gives the feeling of burning, which is actually an acute and temporary irritation (the pepper hasn't actually burned you; it just feels like it has). Some beers will ignite the fire of hot chili while others can help to cool it down. You want something smooth and full-bodied to try to balance and cool down the spice, with sweeter Stouts and Wheat Beers being good choices, while a classic and simple Pale Lager is often pleasingly refreshing with moderate heat. High carbonation and bitterness can both irritate and increase the burn sensation.

The Three Bs of Beer and Food

Bridge, Balance, and Boost are the three concepts you should consider to help you achieve the best beer and food combinations.

Bridge

By connecting similar flavors in the drink and the dish you can naturally create a bridge to hopefully enhance the combination. You don't necessarily need to make the bridge with the primary flavors and sometimes a subtle similarity can be as impactful. Here you need to think about the main qualities of the beer. Is the grain bready or toasty, like pizza or a burger bun, or is it roasted like chargrilled meat or chocolate? Are the hops herbal or tropical, light or strong? Is the yeast fruity, tart, peppery, or neutral? Have any additional ingredients, like spices or fruit, been added?

Pale Ale and pizza

Some good examples of flavors that bridge:

• **American hops** with garlic, roasted onion, hard herbs (such as rosemary and thyme), tomato (think ketchup's sweet tomato flavor), lemon and lime

• **European hops** with lemon, white pepper, endive and arugula (rocket), soft green herbs like parsley and cilantro (fresh coriander)

• **Belgian yeast** with pepper, woody and aromatic spices like cinnamon and clove, cumin and ground coriander, ginger, aniseed, and fragrant greens such as fennel, basil, dill, and tarragon

• **Pale to amber beers** with bread and pizza, caramelization (think of the flavor of grilled food versus poached), starches like potatoes, wholegrain rice, beans, and pulses, nuts, butter and light dairy

• **Dark beers** with barbecued foods, smoke, chipotle chili, chocolate

Some of my favorite bridge pairings:

• Belgian Witbier, infused with coriander seed and citrus, with a Southeast-Asian salad

• The aniseed and fragrantly spicy flavors of a Belgian Dubbel with barbecue beans

• Porter with blackened salmon

• Dunkelweizen with spiced and roasted cauliflower

• Smoked pork with a Rauchbier

• Pale Ale's citrus and resinous flavors with a garlic and herby roast chicken

• Raspberry Sour Beer with lemon cake

• Quadrupel and its bready, raisin-y, festive spiciness with apple pie

Balance

When drinking a powerful-tasting beer or eating a full-flavored dish, it's not always easy to match their intensities, so sometimes it's more effective to find a way to create a balance of flavor. This might involve cooling down the heat of chili; using food to balance the bitterness of a beer, or the saltiness of a snack; or using a light, bubbly, dry beer to balance and refresh heavy or fatty food. This approach is most successful when you've got strong flavors, so while you might not need to do this with a cheese sandwich, you probably will want to with a double cheeseburger.

Amber Ale and quesadilla

Some simple rules of balance:

- **Saltiness balances bitterness** Think fries and IPA

- **Fat balances bitterness** Think guacamole and Pale Ale

- **Spice is cooled by sweetness and texture** Think Mexican chili with Milk Stout

- **Sweetness balances sweetness** Think chocolate brownie with Imperial Stout

- **Fat balances alcohol** Think mature cheddar with a Double IPA

- **Carbonation balances richness and fat** Think Tripel with pork belly

Some of my favorite matches for strong-tasting food and beer:

- Hefeweizen with spicy Thai red curry or pad Thai

- Milk Stout with jerk chicken or sweet potatoes

- Saison with salt and pepper squid or tofu

- Dunkel with al pastor or grilled mushroom tacos

- Weizenbock with a crème brûlée

- Quesadilla with Amber Ale

- A salty pretzel with German Pilsner

- Blueberry muffin with Imperial Stout

Boost

This is the ultimate dream of a beer and food pairing—but not necessarily something that you will aim for every time you eat and drink. This is typically the reserve of the special-occasion beer pairing, although sometimes it's also intrinsically linked to a local pairing, as you'll see below. The idea here is that the beer and food combine in a way that boosts their deliciousness.

Double IPA and carrot cake

Some tasty boost suggestions:

• A sour-sweet cherry beer with a dark chocolate mousse

• Carrot cake and Double IPA

• Barley Wine like a sweet chutney with blue cheese

• Rauchbier with grilled salmon and lemon

• Dubbel with spaghetti and marinara sauce

• Witbier with steamed mussels

• Pale Ale with grilled cheese

• Quadrupel with a cinnamon cookie

Look beyond the Bs and think local

Look at the most popular and classic beer styles produced in a place and you'll typically find they naturally work with the common dishes of that region, especially if you're in a traditional brewing country. Examples include British Bitter with a Sunday roast, West Coast Pale Ale with fish tacos, Munich Helles with schnitzel, Fest Bier with spit-roast chicken, Amber Franconian Lager with Käsespätzle (a German mac 'n' cheese), Italian Pilsner with pizza, Japanese Lager with yakitori, Trappist ales paired with the monastery's cheeses, Pacific Pale Ale with fish and chips, Hefeweizen with Weisswurst and sweet mustard, and Witbier with fries and mayonnaise.

POPULAR BEER STYLES AND WHAT TO EAT WITH THEM

Pale Ale, IPA, and DIPA

Hops dominate these styles with bitterness and lots of aroma, but there's usually a background of grain to support them. The hops are most often going to be citrus, tropical, and stone fruits, with grapefruit, lime, pineapple, mango, melon, and apricot, while they might also give resinous herbs or an allium character (garlic or onion). The grain will typically give you bread, toast, and sometimes caramel. A good match is dependent on the strength, bitterness, and carbonation, which vary between the beers.

Think about American bar food and you're in a good starting place: burgers, fries, pizza, grilled cheese, quesadilla, mac 'n' cheese, and ribs. High fat or salt can help cut the bitterness: guacamole, pork belly, Cheddar cheese, onion rings, and garlic fries. Smoked food and hops can work really well together—think brisket, smoked turkey, and smoked mackerel. A foundation of sweet onion and garlic, especially roasted garlic, can be very good—consider roast

garlic hummus and flatbreads, herby roast meat or vegetables, and onion and garlic in a pomodoro sauce. Sweet Hazy IPAs are good with tacos, kimchi fried rice, and fried chicken or fried tofu. You can also drink your DIPAs with dessert, with citrus cheesecake and carrot cake being good matches—just don't go too sweet and use plenty of mascarpone to balance it.

Pale and Dark Lagers

Lagers bring their balance of gentle malts, crisp bitterness, and carbonation to the dining table. More bitter examples, like Pilsner, go well with hard herbs, garlic, grilled meats, fragrant spices, pepper, chili, and more, while aromatically hopped lagers can be looked at like gentle IPAs. Maltier brews, like Helles and Dunkel, act like a liquid bread with food, offering toasty, nutty sweetness, while strong lagers, like Doppelbock, have a sweet, raisin-y, fruity depth that goes with richer foods. Dunkel is one of the most versatile beer styles to go with food.

Simple lagers are broadly good with light foods: grilled fish and chicken, especially with a butter or cream sauce; cream-based pasta dishes; pork schnitzel

IPA and a burger

Hoppy Lager and Indian curry

and grilled sausages; spicy seafood; Indian curries and Thai noodles (Thai food is especially good with Hoppy Lagers). Amber Lagers go well with chicken or cauliflower wings, quesadillas, most sandwiches, most pizza, and mac 'n' cheese. Dark Lagers are great with a very broad range of foods: ramen and other Japanese noodles; tacos and Mexican food (meat- or vegetable-based); tomato-topped pizza and pasta; mushroom burgers and mushroom pasta; Middle Eastern salads and stews; barbecued meat and vegetables; plus classic German beer-hall food. Doppelbock is good with richer meats, like game, or with desserts such as apple cake.

Wheat Beer

Wheat Beers are typically food-friendly, thanks to their full texture, savory spiciness, and refreshing carbonation. Belgian-style Witbier is usually dry, peppery, and citrusy, often brewed with coriander seed and orange peel, and it's lighter in body than a German-style Hefeweizen. The German brews, which range from pale yellow to dark brown, are usually fuller-bodied, which gives a perception of sweetness, with a fruity, banana-like aroma. Wheat Beers naturally work well with spicy foods but aren't limited to their heat-extinguishing powers.

Witbier and mussels is a classic combination, especially if the mussels are cooked in beer. Witbier is also good with Thai and Vietnamese salads, with flavors like lemongrass, garlic, chili, cilantro (fresh coriander), and Thai basil all working well. Falafel and other Middle Eastern flavors can also be great. Hefeweizen's classic pairing is with Weisswurst—white sausages—for breakfast. It's also good with flatbreads and dips, bean and avocado tacos, fried rice, roasted cauliflower, and coconut-based curries and dal—it likes creamy and nutty flavors. Strong Weizenbocks suit tagines, Middle East baked eggplant (aubergine), and desserts like banana cake, baked custards, and apple strudel.

Witbier and mussels

Saison and Belgian Pale and Tripel

A group of pale, dry, aromatic, Belgian-style beers that are typically excellent choices for food. They range from moderate in alcohol to strong (5.0–10.0% ABV), have a simple malt base, and are often not sweet, despite an underlying richness of malt, and they finish very dry with a lively carbonation. They all share a depth of peppery spice, and might also have aromas like banana, almond, apricot, or lemon.

Saison is as good with a local farmhouse cheese as it is with an exotic Southeast Asian noodle dish. It can do slow-roasted pork as happily as quickly grilled sardines or shrimps. Falafel and hummus are good, as is a herby roast chicken or loin of cod in a butter sauce. Fragrant aniseed flavors like fennel and basil are complementary; roasted mushrooms can be refreshed by Saison; and herb-roasted vegetables also work very well. For Tripels and Strong Golden Ales you can have even more intensity in the dish. Roasted pork belly, jerk salmon, asparagus risotto with lots of Parmesan cheese, French cassoulet, or just a really good aged cheese like Gouda or Comté. Saison is a very versatile beer with food.

Belgian Dark Ales

Like the Pale Belgians, but with more warming spice, dark fruits, and a little toastier sweetness, these beers range from bready Browns to teacake Dubbels to Christmas-cake Quads, with the spices becoming more festive (think cinnamon, nutmeg, and clove) and the base brews being more raisin-like as the beers get stronger. These flavors naturally work with roasted meats, especially game and strongly flavored sausages. They are good with hard herbs, pepper, tomato or spicy pasta dishes, and strong ones can work well with desserts, too.

A Belgian carbonnade of slow-stewed meat in beer is a classic match here. I usually have a Dubbel or Quad with my Christmas dinner (and it's great for Thanksgiving). The spicy, smoky flavors of pulled pork like the sweetness of Dubbel, and Dubbel is also great with tomato-based Italian dishes like lasagna or ragu (meat or veggie). Try Mexican mole or bean tacos, a smoked bacon sandwich, mushroom burger, miso-roast veg, bao buns, mushroom and blue cheese risotto, nasi goreng, or fried rice. Quadrupel is a beer for cheese or dessert, being great with blue cheese and figs, cinnamon cookies, or lighter chocolate cakes.

Belgian Dark Ale and carbonnade

Sour Beer

There's a vast difference in complexity and characteristic between a fast-brewed Gose and a three-year-matured Gueuze. The Fast Sours have a lactic tartness to them and a general lightness, often with added fruits to give more depth, or dry-hopped for more aroma. These beers can almost be thought of as a squeeze of citrus on the side of a dish. Slow Sours and Spontaneously Fermented beers have much greater complexity, texture, tannins, and depth, and they want more mature flavors, while an aged Red or Brown Ale will give more of an acetic, umami flavor.

The Champagne-like quality of Gueuze means it's good with aged soft-rind cheese, goats' cheese, pâtés, and cured meats. Fruit Lambics are good with oily fish and goat's cheese. The Belgian Reds and Browns are almost like an addition of tomato with their sweet-sour-acetic balance, so they can be great with grilled sausages or steaks, or with a ragu. The Fast Sours can be good with spicy Mexican food or Thai curries, but don't drink anything too acidic or strong. Sweeter, fruitier Sours can work with light cheesecakes (peach or apricot) and lemon cake, while chocolate mousse or chocolate with a sweet-sour cherry beer is a classic match.

Dark Ales

From toasty Bitters to malty-roasted Brown Ales to chocolatey Porter and coffee-like Stout, here we're looking at the flavors of grain to go with food. The process of making the beers darker comes from the roasting of malts and that roasting process is the same as the cooking process, with more sweetness developing first before the beer/food becomes darker and more burned (think of a slice of bread as you heat it). Some versions are creamier or sweeter, like Oatmeal Stout, and these are good choices with spice. And if you've got a smoked beer, that smokiness is an injection of savory flavor which can enhance a lot of different dishes.

The amber to brown beers like toasted bread flavors, so quesadilla, pizza, and grilled sandwiches are good. They also like the earthy flavors of mushrooms, so try a mushroom burger, risotto, or biryani. Classic British bar snacks are also good here. Darker beers are good with braised meats, stews and pies, spicy lamb chops, steak and pepper sauce, roasted cauliflower, roasted squash or pumpkin, and Korean dishes like bibimbap, and they can often handle acidity, so try tomato pasta dishes or buffalo wings. Oily fish is good with smoother Stouts, but I've never personally understood the combination of Stout and oysters (unless the oysters are fried and served in a Po' Boy). Smoked beers are almost universally great. Try with pasta dishes as wide-ranging as ragu and carbonara, brothy noodles like ramen, seafood chowder, grilled vegetables, meat, or fish, Mexican dishes, especially with beans and chipotle, and most things cooked over wood. Smoke doesn't often go with dessert, though.

Dark Ale with buffalo wings

Imperial Stout and other Strong Ales

The strength and sweetness in an Imperial Stout make it a natural choice for sweeter foods, especially with its flavors of chocolate, coffee, and dried fruits. Sometimes these beers are also barrel-aged, picking up vanilla, caramel, and other sweeter flavors. These beers are not limited just to dessert, though, and Baltic Porters or Stouts with an ABV of less than 10.0% can work well with dark meat, game, and barbecued flavors—although you have to like big flavors to want those combos. Barley Wines are strong, dark, malty ales with a dried-fruit depth and sometimes a high bitterness, which naturally helps them work with richness and high fat.

With Imperial Stout, think chocolate puddings, crème brûlée (especially with barrel-aged beers), chocolate cookies and muffins, cheesecake, or blue cheeses. Pulled pork or slow-braised beef ribs can be great with a lighter Imperial Stout, adding a depth of umami and sweetness almost like an enriched sauce, while jerk pork can also work. Barley Wine is great with a board of strong cheeses, or apple pie.

Imperial Stout and chocolate mousse

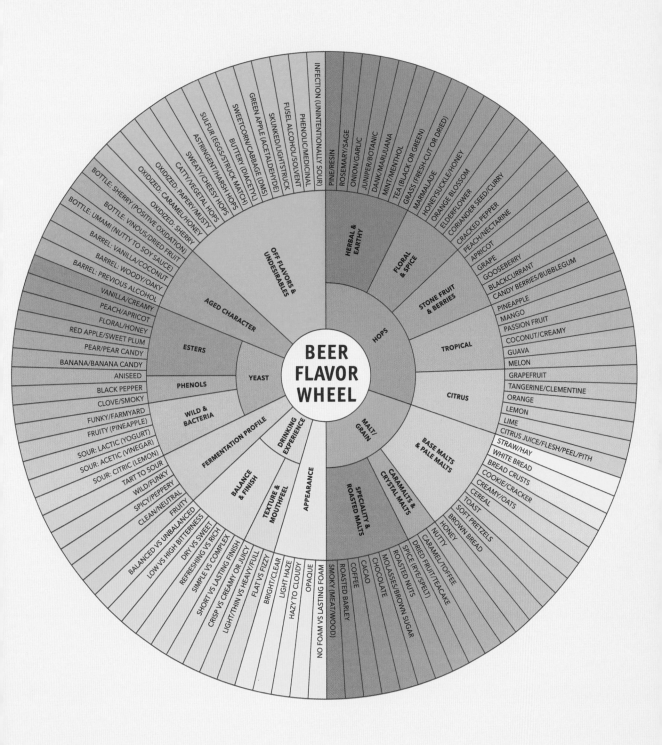

THE WORLD'S GREATEST BEERS

PALE ALE

Pale Ale is the style that grew craft beer from a quirky bunch of basement brewers into a global industry. It's a beer style that helped build thousands of breweries. It's a beer style that has converted millions of drinkers to craft beer, becoming an automatic order without anyone even looking at the taps: "I'll have a Pale Ale, please." It's a beer style built on its essential difference from light lagers, with its toasty malts and impactful citrusy hops. It's a beer style that's been around since the beginning, and today it's a beer style in flux. A beer style that needs to be ever evolving to suit new drinkers, getting hoppier or hazier, while also being muscled to the side by Session IPAs. The beer style which built craft beer is still of fundamental importance, but it's having to modernize, and that's created a large variation in what Pale Ale is today.

Typically, a classic-tasting American Pale Ale (because when we talk about Pale Ale it's almost always American Pale Ale) will be less aromatic, less bitter, and weaker than an IPA, but it might have more malt flavor. But this is where the variations begin, because Pale Ale could be bright, hazy, or cloudy; it could be citrusy, piney, or tropical, and either subtle or impactful; it might be 4.0% ABV or 6.0% ABV; the malt could be light and bready, or more caramelized and fuller. What's important is that nowadays almost everyone—whether they are craft-beer drinkers or not—knows Pale Ale and IPA, and most breweries make one as a flagship year-round beer. The beers gathered together here are American Pale Ales, meaning they are predominantly hopped with American varieties. They might be hazy, but they aren't totally juicy—those beers have their own chapter (see pages 64–67).

Sierra Nevada Pale Ale

Chico, California, USA
ABV: 5.6%

This is the original American Pale Ale. It's the beer that essentially invented the American Pale Ale and it's still the classic example. It was first brewed in 1980 and took an English Pale Ale recipe, bumped up the ABV, and, crucially, used bitter and aromatic American-grown Cascade hops. It was very different from anything else at that time and it helped to forge the beginnings of a whole industry. Sierra Nevada use whole-flower hops in their Pale Ale, which gives it a delicate, floral, grapefruit-peel aroma (their hop store is the best-smelling place in the whole of the beer world). The malt is toasty, with some toffee and bread, and the bitterness is peppery and pithy. Forty years ago, this beer was challenging and intense, whereas today it has a kind of comforting quality and is unquestionably one of the world's most important beers—drinking it fresh at the brewery in Chico is an essential beer experience.

Pressure Drop Pale Fire

London, England, UK
ABV: 4.8%

I remember visiting Pressure Drop soon after they'd started, and I was surprised to see that they were making beer in a shed on a single-vessel, 50-liter Braumeister kit. Soon after, they moved into some railway arches in Hackney with an 800-liter brewery. Then, a few years after that, they grew into a much bigger space with a 3,200-liter brewhouse, retaining the railway arch as a bar. I lived a short walk away, so I often drank there and always had a Pale Fire, which is an impressive flagship beer and one that I think is the best core Pale Ale in London. It's hazy yellow, brightly aromatic with stone fruit, tropical fruits, and citrus, and a little savory-resinous hop, with a crisp bitterness cutting through it to give a refreshing finish. It's fresh, fun, unchallenging, and, being local, it was an ever-present in my drinking for many years.

Half Acre Daisy Cutter

Chicago, Illinois, USA
ABV: 5.2%

If Sierra Nevada Pale Ale is the original Pale Ale, and Hazy Pales are the contemporary ones, then Daisy Cutter signifies the middle years of American Pale Ale's growth. It's not like the malty West Coasters and it's not the full juice of the modern East Coast; instead, it's a moderate Midwesterner, a beer that's both bitter and tropical, with some pine in the background. The malt is bread, instead of toffee. The aromas are on the subtle side, relatively speaking. It's impressively balanced. And it's also relatively low in alcohol compared to other American examples, meaning you can happily drink a few of them. It brings back great memories of my first trip to Chicago, and I now always return when I'm back in the city to get a pint of Daisy Cutter.

Blackman's Mervyn Pale Ale

Torquay, Australia
ABV: 4.6%

Blackman's is run by husband-and-wife team Renn and Jess Blackman, and Mervyn was first brewed as a one-off wedding beer for their friends and named after the couple's dog (and I happened to be at the brewery that day to help out). The beer was so good that they kept it around. A great marriage of Cascade, Mosaic, and Simcoe hops go into this one to give a mix of juicy grapefruit, pine, orange, and tropical fruits, which are sweetened by a beer that's lightly hazy and has some toasty malts. The result is one of those endlessly enjoyable pale beers, the sort that makes sense in the sun, on the beach, in the beer garden, or just your back garden. There's something essentially Aussie about the balance of flavors, which puts it somewhere between an American Pale Ale and a Summer Ale.

Pivovar Matuška Apollo Galaxy

Broumy, Czech Republic
ABV: 5.5%

In a country known for making a diverse range of high-quality lagers, Pivovar Matuška have stood out since 2009 as a brewery who make a full range of ale styles alongside their lagers. Over time, they've become best known (at least to craft beer fans) for their Pale Ales and IPAs. Apollo Galaxy is golden and has a nice backbone of malts, as you'd expect in a pale Czech beer. It's brewed with Apollo, Galaxy, and Citra hops, and these are tropical, pithy, resinous, and tangerine-like. The bitterness is strong and lasting, but sweetened by the malt. What makes this beer so good is how it's balanced like a powerful Pilsner while still being packed with all the most aromatic hops—it's a great skill of brewing and a quality of the Czech palate. Try this one with some Czech fried cheese for a good beer snack.

Track Brewing Co. Sonoma

Manchester, England, UK
ABV: 3.8%

Sonoma is a good example of the modernization of British small-scale brewing and how the influence of hops and Pale Ales has evolved the classic cask ales. This one is sold in cask, on keg, and in cans, and it's equally enjoyable in all formats. The malt base is very light, almost electric yellow in color, and will be hazy if it's kegged or canned and brighter from the cask. The hops in this beer are Centennial, Citra, and Mosaic, and these all add their own expected fruitiness, giving juicy and fresh aromas. It's the ideal ABV for drinking all day in the pub, but it also has enough hop flavor that opening one at home while watching TV will leave your hop thirst properly quenched. Track are great at making hop-forward Pale Ales and IPAs, and they have a good taproom at their brewery in Manchester.

Gorilla Brewing Company Busan Pale Ale

Busan, South Korea
ABV: 4.5%

In a craft beer world that's pulpy with hops and with beers which look like juice, it's brilliantly refreshing to see and drink something like Gorilla's Busan Pale Ale. It's golden, it's bright, and it's crisply bitter, with tangy and grapefruit-y American hops—it's my kind of Pale Ale, the kind that's bold with hop character, where the malt is merely there to support the oily hops and provide something to balance the bitterness. Gorilla also brew KPA, or Korea Pale Ale, which is lighter in bitterness but with a more tropical character, and it's designed to go with Korean food. Gorilla have a large, open taproom in Busan where you can try all their beers, including their British Stout, an ode to home from the brewery's two British founders.

Suarez Family Brewery Homespun

Hudson, New York, USA
ABV: 4.5%

As well as their phenomenal lagers, Suarez Family Brewery make some of the best pale hoppy beers in America. These aren't the kind of stupidly over-hopped, thick, juice brews; instead, they are judiciously hopped, refreshingly light, beautifully carbonated, and gracefully balanced. Homespun is the type of beer that makes you thirsty just by looking at it. The hop aroma teases gracefully with some fresh-cut grass and orange-peel fruitiness, while the malt base (which includes some spelt) is layered, nutty, and a little bready. It's beautifully balanced, crisp, and light. There's a rare pinpoint precision in this, as there is in all the beers made at Suarez Family Brewery. They are wowing kinds of beers, not in the wowing way of watching a firework display, but wow in how they draw you in and keep you interested, then excited, then enthralled by their elegance. Spectacular.

Young Master Classic Pale Ale

Wong Chuk Hang, Hong Kong
ABV: 5.0%

Classic certainly is the right word to describe this Hong Kong-brewed Pale Ale. It's a bright golden color and the malt is biscuity and toasty, edging toward some caramel. The hops are grapefruit-y, zesty, citrusy, grassy, and floral, and they give a dry tonic-like kind of botanic bitterness, which combines well with the carbonation to give the beer a bracing bite. Young Master started brewing in 2013 and have led the Hong Kong beer scene ever since. Alongside their Classic they also make 1842 Island Imperial IPA, plus some beers with a local inspiration, such as adding salted lime to a Gose, or their Witbier, which is made with mandarin orange peel and spiced with zedoary, coriander seeds, chrysanthemum, chamomile, and white pepper.

AF Brew Hoppy Surf

St. Petersburg, Russia
ABV: 5.3%

AF Brew's taproom is in an impressive old red-brick factory in what used to be the Stepa Razin Brewery. On tap you'll find around 20 different beers—most from AF Brew, plus some guest taps—in a full mix of modern styles, often high in alcohol and with adjuncts, as is the Russian trend. Their main beers include several IPAs and strong dark ales, while Hoppy Surf is a solid, go-to American Pale Ale that's got a good foundation of toasty malts, some caramel flavor, plenty of piney and grapefruit-y hops, and a decent bitterness—it's a great beer to go with pizza and, in fact, AF Brew run a small chain of pizzerias called Camorra. They also run a popular bar called Redrum, for which they brew a house Red Double IPA that's intensely hoppy.

Cervecería Barbarian Lima Pale Ale

Lima, Peru
ABV: 6.1%

One of Peru's first craft breweries, and now one of the biggest, Cervecería Barbarian are inspired by American craft beer and you can taste that best in their Lima Pale Ale. It's hazy gold in color and lots of Simcoe hops come through, giving it some pine and tangy citrus. The malt is a little bready and sweet, kind of old-school West Coast, and, overall, it's a little unrefined and rough at the edges, but there's some charm in that. Their other beers include an IPA, a malty Red, a hoppy Wheat, and lots of seasonal specials, some of which use local ingredients. The brewery has a bar in Lima with loads of taps and a kitchen slinging loaded burgers.

Bale Breaker Field 41

Yakima, Washington, USA
ABV: 5.2%

Bale Breaker is a family-run brewery and hop farm situated right in the middle of the Yakima Valley. The hop-growing business is into the fourth generation and they added the brewery in 2013. Field 41 is so named because the brewery and its taproom are on field 41 of the hop farm. The beer is fronted by piney, herbal, and orangey Simcoe and backed up by some grapefruit-y Cascade, some mango and berry-like Mosaic, and some lemony, pithy Loral. It's in the bright, oily, dry, refreshing, and bitter style of Pale Ale, with the sort of malt that doesn't interfere with the hops, instead just adding some toast and texture. Bale Breaker's Topcutter IPA gives even more hop aroma and flavor, and marks out the brewery as one of the finest users of hops you can find, as you'd expect given how close they are to them.

Stigbergets Bryggeri American Pale Ale

Gothenburg, Sweden
ABV: 5.2%

Stigbergets's APA is a bridge between classic bitter West Coast Pales and contemporary juicy Hazy Pales. It's golden and lightly cloudy. The hops are both tropical and tangy citrus, with some melon, apricot, guava, and grapefruit all mixing together. The malts are what you'd expect in a Pale Ale, being toasty and a touch caramelized, leaving a little residual sweetness on the lips, although it ends dry with a long bitter finish. It's the sort of beer that gets more interesting and excellent as you drink it, with more depth and complexity revealing itself. Stigbergets make a lot of excellent hoppy beers, from their West Coast IPA through to several Hazy DIPAs, including the modern mandarin and melon-y Muddle.

The Piggy Brewing Co. Pick Me Up

Liverdun, France
ABV: 4.5%

Pick Me Up is a cloudy and tropical Pale Ale, showing the style's transition toward the modern taste for juicier beers, where it's becoming more normal to see Pale Ales which look and taste like this. This one is juicy in the melon-guava-peach sense, but it's not full fruit juice, retaining a light and refreshing body and also a softness to its character, which helps to emphasize all the Citra hops used in the beer. Pale Ale is always a good choice with pizza, but if you're in the Lorraine region of France, then you're close to where *Flammkuchen* is from, and that'd be a great beer snack for Pick Me Up, being a crispy, thin, baked dough topped with cream cheese, onion, and smoked lardons—those flavors love the fruity hops.

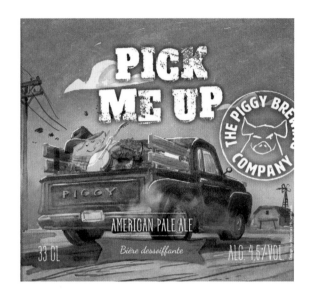

Behemoth Brewing 'Murica

Napier, New Zealand
ABV: 6.0%

'Murica is a good old West-Coast-style American Pale Ale, the kind that's golden orange in color, with Amarillo, Centennial, and Simcoe hops, which combine to give orange, grapefruit, pine, and peach, and a herbal and resinous bitterness that really grips and lingers on the way down. It's the lasting bitterness that makes this one stand out for me; increasingly, Pale Ales are getting sweeter and more tropical, leaving behind the bitter citrus with which we were so familiar in American Pale Ales, so I always like to get that punchy bitter finish. Behemoth's IPAs are also really good, as is their NZ Pilsner, which is fresh with stone fruit and tropical fruits, with a lasting, crisp, dry bitterness.

Graff Brygghus Portland Pale Ale

Tromsø, Norway
ABV: 4.7%

Marius Graff and Martin Amundsen started their brewery in 2015 in a 100-year-old wooden house which had been in Martin's family for generations. When the two met, Martin was working in a bank in Oslo and Marius was a young homebrewer who was blogging about his brewings. They met, discussed the idea of opening a brewery, and traveled to Portland to visit breweries, where Marius—then only 19 years old—got to intern and learn, before they returned home and built Graff. Portland Pale Ale is inspired by their pre-brewery beer trip. It's Citra-hopped and has lots of orange and pineapple in the nose; there's a little sweetness and a lasting bitterness, while the city's naturally soft water comes through in the beer's clean clarity of flavor. Their Session IPA is also very good and at Christmas, in the Norwegian tradition, they make a few Jul beers, including an excellent Black IPA.

AMERICAN IPA

If American Pale Ale was the foundation style for the emergence of craft beer, then American IPA is the style which became its defining monument. Speak to anyone around the world about craft beer and ask them to describe it, and even those with little knowledge will likely give you a synonym of IPA: hoppy, bitter, fruity, strong. It's been brewed for a few decades, but it took a while for it to become the most popular—or defining—beer type, in the early 2000s. It's been unstoppable ever since and, as its popularity has increased and spread, IPA has become a family of beers and requires a prefix to tell you more about what to expect: it could be a Session IPA or a Double IPA, a Hazy IPA, a Black or Red or White IPA, a Sour IPA, or one with fruit in it, or the classic American-style IPA. The American IPA is the one that started it all and it's now sometimes referred to as West Coast for its clear and bitter origins compared to the cloudy and smooth East Coast-inspired Hazy IPAs. As more Hazy IPAs are brewed, we're seeing a resurgence of bright, bitter American IPAs.

An American IPA can be many things: as pale as Pilsner or almost red in color; somewhere between very dry, and caramelized and sweet (a West Coast-style will usually be lean and dry); it could be deeply bitter or just gently hopped at the end; perfectly bright or hazy; anywhere between 5.5% ABV and 7.5% ABV; hopped with classic American varieties like Cascade and Centennial, giving grapefruit and pine, or it could be more tropical and melon-like with newer hops. For me, the defining qualities of a classic-tasting American IPA are an aroma of citrusy hops, a clean malt base (usually in an almost-bright beer), and a deep, lasting bitterness.

Duration Brewing Dripping Pitch

West Acre, England, UK
ABV: 6.7%

Miranda Hudson and Derek Bates—who's just known as Bates—have built themselves a special brewery in the Norfolk countryside. A culmination of beer experience and a desire to have something lasting and sustainable led them to convert an old farmhouse into their impressive modern brewery. They make a mix of clean, fresh canned beers and wild and aged bottled ones, both reflecting time and place—in their words, they are "beers that belong." Dripping Pitch is one of the best West Coast IPAs brewed in Britain. Columbus, Amarillo, and Citra give the beer a pleasing stone fruitiness and some lemon pith and orange, with a little malt sweetness having the ability to make those hops taste fruitier, plus an underlying greener, herbal kind of bitterness. Be excited for what Duration are doing and seek out their beers.

Heart of Darkness Kurtz's Insane IPA

Ho Chi Minh City, Vietnam
ABV: 7.1%

I'd been traveling through Southeast Asia for over a month by the time I got to Ho Chi Minh City. I'd drunk a lot of pale lager and, as much as I like that, especially with the local food, I was craving something devastatingly hoppy and bitter. I found that exact beer at Heart of Darkness with Kurtz's Insane IPA. It was lightly hazy gold, and exploding with grapefruit, citrus, pine, and pineapple. Dry in the body and very bitter at the end, and all balanced and crisply refreshing for such a powerful beer. It's the best IPA I've drunk in Southeast Asia and brewed by one of Vietnam's best breweries. Heart of Darkness was started by Englishman John Pemberton. He had lived in the US before moving to China, where the lack of beer variety led him to start homebrewing. John's job then took him to Ho Chi Minh, where he converted most of his apartment into an advanced home-brewery. Eventually, he quit his job and started the brewery just outside the city, opening a taproom downtown.

Dogfish Head 60 Minute IPA

Milton, Delaware, USA
ABV: 6.0%

There were many classic American IPAs that I could've listed here. I thought about Bell's Two Hearted, Bear Republic Racer 5, Russian River Blind Pig, and many others, but I picked 60 Minute IPA because it's an IPA which everyone should try so they can see where craft beer evolved from and why the classics remain important. Before New England IPAs (NEIPAs) and Hazy IPAs were a thing, there was a distinction between West and East Coast, with the West typically being leaner, more grapefruit-y, and more bitter, and East Coast having a bit more malt sweetness to them. This beer is one of those East Coasters. When I went to Dogfish Head, I knew I wanted to try a 60 Minute IPA, but I also wanted to try everything else, so I got a pint of 60 and a couple of flights, but I was so enamored of the 60 that I ordered another pint. Orange, grapefruit, and pine aroma, toasty malt, a little caramel, and a crisp, refreshing, balanced bitterness at the end. The flavors were so clean and precise that I could taste everything in high-definition, and while it's not one of those "Woah!" kinds of IPAs, it is one which is deeply satisfying, unchallenging, and pleasing to drink. A classic American IPA. (See image on page 54.)

Breakside Brewery Breakside IPA

Portland, Oregon, USA
ABV: 6.2%

Breakside IPA is golden in color, but don't expect much malt sweetness. Instead, those grains add a juicy character, something a little toothsome and moreish, which heightens the hop flavors. Those hops are bright with grapefruit and tangerine, pine, and resin, and the beer's bitter. It's a great showcase of the hops grown close by and it's so good because it has all the flavors you want in an IPA, while also being elegant and light, not overdone and intense. Breakside brew lots of different IPAs and all of them are very good, but then Breakside are almighty brewing all-rounders and are good at everything. They have a couple of sites in Portland and you should dedicate at least an evening to really getting to know and enjoy their beers.

Driftwood Fat Tug IPA

Victoria, Canada
ABV: 7.0%

This beer should be considered a modern classic Northwest IPA. It has a clean malt body and a hefty hop addition, giving a high bitterness and a strong aroma. It pours a bright gold with a creamy white foam. You get classic grapefruit, orange, lemon, apricot, and citrus pith. It's very clean to drink, with the malt holding it all together without adding much sweetness, and then all those hops give it an oily, citrus-peel depth, some spicy resin, and a firm, clean bitterness. It's a superb American-style IPA. They call it a Northwest IPA and that may help highlight a few differences with, say, a San Diego IPA, where the Northwest might be a little lower in alcohol and have a little more malt; it's often slightly hazy (but not cloudy); and the bitterness might be more balanced with the sweetness overall.

Reuben's Brews Triumvirate

Seattle, Washington, USA
ABV: 6.0%

I went into Reuben's Brews taproom while on a big brewery crawl around Seattle. I had several more stops planned, but a taster of Triumvirate immediately wrote off those plans. It's very pale, sensationally bright, almost salaciously bright, in a world where haze is prized. It's hopped with a triple-header of Citra, Amarillo, and Mosaic to be a mix of tropical fruits, orange, grapefruit, and mango, and there's a deep, deep, deliciously crisp bitterness, all with a body that's as lean and dry as a classic Pilsner. The balance was immaculate, the aroma was ambrosia. I drank it again a week later at the Great American Beer Festival and just kept passing them my glass for 1oz (30ml) hits at a time. This is the kind of IPA that I want to be able to drink all the time.

Hammer Wave Runner

Villa d'Adda, Italy
ABV: 6.5%

I have really powerful memories of Wave Runner—some good, some less so. I was on vacation in Italy and we'd had a few days in Naples eating pizza. While there, I'd found a small craft beer store and had a bottle of this, and I loved it. It's the kind of IPA that's brilliant yellow, intensely aromatic with grapefruit, mango, and stone fruit, with a very lean and clean body and a long bitter finish. I bought as many bottles as I could carry home and took them with me when we went to the nearby island of Ischia, where I drank more of this beer while watching the sunset and looking over the bay of Sant'Angelo. Those were the good memories. The bad memories come because I watched England lose to Croatia in the semi-final of the 2018 World Cup while in Ischia and drinking this beer. Still, the good memories of the beer have (just about) outlasted the bad ones from that moment as this is a world-beating American IPA.

Seasons Craft Brewery Green Cow IPA

Porto Alegre, Brazil
ABV: 6.2%

Sometimes simple is best, as is the case with Green Cow IPA, which just uses Pilsner and Munich malts and Centennial hops. Inspired by classic American IPAs in which Centennial leads (think Bell's Two Hearted), with orange, lemon, orange blossom, some resinous pine, florals, and pepper, it's a slightly hazy golden beer and the base brew is pretty light. There's some malt character with a little toffee sweetness which edges through, and that's able to balance the bitterness. Seasons also brew Holy Cow, which bumps the booze up to 7.5% ABV and adds more and different hops. They also make Moosaic, a West Coast Double IPA. And, for something a bit different, they make Basilicow, a Witbier with added basil.

Brassneck Brewery Passive Aggressive

Vancouver, Canada
ABV: 7.0%

Brassneck call this one a Pale Ale, but at 7.0% ABV I'm putting it with the IPAs (it's at least a Strong Pale Ale...). This brewery has a rare ability to be brilliant at whatever style they choose to make, and they make a lot of different beers. However, they will always have two core beers available at their taproom: Brassneck Ale, which is an English-ish Pale Ale, and Passive Aggressive. This is an almost-bright beer and it's layered and rich with hop flavor, giving depth rather than just a wallop of aroma. It has a fresh, fruity hop character with some tropical fruits and mandarin, plus a little evergreen pine. At the end, the bitterness and alcohol combine to give it a clean finish. It might be personal preference, but I get so much more enjoyment from an IPA like this than from any hazy juicy IPA.

The Booth Brewing Kukmin IPA

Seoul, South Korea
ABV: 6.5%

The Booth is an ambitious Korean brewery which has expanded into numerous bars in the city (where they serve huge slices of pizza alongside the beers). They have also taken on a defunct brewery in Eureka, California. They've been responsible for leading a change in their home market by introducing a totally refrigerated distribution system and they also host one of Seoul's biggest beer festivals. Kukmin IPA is their flagship beer. It's a golden IPA with a little haze. The hops are a pleasing mix of citrus, melon, fleshy tropical fruit, and gummy candies. It's on the subtle side, with a gentle aroma, a clean body of malts, and a gentle dry finish. The brewery's tagline is "Follow the Fun" and that's what saw a doctor, a financial analyst, and a journalist quit their jobs and change careers to set about transforming Korean craft beer.

Cervejaría Wendtland Perro del Mar

Ensenada, Mexico
ABV: 7.0%

Ensenada is a hotspot of Mexican craft beer, with over a dozen breweries making it like a mini San Diego. There are a lot of bars and taprooms, all within walking distance of each other, and with a high overall quality. Wendtland is one of the best in the area, and in 2019 they won Best Large Brewery in Mexico at the Copa Cerveza, a Mexican beer competition. Their Perro del Mar is a light orangey-amber color and it's perfectly bright in the West Coast style, as you might expect from a brewery this close to California. It's got peaches, pine, and pith, and a high level of bitterness. Their small brewpub is in the middle of town, but it's worth heading up to their taproom which overlooks the Pacific Ocean. A pint of Perro del Mar, a plate of tostadas, and the sunset is a perfect beer experience.

Roosters Brewing Co. Baby-Faced Assassin

Knaresborough, England, UK
ABV: 6.1%

Baby-Faced Assassin is an all-Citra-hopped IPA. It's almost bright gold and the Citra hops give it a peachy and sweet citrus fruit aroma. It's a beer that's got a lot of bitterness behind it, giving some bitter grapefruit, plus something more floral. It has an old-school quality, but also lots about it that is modern and bright. It's a beer that I seem to open and drink within just a few minutes. It's excellent. Rooster's Yankee is another beer to look out for, especially on cask, and it was one of the first British beers to use Cascade hops, which it combines with soft Yorkshire water and English Golden Promise malts. It's a modern classic British beer.

Liberty Brewing Knife Party IPA

Helensville, New Zealand
ABV: 7.1%

A bright, golden-colored brew, Knife Party is packed with American hops, but not in a one-dimensional, top-heavy, all-for-the-smells kind of way, and it's brewed to have hops all the way through it, layered and complex, mixing all the orange, marmalade, floral, grapefruit, sweet lemon, and piney, dank, earthy aromas with an oily, citrus-pith mouthfeel, then there's a firm grip of bitterness at the end. It's a proper West Coast-style American IPA with just a little malt holding it together and allowing the hops to be the superstars. Liberty are renowned for their hoppy brews, with Halo being a fresh and aromatic NZ Pilsner, while Yakima Monster is a super Pale Ale, and their C!tra a perennial favorite Double IPA.

BentSpoke Crankshaft IPA

Braddon, Australia
ABV: 5.8%

The bright orange can is a color cue for when you crack back the ring pull. The beer pours a bright orange in your glass, the kind of orange-gold that you look at and know immediately it is going to be good. The beer is hopped with Ekuanot, Simcoe, Citra, and Centennial, which are some of the most orangey hops you can find. And altogether you get a fruity, tangy, tangerine-y, orange blossom-like West Coast-style IPA that has some nice juicy sweetness and a bitter, pithy finish. BentSpoke's whole range is well made, well balanced, and consistent, mostly with hop-led styles. In the annual Hottest 100 Craft Beers, it was named the best beer in Australia for 2020.

WarPigs Brewpub Lazurite

Copenhagen, Denmark
ABV: 6.8%

The WarPigs brewpub is in Copenhagen's revitalized meatpacking district. It's a collaboration between Mikkeller and Three Floyds, and they brew beer down one end of the large space and have a Texas-style barbecue smoking at the other end. Lazurite is the brewpub's flagship IPA. It's golden and lightly hazy. The hops are bursting out of the glass with tangy citrus, lemon, and pineapple. The malt is a little toasty and that helps balance the powerful bitterness—it's a faultless IPA and a great beer to go with smoked and fatty foods. Copenhagen is a must-visit beer destination and Mikkeller have been central to the city's beer development. What I think is most interesting about Copenhagen and Mikkeller is how they have so many bars and restaurants and yet each is worth visiting because they are all different: a taco restaurant, a bar specializing in Lambic, a ramen joint, a warehouse of barrel-aged beers, some fine dining, a 40-tap beer bar, plus beer and smoked meat in WarPigs.

Societe Brewing Co. The Pupil IPA

San Diego, California, USA
ABV: 7.5%

This one deserves to be considered a new classic American IPA. It's a perfect example of the San Diego or West Coast style of IPA, meaning a simple, light malt profile and a strong bitterness. It's gold in color and has none of the specialty or caramel malt sweetness that you might find in other American IPAs. The hops are brightly aromatic, as if you're smelling and tasting them in high definition, with lots of grapefruit, tangerine, pineapple, and a little pine. It's light, crisp, and refreshing despite its 7.5% ABV (which you'd never guess without knowing it), and it's refined with a dry, tonic-like bitterness. This beer will always be on tap at the tasting room alongside other excellent hoppy beers, including a crisply bitter Session IPA, plus they also make some very good Belgian-style ales.

THE REGIONAL IPAS OF AMERICA

IPA might be America's—and craft beer's—flagship style, but drink around and you'll taste a lot of variation. Here is an attempt to find differences in American IPAs based on a time period or place, where it's relevant to consider the natural fluidity of styles and inspiration, and to bear in mind that the physical location of a brewery doesn't necessarily reflect the beers they brew. Consider this a discussion point, and it's updated from my book *The Best Beer in the World*, where all these sub-styles tend to have Session and Double versions.

The Original American IPA

(mid-1990s onward)

Try: Lagunitas IPA, Bear Republic Racer 5
Golden-amber with toffee-like malt in the background and orange, floral, and grapefruit-y hops in the aroma and flavor. The moderately high bitterness is balanced against the malt sweetness. Very important in all the West Coast IPAs is that it has a neutral ale yeast which doesn't produce many esters. These are the early defining American IPAs and many remain as loved examples of the style.

The West Coast IPA: The Bitter Early Years (circa 2000 onward)

Try: Green Flash Palate Wrecker, Russian River Blind Pig
The hugest of hop hits, resinous, pithy, and citrusy, with a very high bitterness, and often with very little malt body or malt flavor. A dry finish is characteristic. Typically bright and clear. Blind Pig is an enduring and excellent example with a more pronounced aroma than some of the earlier bitter-focused brews.

The West Coast IPA: The Less Bitter Middle Years (circa 2007 onward)

Try: Ballast Point Sculpin IPA, Firestone Walker Union Jack IPA
There was a shift from bitterness to flavor. Bitterness has come down a bit and there's more aroma and hop flavor. Some examples have a richer malt flavor, though they are not malty or sweet, and are usually bright. Hop aromas are now citrus pith and peel, orange, and pine. From 2020 there's been a resurgence in West Coast IPA, a kind of nostalgic thirst for it, and most of the beers (in my experience) tend to have these qualities, perhaps being unfiltered.

The West Coast IPA (circa 2010 onward)

Try: Societe The Pupil, Pizza Port Swami's
The hops have shifted a little from the bittering addition and have been added as late or dry-hops. Bodies have slimmed, bitterness is reduced slightly (though it still dominates), and aromas use a mix of classic C-hops alongside newer varieties. Typically bright. And perhaps most important in all the West Coast IPAs is that it has a neutral ale yeast which doesn't produce many esters.

The West Coast Hazy (circa 2018 onward)

Try: Cellarmaker Dobis, Sante Adairius Simpleton
Hazy is cool now, so it makes sense that all of the impact of the New England-style IPA has eventually reached the West Coast style and given us a mix of bitterness, classic C-hops plus some modern fruity ones, a little malt character, a neutral yeast, and a hazy appearance (though not full juice).

The East Coast IPA

Try: Dogfish Head 60 Minute IPA, Brooklyn East India IPA
Another early form of the style, but still around today, these are maltier than the West Coast IPAs and there's some caramel and toasty depth. Floral and citrusy instead of resinous (maybe as a result of using British or European hops as well as American ones), rounder mouthfeel, and less pronounced bitterness. These beers still exist, though the naming convention of East Coast has disappeared; today, if we see East Coast, it's more likely to mean New England-style.

The Northwest IPA

Try: Boneyard RPM IPA, Breakside IPA

These IPAs are all about the hop aroma and flavor, where the beers are top-heavy with fruity, citrusy, piney hops from the Pacific Northwest. Importantly, they are also often lightly unfiltered, which adds to the simple grain bill and gives body and a general malt richness without sweetness. Bitterness could be powerful or balanced. Modern West Coast IPAs seem to be becoming a bit more like this kind of Northwest IPA.

The Midwest IPA

Try: Bell's Two Hearted IPA, Three Floyds Alpha King

Think oranges, marmalade, orange soda, and floral hops, where a sweetness of malt gives a richness to the brew and balances the bitterness. These likely use the classic American C-hops rather than newer varieties. Most IPAs in this category are classic rather than modern.

The Colorado IPA

Try: Oskar Blues Gubna, Great Divide Titan IPA

Lots of caramel malts pack the body with a lip-sticking sweetness and a toasty, toffee-ish flavor, while the hops aggressively come in to balance that bitterness and then throw out some dank, pithy aromas. This kind of IPA has largely evolved to have a tauter malt profile, while some examples have disappeared from beer line-ups in place of modern Hazy IPAs.

The Vermont IPA

Try: The Alchemist Heady Topper, Hill Farmstead IPA

These are very aromatic with citrus and tropical fruits, and lots of floral aroma, and the hop flavor is loaded throughout. Expect a hazy and relatively full body because these beers are unfiltered, where there's a juicy mix of hop and malt to balance the brews before a dry and relatively bitter finish. These beers inspired the New England IPA but should be considered separately.

The New England IPA

Try: Tree House Julius, WeldWerks Juicy Bits

Very hazy and very full-bodied and smooth, these beers are also very aromatic, with a mix of modern and classic hops plus—importantly—a yeast which produces a lot of fruity esters. We expect lush, intense citrus and tropical fruit aromas in these beers with mango, mandarin, stone fruit, pineapple, and more. Bitterness is often medium to low. They look and taste like fruit juice.

The Modern IPA

Try: Bearded Iris Homestyle, Sierra Nevada Hazy Little Thing

In many ways this has become the new standard IPA. Lighter-bodied than a New England IPA, these are cleaner, drier, and brighter beers with an aroma that's tropical and juicy like melon, guava, passion fruit, mango, mandarin, and some pine. They often use a mix of modern and classic hops, and have a clean, dry, refreshing finish. This IPA style is hazy and intense with hops, but still balanced and the kind of beer you want several of. It seems that if we now order a beer called an "IPA," it'll be something like this.

The Flavored, Soured, or Culinary IPA

Try: Hudson Valley Amorphia, any Milkshake IPA

Not regional IPA but a sub-style that uses adjuncts to flavor the beer. It could be lactose (milk sugar) and vanilla in a milkshake IPA; it could be fruits and lactic acid in a Sour IPA; or it could just be some citrus or tropical fruits. Hops are present primarily in their fruity aromas and the bitterness is typically very low. These beers might just be a short-term fad.

SESSION IPA

"Session" is a word that's been adopted and adapted for beer's dictionary. It came from a colloquial British term used to describe drinking multiple pints of the same beer in a row—you were "having a session" or "on a session" of the same beer, usually always sub-4.0% ABV and typically a dry, bitter ale (though you'd go on a lager sesh, too). Americans took the word "session" and applied it to mean a low-alcohol beer, which evolved to become used like the word Double or Imperial; where Double means a stronger version of any beer style, Session means a lower-alcohol version. The name stuck to IPA and it became an important sub-style in the IPA category (to the detriment of Pale Ale, which was less cool than these new Session IPAs), growing enormously since its emergence, in earnest, in 2013.

Today's Session IPAs are typically between 4.0% ABV and 5.0% ABV. They represent everything that is good about an IPA—big hoppy aromas, dry body, bitterness—just with less alcohol, and they've become core beer styles for many breweries. However, considering the British usage, ironically many of these beers are unsessionable because they are intensely aromatic and bitter, meaning one or two is enough in one sitting. But, then again, the idea of the "session" has been adjusted so much that it's now become a specific style without connotations of "sessioning" the beer—it's simply an IPA with a bit less alcohol. Session IPAs are usually lighter in body and have more aroma and bitterness than a Pale Ale.

Lawson's Finest Liquids Super Session #2

Waitsfield, Vermont, USA
ABV: 4.8%

Super Session is part of a series of single-hopped Session IPAs that use the same base malt recipe but change up the hop for each version, and several of the brews have been so good that they've become regular beers in the brewery's line-up. #8 (pictured left) is brewed with Mosaic. #2 is all Amarillo and those hops give orange candy, orange peel, grapefruit, ripe peaches, and some floral aromas. The base brew is a hazy deep gold. It's got some breadier malts, which fill out the flavor, before a pronounced and lasting piney, resinous bitterness. It's a Session IPA that fully satisfies in hop flavor for the lower ABV, but, if you want more hops and more booze, then Sip of Sunshine is the brewery's best-known Double IPA. It's often talked about alongside other Vermont IPAs or NEIPAs, but this isn't a cloudy beer and it has some chewy malt, an oily citrus depth, dank and piney hops, and some juicy aromas—it's becoming a modern classic. Go to the brewery's spacious, barn-like taproom and drink through their excellent IPAs (American, Session, Double, Triple... go for all of them) with a plate of local Vermont cheeses.

Cierzo Brewing Mosaic Session IPA

Zaragoza, Spain
ABV: 4.5%

It's in a beer like this that Mosaic hops can really be showcased. Sure, they taste great when overloaded into a Double IPA, but Mosaic have a subtle side, one which is revealed when they are used moderately in a light-bodied beer. Cierzo's Mosaic Session IPA is a light yellow color with a little haze to it. Right away, the hops give you some of the fruit you expect in Mosaic: there's some fermenting mango, some over-ripe tropical fruits, apricot, and lime, then they come through with some berry notes and a little spice. The base beer is crisp, light, and refreshing, and it all ends with a long-lasting peppery bitterness. If you're in Zaragoza, then they have a taproom where they pour 24 beers. You'll also likely see their Citra-hopped IPA and a super-fruity Double IPA with added peaches.

Minoh Kozura IPA

Osaka, Japan
ABV: 4.8%

Minoh is one of the original Japanese craft breweries, founded in 1997 by Masaji Ohshita and now run by Ohshita's three daughters. There's a clarity and precision of flavor in their beers, with exceptional balance and quality across all styles, from Pale Ales to Hefeweizens, Yuzu-infused Witbier to Imperial Stouts, Pilsners to Double IPAs, and the beers all pour and present really well, with a thick creamy foam that holds its structure. Kozura is a yellow-colored Session IPA. It's light and crisp, dry like Japanese lager, with a pithy bitterness, and all through it there's a nice citrus flavor and aroma, with some stone fruit and floral hops. It's simple, unchallenging, and excellent. Also excellent is the brewery's Boss Zaru Black IPA, which manages to get a very fresh orange character into the dark brew—it's one of the best Black IPAs I've had.

Balter Brewing XPA

5.0% ABV
Currumbin, Australia

XPA has become a popular and important beer style in Australia. It's interpreted differently by different brewers, but the X part references "Extra" and that typically means "extra pale" and "extra hoppy" (though not extra bitter) when compared with a regular American Pale Ale. For me, that places it in the Session IPA category, sitting between a Pale and IPA, and being nice and bright and hop-aromatic. Balter's XPA is one of the originals of the style and definitely one of the best, routinely coming high up in the annual Hottest 100 list of Aussie brews. This XPA is pale gold; it's heavily American-hopped; and it's got lush tropical fruits, passion fruit, melon, lime, and mandarin, with some refreshingly crisp bubbles at the end. Balter's IPA is also a very good beer.

Malbygg Sopi

Reykjavik, Iceland
ABV: 4.7%

Malbygg have been brewing in Reykjavik since 2018 and they are best known for their hazy and hoppy beers, which is exactly what Sopi is. Lighter than a lot of the full-bodied hazy beers, Sopi is cloudy but crisp. It has lemon, peaches, passion fruit, and mandarin in the aroma; the body is clean and soft, and you can taste a cleanness in the water profile, which allows for a lasting, refreshing bitterness—it'd be great with some freshly grilled seafood and a squeeze of lemon. As in Norway, Finland, and Sweden, in Iceland alcohol is sold in government-owned stores—they're called Vinbudin. Far from limiting selection, these stores tend to have a great variety from local and international breweries. Several of the Malbygg beers are available in the Vinbudin, including their Citra-hopped Humar DIPA and their Galaxy IPA.

ParrotDog Rifleman

Wellington, New Zealand
ABV: 4.5%

Rifleman is a New Zealand-brewed XPA made with tropical Antipodean hops, which give you some passion fruit, papaya, grape, melon, and tangerine in the aroma. The base has some simple crackery malt and a slight chewiness, which enhances the hops, while the finish is the subtle and refreshing kind that makes it easy-going and easy-drinking, ideal for fish and chips or a bowl of kumara fries (they're like Kiwi sweet potato) with spicy mayo. ParrotDog's flagship beer is BitterBitch IPA, one with a foundation of toasty grains, some bread and caramel, a robust English bitterness, then loads of tropical hop aromas. The brewery's bar feels like a retro hotel pub, with booths, '70s wallpaper, wood cladding, old rugs, and a pool table, plus a view through to the brewery.

Woodstock Brewing Slice of Life

Cape Town, South Africa
ABV: 4.5%

Brewed with lemon peel, this light Session IPA is zingy and fresh with citrus, which is enhanced by the addition of grapefruit-y Cascade and Yellow Sub hops to give orange and lemon aromas. The malt is biscuity and simple, perfect for creating the kind of crisp and refreshing flavor that you want in this kind of beer, while the bitterness and some zesty lemon finish it off—it's an ideal summer beer. Woodstock's taproom is modern and bright, and there you'll find Californicator, their main IPA, which is 6.8% ABV with lots of tangy orangey and grapefruit hop, or Happy Pills, their German-style Pilsner, which is floral, lemony, and refreshing.

Hop Notch Brewing Hello World!

Stockholm, Sweden
ABV: 4.7%

Hop Notch started out at the end of 2018 and is a project between Jessica Heidrich and partner Magnus Karperyd. Jessica is one of Sweden's best-known brewers and a much-loved figure on the beer scene, so it's no surprise that Hop Notch has quickly seen a lot of success. Hello World! was their first beer and it's a Citra and Mosaic-hopped Session IPA. It's unfiltered for flavor and not for trendy haze, and it's a hop-led beer with grape, passion fruit, mandarin, and some citrus peel, with a lasting, refreshing bitterness. They also make Hopstart, an Amarillo-hopped IPA, which is inspired by West Coast IPAs. It immediately reminded me of the kinds of IPAs which first made me love that style. They're top-notch hoppy beers.

Whiplash Northern Lights

Dublin, Ireland
ABV: 2.8%

Whiplash call this one a Micro IPA and while it might be small in alcohol, it's definitely big in flavor. The base brew uses Vienna malt, Caramalt, oat malt, and wheat malt to combine toasty and sweeter notes with the texture and body brought by oats and wheat. It's hazy and golden. The hops are Mosaic and Vic Secret, and these both like a lighter-bodied beer and give out loads of tangerine, pomelo, apricot, melon, and blood orange, an aroma that suggests a much stronger beer. The body is light, yet satisfying, and it's not thin, with a pithy and herbal bitterness which clings, making it the sort of beer that's ultra-refreshing when you want a hop hit without the heavy alcohol.

Hoppy Road Ad Lib

Maxéville, France
ABV: 4.0%

The French palate for beer tends toward dryness and bitterness, and this beer has both those qualities. It's very lean, it cuts down to almost complete dryness, then the hops punch in and give an herbal, peppery, long-lasting finish. It's only 4.0% ABV, and the dry and bitter finish makes it extra refreshing. The hops are aromatic with lemon, orange, peach, pineapple, and some spicy, peppery qualities. Hoppy Road's Dhaki is their Double IPA and it's a clear-ish West Coast version that's pithy and very bitter, with a clean depth through the middle. Either beer would be great with a croque monsieur or a grilled cheese.

DOUBLE IPA

I remember the bitterness arms race. 120 IBUs! 180 IBUs! 1,000 IBUs! It was around 2010 and there was a general ongoing exploration of what was possible for beer: more malt, more alcohol, more barrel-aging, more hops, more bitterness. Brewers were making a statement— craft beer means flavor—and those brews were the antithesis of the light lagers they were fighting against. Double or Imperial IPAs, essentially a stronger and hoppier version of a regular IPA, were one of the first bigger beer styles to gain notoriety. Some of these were extraordinarily bitter in a way that we rarely get to taste today, thanks to a general trend toward sweeter or less bitter beer. The earliest Double IPAs were brewed in the mid-1990s, but it took until around 2010 before more Double IPAs were being brewed as core beers, with some famous names (Pliny the Elder, HopSlam, Nugget Nectar) popularizing the style. Double IPAs have become one of the most important craft-beer styles, with Hazy DIPAs extending that style and further increasing its popularity. The Hazies feature in another chapter (see pages 64–67); here, we have more of the classic, brighter, more bitter "West Coast" style of beer.

Most Double IPAs are 7.5–10.0% ABV (a sweet spot is anything in the 8.0% range). They are intensely aromatic with American hops, which could be the grapefruit and citrus of C-hops (Cascade, Centennial, Columbus) or the tropical aromas of more modern hop varieties (Mosaic, Citra). Most have a high bitterness and also a noticeable malt presence, though they shouldn't be sweet or caramelly; the best and most drinkable maintain a balance between the malt (flavor and texture), hop bitterness, and alcohol.

Russian River Pliny the Elder

Windsor, California, USA
ABV: 8.0%

I still get excited when I see Pliny the Elder. It was the beer that came to define my early curious enthusiasm for American craft beer at a time when it was almost impossible for me to drink anything like this, and it became the beer that I most wanted to drink. When I finally had the money and opportunity to travel to America, I went straight to San Francisco, straight to a bar which had it on tap, and I ordered it as my first beer. It was remarkable: a brilliant, bright gold; oily and resinous with hops; intensely aromatic and pithy, like biting into a grapefruit; then very dry, lean, and very bitter. I had two, got very drunk, and had to go to bed early, but I'll never forget that first taste, and now when I see Pliny, I order one (just saying the words: "Pint of Pliny" is exciting). Pliny the Elder is a beer that has come to define the best of what Double IPAs can be, and it's better than everyone says it is.

Magic Rock Human Cannonball

Huddersfield, England, UK
ABV: 9.2%

Human Cannonball is a bigger version of Magic Rock's regular IPA, Cannonball. It's a deep gold-amber with a light haze. The aroma is all orangey and oily in an old-school, West Coast way. As you'd expect for a beer over 9.0% ABV, it's relatively full in body, a little sweet like pound cake, but very bitter to balance it—it's bitter-sweet in a way that not many Double IPAs are today, and I love it for that reason. There's loads of orange, roasted pineapple, and peaches, pithy citrus peel, orange soda, and apricot, and it gives you a woozy mix of heady hops and warming alcohol. They also make Unhuman Cannonball, an 11.0%-ABV Triple IPA, which is dense and intense with hops.

Epic Brewing Hop Zombie

Auckland, New Zealand
ABV: 8.5%

This is one of those beers that I wish I could drink more often. It's a ripper of a DIPA, one that's a bright golden color, with a blasting aroma of pithy, dank, oily, resinous American hops, the kind that give loads of tangy grapefruit and orange. The malt is a little toasty and gives the beer a good texture, but it's mostly there just to amplify all the fruitier flavors in those hops. I really like how this one has a driving, forceful kind of bitterness, one that's prominent but never overwhelming. Epic have been making American-style IPAs for longer than any other Kiwi brewery and they remain one of the best at what they do. Also look out for their excellent all-American-hopped Armageddon IPA.

Cellarmaker Dank Williams

San Francisco, California, USA
ABV: 8.2%

I once described a beer as "dank" during a beer training session with some bar staff in Birmingham, England, and almost everyone either laughed or looked at me curiously, and it turned out that for them dank meant "cool," so my "This beer is dank" comment sounded odd to them.... The beery meaning of dank is a marijuana-like quality, a resinous, herbal, funky bitterness that sits between the familial plants of hops and cannabis. In Dank Williams, the hops are a mix of American and New Zealand varieties and they give citrus, stone fruit, and juicy tropical fruits, and then some dankness at the end, all in a bright and dry Double IPA with a load of bitterness. It's dank in both the Brummie sense and the beery one. Cellarmaker have a great taproom in SF, plus House of Pizza, where they serve up fat Detroit-style pies, which are very good with big IPAs.

Jing-A The Airpocalypse

Beijing, China
ABV: 8.8%

Because of Beijing's concerning air quality, local brewery Jing-A decided to make a Double IPA with a price exception based on the Air Quality Index (AQI), so if the AQI goes above 200—which is considered "very unhealthy"—then there's a 20 percent discount on this beer in the brewery's taprooms, and that discount goes up by 10 percent for every additional 100 points on the AQI. It's a silver lining on the smothering smog. The Airpocalypse is an amber color. It's got lots of sweeter malts, but the beer isn't sweet overall, and all the resinous, pithy, piney hops cut through it and lead into a really long, bitter finish. The air quality in Beijing is gradually improving, although I don't think any of the locals will resent reverting to full-price pints, especially for a Double IPA as good as this one.

Block 15 Brewing Sticky Hands

Corvallis, Oregon, USA
ABV: 8.1%

Sticky is a good word for some of the Pacific Northwest Double IPAs. If you've ever held handfuls of American hops, then you'll know how resinous they can feel and how they leave your fingers gummy with hop oils. When used heavily in strong beers, those hops combine with the sweetness from the malt and the slickness of alcohol to give an overall rich, oily depth that's almost tacky on your tongue. In Sticky Hands, that complex layering of hops comes from several heavy additions of hops in a beer that has a tight, lean body with a hint of sweetness, a crisp dryness, and a long bitter finish—the kind of finish that makes you smack your sticky lips. I drank a couple of these in The Pine Box, in Seattle, a brilliant bar in a former funeral home, where you sit in what used to be the chapel, and the bar and tables are made from reclaimed oak coffin cabinets.

Cervejaria Dogma Rizoma

São Paulo, Brazil
ABV: 8.3%

In 2015, three separate Brazilian gypsy brewers came together and formed Dogma. They were one of the first Brazilian brewers to put their beer in cans (it was Rizoma) and, once legislation changed in São Paulo, they were one of the first brewpubs to open in the city. They've won many awards and are rightly celebrated for their beers and their bar. I can't speak or read Portuguese, but Cervejaria Dogma's description of Rizoma tells me everything I need to know: *Uma quantidade absurda de Mosaic e Citra*. Those hops are all used late in the process for maximum aroma, and they give lots of tropical fruits, mandarin, mango, pomelo, peach, and pepper, plus a spicy kind of bitterness, all in a beer with a toasty, clean body of malt. Rizoma is a seasonal release, so might not be available all the time, but their Hop Lover is a year-round Double IPA which is also good, or look for Cafuza, their Imperial Black IPA.

Jester Luptopia

Rancagua, Chile
ABV: 9.0%

This is an unapologetically bitter and boozy West Coast Double IPA. It's a lightly hazy deep golden color. The aroma is a mix of classic American grapefruit, pine, and orange peel, plus some modern mango and tropical fruits, all intensified and amplified by the high alcohol content. The body is light for its strength, robust but not sweet, and it has some brioche-like flavor before all the hop bitterness comes through at the end, along with some boozy warmth. A decade ago, the evolution of Double IPAs was toward being as bitter as possible, whereas today's Hazy IPAs have gone in the opposite direction toward sweetness. Long live beers like Luptopia which remind us just how thrilling a heavily bittered Double IPA can be.

Pirate Life IIPA

Port Adelaide, Australia
ABV: 8.8%

Brewed early in 2015, IIPA was Pirate Life's first beer—and what a beer to start out with. Simcoe, Centennial, and Mosaic give this beer lots of juicy citrus, some tropical fruits, and some of the mango of Mosaic, as well as a strong bitterness which measures over 100 on the IBU scale. The malt is a foundation for the hops and provides balance against that bitterness. Pirate Life's Mosaic single-hop IPA is also exceptional, while their 3.5%-ABV Throwback IPA is a more moderate hoppy brew. Pirate Life have a very impressive brewery and taproom in Port Adelaide, which is big, bright, and open with 24 taps of fresh beer, a food truck, large garden, a big merch store featuring things like stubbie holders and skateboards, and there's even a barbershop. They added a Perth venue mid-2020. The brewery is now part of Carlton & United, a subsidiary of AB InBev, but that should not deter any drinkers as these beers are superb.

Boneyard Notorious IPA3

Bend, Oregon, USA
ABV: 11.5%

Notorious is a remarkable Triple IPA. I was in the brewery's tasting room when it was like an old garage (perhaps because it was in an old car workshop... they have a new pub now which is much bigger). I was passed a taster of Notorious without knowing what it was. I took a sip and loved it, and I chugged the rest of my glass, all without any clue that it was 11.5% ABV. It's honeyed and toasted, and the amount of malt in there makes the hops taste over-ripe or as if they've been stewed and cooked. It's got roast pineapple, grapefruit marmalade, sticky pine resin, Cointreau, and apricot liqueur, and while you definitely know it's strong by the time you've drunk half a glass of it, it has a dry and bitter finish which allows it to be balanced. It's a good beer to have with food and would work well with a hearty mac 'n' cheese or with some carrot cake for dessert. Boneyard's RPM IPA is their flagship beer and it's big, bright, heavy on the aroma, and light on bitterness.

HAZY PALE ALES AND IPAS

Hazy hoppy beers were the great emergent beer category of the late 2010s, and I don't think anyone could've or would've predicted that. Today, you can rarely go to a brewery or beer bar and not see a glass of cloudy orange beer. In fact, many breweries have built their business on a constant flow of juice. Juicy and hazy are two common words that are used when talking about these beers and while many of them are both juicy (in look, smell, and flavor) and hazy, the word juicy is now more widely used to describe a beer with a modern hop aroma—think melon, guava, ripe stone fruits, and a general fruitiness that's different from the grapefruit pith and pine of more traditional American hops. I call these beers "Hazy IPAs," but they are also called New England IPAs or NEIPAs, in a nod to their Northeast US origins.

Pales and IPAs range from 5.0% ABV to 7.0% ABV. Their appearance has become a defining part of their appeal; they are pale yellow to deep orange and the haze can range from cloudy lemonade to opaque orange juice. The bodies can be light and crisp, or thick and smooth, but generally the stronger the beers get, the fuller they become. The haze and the texture of these beers are a result of the wheat and oats used to make them and their high hop contents, plus they are unfiltered. These beers are impactfully aromatic with hops, usually toward the most juicy and tropical fruits, but sometimes with some danker, more resinous hops. The yeast used in these beers is usually high in esters, which adds its own fruitiness or the suggestion of sweetness—stone fruits, bubble gum, vanilla. The best are incredible, but there's a chasm between the ones that are great and the ones which are trying to approximate the look and experience of these beers. Freshness is very important—keep these beers cold and drink them fresh.

Boréale IPA du Nord-Est

Blainville, Canada
ABV: 6.0%

Brewed outside Montreal, and not far from the influence of their New England neighbors, Boréale's IPA du Nord-Est looks full and juicy, but it's not a full-fat, sticky Hazy IPA. Instead, it's in the progressive style that's light in body and dry, with a soft, cordial-like quality. The aroma is ripe with melon, mango, sweet-citrus pulp, and stone fruits, and it finishes with a dry bitterness to cut through the juiciness. Boréale's IPA is a modern beer from a brewery that started in 1987. Their classic range of beers still shows us what the early years of craft brewing looked like, with a red ale, a white beer, a blonde, a malty IPA, and a strong ale. All are good, and they have a clean, subtle balance, but it's the Hazy IPA which is becoming a new favorite.

SOMA Beer Combo

Girona, Spain
ABV: 6.0%

SOMA is a modern Spanish craft brewery who find themselves at a lot of the best European beer festivals, where their IPAs are very popular. Combo is their American-hopped Hazy IPA and it has lots of the softer exotic fruits like guava, papaya, melon, peach, sweeter mango, and mandarin, and a zesty hop depth which adds bitterness. It succeeds in plumping up the juicy fruits with an oatmeal-smooth body and still has a refreshing finish. SOMA also brew with Spanish hops and they've made a Catalonian-grown Chinook-hopped Hazy DIPA called This Chinook is Different. It looks the part and has a gentler floral, cantaloupe, and peach character compared to its in-your-face American equivalent.

Deya Brewing Steady Rolling Man

Cheltenham, England, UK
ABV: 5.2%

This should be the template for all Hazy Pale Ales. It's vibrant, verdant, exciting, and refreshing, with a brilliant balance of hop flavor and a crisp bitterness, and the brewery have nailed the difficult skill of making beers that are saturated with hops but retain an essential balance, with their Hazy DIPAs being just as good as the Pale Ales (ruinously so, in fact...). Steady Rolling Man pours a cloudy yellow. It's fresh with mandarin, mango, lemon, pithy citrus, and general tropical fruits, with those hops deeply infused all the way through to the dry, more-ish finish. Deya regularly release new brews, often hazy and hoppy, and don't overlook their excellent Hokum Stomp, a lush and delicious Porter, and the very good Tappy Pils.

Salt Citra NEIPA Jnr

Saltaire, England, UK
ABV: 4.3%

This is a Session New England IPA (a SNEIPA?) and a junior juice bomb that's exploding with Citra hops. It's a very pale lemonade-yellow in color, close to the lightest yellow you can make a beer. The Citra hops are big for such a little beer, giving loads of mango, mandarin, lychee, peach,

and passion fruit, plus a tanginess of citrus. The body is light and zings with a refreshing carbonation, yet it's also somehow full and smooth—it's a clever bit of brewing to combine the lightness and the hop depth while also being dry, satisfying, and quenching. It's also a perfect example of how the hazy style can work with a low alcohol content, and British brewers are better than anyone at getting flavor at 4.0% ABV. Salt Beer Factory have an impressive brewery taproom in an old tramshed, where you sit surrounded by the brewing vessels—there aren't many places like that to drink in Britain.

Bearded Iris Homestyle

Nashville, Tennessee, USA
ABV: 6.0%

This single-hopped Mosaic IPA is a joy of a beer. It's got the full range of Mosaic's mega fruitiness. It's soft and gentle, thanks to an addition of oats, with a finish that's dry and refreshing with a hint of fresh citrus peel. Being on the lighter side of hazy (instead of opaque juice), with a fresh tropical aroma, it seems to me that Homestyle is the perfect example of the evolution of Hazy IPA, from the initial uncontrolled hop soup excitement to a more consistent, long-term appreciation of the style. I love Homestyle (really, I do: it's one of my favorite everyday Hazy IPAs) for its full mix of Mosaic's wonderful aromas and its easy balance, which means I always want a second one. The brewery's taproom is a great place to drink: one side is like a parlor, with tiled floors, a pool table, armchairs, stools, and a wooden backbar, while the other side looks over the shiny, stainless-steel brewhouse.

O/O Brewing Naranghi

Gothenburg, Sweden
ABV: 6.8%

Naranghi is one of Sweden's top IPAs. It's got sweet apricot, orange zest, freshly squeezed orange juice, melon, stone fruits, and even a little minty, herbal character at the end. This beer is good because it's on the restrained side of the style in terms of body and richness, giving you lots of fruit without being overly sweet or heavy, and having a satisfying texture while being dry. The finish is also really nice, achieving a perfect intersection between booze, bubbles, and bitterness. If you prefer a piney IPA, then O/O Brewing's Evergreen has a similar balance and lightness to the Naranghi and then a danker, more resinous, and more herbal kind of hop character.

Hop Nation Jedi Juice

Footscray, Australia
ABV: 7.1%

In this Aussie-brewed Hazy IPA, the usual hop duo of Citra and Mosaic are joined by a couple of Kiwi hops, Riwaka and Nelson Sauvin. Together they give some complex tropical aromas with grapes, pear, papaya, guava, passion fruit, orange, and pineapple. The beer has a cloudy orange appearance, but maintains a lighter body, and isn't thick and smooth, making it more refreshing, which is also helped by having a clean and dry finish with a zing of citrus pith. Hop

Nation brew in what was once a factory where whale fat was made into candles and wax. Today, it's a large, open space with bright, spray-painted murals, where the silver tanks are in striking contrast to the old, red-brick warehouse walls. They have 15 taps of their own beer available, including some mixed-fermentation beers, inspired by the fact that the brewery founders started out as winemakers before switching to beer.

Uchu Brewing Uchu IPA

Hokuto City, Japan
ABV: 6.0%

Before they started brewing beer at Uchu, they started growing hops. To most, this would seem like an extravagant long-term plan, but the team behind the brewery were already farming. When they started adding hops (including Cascade) to their fields, they learned that their region was once known for hop-growing and that reawakened the soil as the bines began to bloom. That was in 2016 and the brewery was built next door the following year. Most of the Uchu beers are hazy hoppy brews, made mainly with modern American and Australian hops. Uchu IPA, or Space IPA, is one of the brewery's main beers and it's a Mosaic-led Hazy IPA with a rich texture of malt, a crisp and dry finish, and lots of the tangy tropical fruits and tangerine that you expect from the hop, while some of their homegrown Cascades are also added here and give some softer citrus and floral aromas.

WeldWerks Brewing Co. Juicy Bits

Greely, Colorado, USA
ABV: 6.7%

It's the concentration of hop flavor in Juicy Bits that makes it stand out. It's as if all the fruitiest hop oils have been extracted and enhanced, yet this beer has an elegance to it, a lightness for its strength, a gentleness for its body weight, and a character somewhere between orange soda and tropical juice. It's brewed with Mosaic and Citra, like most hazy beers, plus they also add El Dorado, and it's really orangey with tangerine and mandarin and some sweet pomelo, as well as creamy mango. Weldwerks also make a DDH Juicy Bits, which is even more concentrated in hop flavor, plus Extra Extra Juicy Bits, a DIPA. They are all beers worthy of their hype. (See image on page 55.)

Stamm Brewing Nevermont Magic Dust

Moscow, Russia
ABV: 7.0%

Hazy IPAs are everywhere now. It's a sign of the influence of American brewing that no matter where you find a craft brewery, you find a Hazy IPA. It makes sense: the classic West Coast IPA is intense and bitter, whereas these modern IPAs are sweet, smooth, and juicy, obvious in their citrus fruitiness. Stamm's Nevermont Magic Dust suits that smooth and juicy description perfectly. It's got a lightness to the body, plenty of tropical fruits, some sweet pineapple, and a quench of bitterness at the end. Stamm's My Three Hops (those being Idaho 7, plus Citra and Mosaic) is their Hazy DIPA.

Abyss Brewing Zen NEIPA

Lewes, England, UK
ABV: 6.0%

In the time between starting to write this book and finishing it, a lot happened. Mostly there was the global pandemic, but from a personal perspective, I moved from East London to go and live by the sea in Eastbourne. That's given me a whole new choice of local brewers, and at about the same time I was decorating my new place, Abyss were building their new brewery up the road from me in Lewes, East Sussex. I'm very excited to have Abyss nearby as I love their beers. Zen has lots of pink grapefruit, tangerine, fermented pineapple, and creamy coconut, and it's all so nicely balanced and smooth. I also really like their Super Pale, a low-ABV, full-flavor Pale Ale. Lewes has become a small beer destination, being home to Abyss, Beak, and Harvey's (for a classic Bitter) and with Burning Sky nearby, too.

Seoul Brewery Pale Blue Dot

Seoul, South Korea
ABV: 7.0%

Pale Blue Dot is Seoul Brewery's main IPA and it's on the juicy side of the hazy style. It has a full texture, but isn't at all heavy, and remains light to drink. The haziness in the beer does the important job of plumping up the fruitiness in the hops (these are Citra, Mosaic, and El Dorado), where you get melon, clementine, guava, and a little tangy citrus at the edges, all more restrained than some of the American versions and being really fresh, clean, and vibrant. Seoul Brewery have a smart, dark brewpub where you can sit next to the brew kit while drinking from a range of hop-forward beers, plus a coconut, vanilla, and lactose Porter. Seoul has become one of the destination beer cities in the whole of Asia, a place where the culture of eating and drinking out together has created a city of brilliant beer experiences, as there's now an overwhelming number of craft beer bars and quality breweries.

To Øl CPH Tricerahops

Copenhagen, Denmark
ABV: 6.2%

If Tricerahops were a fish, it'd still be flapping around on the plate when it was served to you, it's that fresh. I wish I could take credit for that line, but it's how To Øl describe this yellow-gold, triple dry-hopped IPA. The hops are Amarillo, Citra, Mosaic, and Simcoe, and they give everything you'd expect in this kind of mega-hopped beer. It's a tropical smoothie with some savory notes in the background. The body is light and a little sweet, and it ends with enough dryness to keep this golden hop juice (another one I can't take credit for) well balanced. To Øl was started by Tore Gynther, who went from homebrewer to gypsy brewer and later opened Brus, a brewpub in Copenhagen (if you see To Øl CPH, then it's brewed at Brus) with super-fresh beer poured from tank and a kitchen that mixes modern European and Asian influences.

HAZY DIPA

Hazy DIPAs have become a craft beer phenomenon. These opaque DIPAs are strong, saturated in hops, ripe with tropical fruit aromas, and thick like juice. Even more so than Hazy Pales and IPAs, the Hazy DIPA—because it's always written DIPA and, yes, you can say "Dipper" if you wish—has come to define a moment in beer's perpetual flow and evolution. A decade ago, IPAs were out-IBU-ing each other, getting ever more bitter; now they're trying to squeeze as much juicy hop fruitiness into the beers as possible. It's a difficult thing to do, to achieve the pure fresh-fruit flavor and aroma that you expect in these beers, so the best deserve to be applauded. They are also a joy to drink: there's something so unbeer-like about them that makes them incredibly appealing, in both appearance and flavor.

Hazy DIPAs are usually between 7.5% ABV and 9.0% ABV. They are cloudy with wheat and oats in the grain bill, plus the density of hops and their natural polyphenols which together leave a haze. Some are celebrated for their soft and "pillowy" mouthfeel, something that's outrageously smooth and almost creamy to drink, while I think that the best need to have balance and finish well, or they can be too sweet and claggy. That ending can come from bitterness, dryness, alcohol, a slight acidity, or carbonation, though it's usually a combo of those elements. Almost all use hops like Citra and Mosaic to maximize the juice, giving soft citrus, stone fruits, melon, and a whole bowl of tropical fruits, and the yeast will be prominent in fruity and sweet esters, such as apricot and vanilla.

The Alchemist Heady Topper

Stowe, Vermont, USA
ABV: 8.0%

Heady Topper is often cited as the archetypal hazy New England-style DIPA, but I don't believe that. Sure, Heady is a hazy Double IPA, and it comes from New England, but have you drunk Heady and compared it to, say, a Tree House DIPA? Heady Topper, to which the name sort of alludes, was inspired by weed. Wafts of heady, green, dank, pungent hops, a hazy appearance, a resinous, bitter finish... plus it has a lot of stone fruit around it, some from hops and some from yeast. Most of the newer DIPAs are thick and abundantly tropical, morphed from Heady (which likely provided some inspiration in the first place) into something way gaudier and attention-grabbing, and pushed to the limits of how much hop can be pulped into your pint glass. I think The Alchemist make some of the best DIPAs in the region and I like them for being refined and restrained.

Verdant Brewing Co. Putty

Penryn, England, UK
ABV: 8.0%

Verdant are one of the great British beer success stories of recent years, growing from a tiny 200-liter system in 2014 into an impressive 3,500-liter system in 2020. Their success has been built on great beer and the demand it's created. Their regular range goes from the 4.5%-ABV Light Bulb via Bloom, a 6.5%-ABV IPA, to Pulp, their 8.0%-ABV DIPA—all are in the modern hazy style and all are very good. Putty is an annual January release which is always cheered and chased by British beer geeks (myself included). Mosaic, Galaxy, and Azacca provide all the hop fruitiness in the beer, which is the expected tropical smoothie, plus some sweeter vanilla cream aromas from the yeast and a soft citrus and stone-fruit middle. The malt bill, which gives a bright orange beer, is made up of Golden Promise malts, wheat, and oats, giving a lush, silky, smooth texture. Get some Putty in your hands whenever you see it.

Tree House Haze

Charlton, MA, USA
ABV: 8.2%

Tree House's beers have come to define the New England IPA, and these are the beers that other brewers all around the world are looking to emulate. They are celebrated for the way they can saturate their beers with hop flavor and also make them bloom with pure fruit aromas. They are celebrated for the way the beers look, with their luminous, rich orange colors. And they are celebrated for the texture they manage to get into their beers. In many ways, it's this texture—a creamy, soft, pillowy, almost silkiness—which others try hardest to get right. Julius is their flagship Hazy IPA and it's like tangerines, peaches, and mangoes blended until impossibly smooth, all with a lush balance and refreshing finish. Haze is their go-to DIPA and it's a mouthwatering basket of tropical fruits, loads of peaches and passion fruit, creamy mango, then it's got a piney or resinous bitterness to keep it easy-drinking for such an intensely flavored beer. Super impressive and worth the hype.

Brasserie Pophin DIPA Mosaic

Vaumort, France
ABV: 8.0%

Brewed in a barn next to his parents' farm, Arnaud Pophin's beers are some of France's best rated and most wanted. Rightly so, as they are exceptional, especially the single-hopped DIPAs. Their DIPA Mosaic was the kind of beer that I kept going back for more of, dumbfounded by how something could smell so damn delicious. I love Mosaic hops, and this is one of the best beers I've had that's made with them: plump mango, dried mango, ludicrous amounts of tropical fruits, something funky like fermenting pineapple, and a beautiful intensity. The body of the beer was incredibly light and soft, made impressive by being 8.0% ABV. Pophin's Icauna makes use of a more local flavor—there aren't many Mosaic hops grown in the middle of France—by using malt grown on his family farm (though it does also add modern, fruity hops).

Brew Your Mind Evermind

Szekszárd, Hungary
ABV: 8.2%

Grams per liter, or g/l, has become one of the new measures used by brewers and sought by beer geeks. It refers to the quantity of hops used per liter of beer, with 20–30g/liter at the high end of what can maximally be mixed into a brew. Evermind is brewed with 24g/liter of both hop pellets and lupulin powder (a powder made from concentrated lupulin resins and oils used to give the freshest aroma), and it's got the sort of hop aroma that makes you chuckle when you take a deep sniff: pure fruit, canned mandarins, over-ripe mango, a mush of tasty tropical fruits, and some honeydew melon. The beer is oily and slick with hops, and the body is full and smooth, with some sweetness giving it extra texture and some residual sticky-lip sweetness, before it ends with a little cut of carbonation.

Hocus Pocus Overdrive

Rio de Janeiro, Brazil
ABV: 8.2%

It's a magic trick how this beer remains so light to drink for its high strength. In fact, all the best examples of this style have a similar lightness and a soft and silky texture. Hocus Pocus were one of Brazil's first breweries to make a New England-style IPA, and Overdrive has become one of the top-rated beers in the whole country. It uses Citra hops and a yeast known for producing fruity esters, and together these give lots of peaches, apricots, sweet orange, some gooseberry, even some strawberry or cherry, and a little pine or herbal bitterness at the end. It's smooth, it's balanced, it's ripe in its fruitiness, it's juicy, and it's delicious. If this one isn't quite enough for you, then they also make some 10.0%-ABV hazy Triple IPAs.

Lervig Supersonic

Stavanger, Norway
ABV: 8.5%

Citra hops lead the way in Supersonic, backed up by some Amarillo, Simcoe, and Enigma, and it's a blast of citrus fruits, some pineapple, mango, and a little tangerine. Wheat and oats fatten out the beer and give it body without sweetness,

and, as is common in these beers, that enriched body helps to enhance the fruitiness from the hops. To cut it with balance, there's a good combination of carbonation, alcohol, dryness, and bitterness, giving you a big DIPA that soars to a supersonic boom of brilliance. If this is your kind of beer, then also look for Lervig's Tasty Juice, a DDH IPA with Citra, Mosaic, and Equinox, or their regular seasonal specials.

Cabin Brewing Company Super Duper Saturation

Calgary, Canada
ABV: 8.0%

I like a brewery that gives me progression in my drinking. At Cabin you can start with Saturation, a juicy and fresh little 4.0%-ABV Session Ale. Then there's Super Saturation, their core Hazy Pale Ale, which is lush and smooth with tropical fruit and a lovely lightness at the end. Then there's Super Duper Saturation, which is fully saturated with Citra, Simcoe, and Amarillo, and they give it a density of fruits—citrus, mango, pineapple, apricot. It's super-duper drinkable, thanks to its lingering dryness and how you just don't want to stop tasting those hops. You can saturate yourself and drink all the beer in their taproom, which is one of the smartest I've seen, and where you might also find Summer Saturation or Single Saturation.

Other Half All Green Everything

Brooklyn, New York, USA
ABV: 10.5%

All Green Everything is a Triple IPA pummeling in with a 10.5% ABV. It's double dry-hopped and uses Amarillo, Citra, Mosaic, and Motueka. It's an astonishing beer, the sort of beer that just wows you with its aroma and flavor, with its insane fruitiness, its thick and smooth body, and its juice-like qualities, and in how it's somehow refreshingly dry at the end. In my (hazy) experience, it's a beer that you'll drink in seconds, gulping joyfully, and it's only when you've nearly finished a glass of it that you'll realize how strong it is and you'll be left woozy, warmed, and lightheaded, as if in a foggy-hoppy daydream. Talking of hoppy daydreams, Other Half make a series of Daydream Oatmeal Cream IPAs which use oats and lactose. These are creamy, but not sweet, unbelievably smooth like a purée, dry, and a little boozy at the end—it's intense and excellent. If you're in Brooklyn, then go to the taproom; just watch out, as almost no one leaves there sober or coherent.

Boneface The Big Unit

Upper Hutt, New Zealand
ABV: 8.6%

The Unit is Boneface's New Zealand-hopped IPA, and the brewery take that and make it much bigger in The Big Unit. That supersizing squeezes loads more pungent tropical fruit from the hops, with strong kiwi, grape, and some tangy grapefruit. It has a great balance for such a big beer and the body is sweet and lush, and it ends with some booze heat and bitterness. Boneface have a large industrial brewhouse with a taproom and full kitchen menu, so you can visit and drink the beers as fresh as possible, which is important with these Hazy DIPAs. While you're there, check out The Unit to see how they went from IPA to DIPA, and then see if Mega Unit is on, as it's a 10.5%-ABV Triple DIPA. Just don't go there expecting gentle, light-tasting beers—Boneface deal in big, bold brews.

ENGLISH PALE ALE AND IPA

If you speak to almost any beer-drinker today and say "IPA," they will think of citrusy, tropical, and piney American or Antipodean hops. Yet it was traditional English-brewed India Pale Ales, originating in Burton upon Trent and brewed with English hops, which created this type of beer in the 1800s, and, as you can read on pages 84–85, it's a style that has been in constant evolution. The original India Pale Ales were robustly bitter and relatively strong, mellowing over the many months between the day they were brewed and the day they were drunk. Over time, and as it was drunk more in Britain as a fresh and unaged beer, it got weaker and less bitter and it transitioned toward everyday-drinking Pale Ales and Bitters, which have continued to get weaker. Today, it's an under-represented beer style, with American hops preferred over English ones, but modern English-hopped beers can have a wonderful complexity to them.

English Pale Ales and IPAs range from 4.5% ABV to 6.5% ABV (there are seldom any English DIPAs, as at that strength they veer toward Barley Wines). They are defined by their ingredients, which will be pale malts (probably from England) and traditional English hops. The malts will give a toasty, bready, chewy, and complex depth to the brews and the best will certainly have a full malt flavor, though shouldn't be sweet or caramelly. The hops used will be names like Goldings, Fuggles, Challenger, Target, and First Gold, and they give dried citrus peel, hop sack, subtle stone fruits, hedgerow fruits, hard herbs, and a spicy or peppery quality. When used well, they give a deep and clean bitterness and also a complex aroma which demands you give it some attention, rather than being immediately obvious like a Citra or Mosaic. They are never as impactful or aromatic as an American IPA; instead, their success lies in how they balance malt and hop and have a rich depth of both.

Ramsgate Brewery Gadds' No.3

Ramsgate, England, UK
ABV: 5.0%

As a Man of Kent, this beer holds a patriotic appeal for me. The dominant initial flavor in this Pale Ale is from the East Kent Goldings hops, which are grown near the brewery. It's a hop that's nowhere near as popular or well-known as names like Galaxy or Citra but is peerless in its own special way. In No.3, it gives an enticing mix of bitter lemon, tangy marmalade, pepper, hop sack, cumin, and honeysuckle aroma and flavor, plus an intense, lasting bitterness like the best kind of West Coast IPA. The malt has just the right amount of toastiness and a fullness to balance the hops—it's the kind of beer that has a focused and refined flavor, uncomplicated and pure in its showcasing of the English hops and malt. No.3 is one of my favorite beers.

Green Man Brewing IPA

Asheville, North Carolina, USA
ABV: 6.2%

I went to Asheville with high expectations and left a few days later considering it one of the best beer cities in America and the world. There's a density of breweries there that you can't find elsewhere, and they're packed in and close to each other, which means you can visit a dozen great places without ever walking for more than a few minutes at a time. They all have their own (often large) spaces and everywhere is busy with different crowds and vibes, so there's a perfect brewery for everyone in Asheville. The vibe in Green Man's Dirty Jack's, the original tasting room, is like a cozy house party with old friends. It's got a lived-in appearance with brewery stickers, TVs, beery bric-a-brac, lots of yodas, 12 taps of beer, and a plaque above the taps reading: "I love this bar." Their core beers are English-inspired with a nice malty ESB and this IPA, which is a tasty contrast to all the tropical-scented IPAs poured everywhere else. It's orange-amber in color with a lacy white foam. The balance is great, with plenty of chewy and biscuity malts, some toffee, a lengthy and powerful bitterness, and a depth of tangy, orangey, tea-like hops. It's a taste of England in a dive bar in Asheville.

LeVel33 India Pale Ale

Singapore
ABV: 4.5%

LeVel33 is the world's highest urban brewery, situated on the 33rd floor of Singapore's Marina Bay Financial Center. It's unquestionably one of the most impressively located breweries on the planet. The beers are all good without wowing, but then it's the surroundings that add the wow factor. Sitting on the smart outside deck, with the stunning view of the Marina Bay Sands and the city's skyline, I didn't expect my penthouse pint of their India Pale Ale to give me a taste of East Kent, but that's exactly what happened, as it reminded me of Ramsgate Brewery's No.3. Hazy amber, some toast and toffee and a rich malt base, then lots of spicy, herbal, orangey hops with a deep bitterness. As I was drinking, I saw a small cricket pitch through a gap in some skyscrapers and felt an odd pang of homesickness.

Nynäshamns Ångbryggeri Indianviken Pale Ale

Nynäshamn, Sweden
ABV: 6.2%

The brewery's website auto-translates this beer's information to tell me that it's a traditional India Pale Ale with "large bumblebees and heavy afterbars" and it adds that the beer is generously "dry-humbled".... What I can more accurately tell you is that this is a beautiful, amber-colored beer, one that glows in the glass and one that, after a single glance, will tell you to expect all of its toasty, bready malt. The English hops in this one give orange, white pepper, apricot, and some piney notes (but no bumblebees...). It's bitter, but the malt balances it well. Swedish brewers are often very good at getting a complex depth of malt into their beers, especially in English styles of beer, and this is a fine example of that, as is Nynäshamns's best-selling Bedarö Bitter.

Carakale Pale Ale

Fuheis, Jordan
ABV: 6.5%

Carakale was Jordan's first craft brewery and they started with the big ambition of creating a beer culture in their country. Yazan Karadsheh studied engineering in Boulder, Colorado, but a chance flick through a beer book showed him that his country had no beers mentioned. It became his mission to change that. It started with homebrewing, then studying brewing, then interning at breweries, and eventually returning home to build his own brewery. Carakale's core beers are a Lager, Blonde, and Pale Ale. The Pale Ale is a rich amber color from the use of colored malts. Those malts dominate the taste with bread, toffee, toasted malts, and honey, almost like a Sierra Nevada or an English ESB, with some sweetness which suits local tastes. The hops are subtle and balanced, being bitter enough and giving a hint of some herbal, peppery depth. Carakale make a wider range of seasonal brews and if you want a beer with a local flavor, then they have a sour with pomegranate and blood orange, and also an Imperial Porter made with dates, Bedouin coffee, and cardamom. Hopefully Yazan will be happy that his country's beer is now represented in the beer books.

The Cheshire Brewhouse Govinda

Congleton, England, UK
ABV: 6.8%

Govinda is a remarkable beer and a heritage recipe of a Burton upon Trent-brewed India Pale Ale from 1843. It uses the heritage malt Chevallier and a lot of East Kent Goldings hops. It goes through a three-hour mash and then a three-hour boil, both processes taking about three times as long as a modern IPA. All that mashing and boiling turns the beer a deep amber color. The malt is caramelized and rich, a little sweet at first, but then the hops power through with marmalade, baked pears, dried stone fruits, some bitter honey, and a warming spiciness. It's the sort of beer that you want to open, pour out, and think about—you don't just open and chug a beer like this, as it gives us the opportunity to consider just how much the IPA has evolved over the past 200 years.

Circle Brewing Archetype Historical IPA

Austin, Texas, USA
ABV: 7.5%

Those old Pale Ales brewed in Burton-upon-Trent or London were matured for months in big wooden barrels, shipped thousands of miles, crossing the equator twice, arrived in India and were then bottled, and that time and the journey markedly changed the beers. To replicate an historical taste of IPA, Circle Brewing worked for months to develop the recipe for Archetype. They sourced a specialty maltster to recreate Burton White Malt. They only use East Kent Goldings hops and add them according to old recipes. They store the beer in oak barrels for four months, to match the length of the voyage to India, and they add some *Brettanomyces* wild yeast to mimic the maturation. It's a pale golden beer. The aroma is of lemony *brett* at first with some barrel and some floral, orangey hops. It has a lightness to the body and a dryness, and a lively carbonation which lifts it. The hops and *brett* give this beer a richness and elegance of flavor, then it's peppery and persistently bitter at the end. As the bottle label says, it's a beer 200 years in the making and it's something that you drink so you can think about it, consider it, swirl and sip it, and wonder: what were India Pale Ales really like?

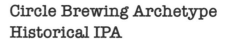

PACIFIC PALE ALE, IPAS, AND SUMMER ALES

The hops grown in Australia and New Zealand tend to be more tropical than the big citrus of American hops, and they are prized everywhere for those aromatics and are often used as a mix with American hops to juice more fruitiness into the beers. By using only their own local hops, Aussie and Kiwi brewers have developed their own kinds of Pale Ales and IPAs, which are distinct from American brews, and we can call these Pacific Pales and IPAs. Those beers are also joined by the Australian Summer Ale, a low-alcohol, light-bodied ale with a fresh, fruity, floral, Aussie-hopped aroma—it's a very popular local style and one of a few homegrown beers developed by Antipodean brewers. Other regional styles include New Zealand Pilsner, "Mids" (3.5%-ABV session beers), XPA (Extra Pale Ales, similar to a Session IPA), and a prevalence in Australia of Red IPAs.

Summer Ales and Pacific Pale Ales and IPAs have similar characteristics to American Pales and IPAs, though they'll be a little lower in alcohol overall, typically ranging from 4.4% ABV to 7.0% ABV. They are usually light in malt, especially the Summer Ales, and this adds to their refreshing quality. It's the hop aroma and flavor that really define these beers, and by using Australian and New Zealand hops they have a mix of mango, passion fruit, pineapple, guava, pomelo, melon, apricot, grapefruit, grapes, and gooseberries. They are usually fresh and vibrant, not thick and smoothie-like.

Bissell Brothers Reciprocal

Portland, Maine, USA
ABV: 7.3%

Reciprocal is a double dry-hopped Australian Hazy Double IPA. Australian hops are prized in the new Hazy IPA styles because they are so juicy and tropical and bring with them passion fruit, ripe mango, and sweet citrus flavors. Hops such as Galaxy and Ella are typically used alongside American hops like Citra and Mosaic, but, in Reciprocal, it's an all-Aussie affair. Ella, Summer, and Vic Secret give this beer an abundantly juicy aroma that's like a delicious, boozy tropical smoothie. There's some sweet stone fruit, a lot of tangerine, some guava and grapefruit, a resinous kind of bitterness, and some alcohol warmth. Bissell Brothers are one of the best Hazy IPA brewers around and their Swish DIPA was one of the beers that convinced me just how good this style could be. The brewery has two locations: one focuses on hops and the other on mixed-fermentation and barrels.

Stone & Wood Pacific Ale

Byron Bay, Australia
ABV: 4.4%

This is the quintessential example of an Australian Summer Ale. It's brewed with Australian barley and wheat, plus loads of Tasmania-grown Galaxy hops. The base of the brew looks like a glass of sunshine—it's a beautiful, hazy yellow. It's both light and textured, making it simultaneously super-refreshing and pleasingly satisfying to drink. The bitterness is low, but the hop flavor and aroma are high, and that's what makes this beer stand out, with the Galaxy hops giving a fresh, tropical, passion-fruit, and mango aroma. It's such a good beer and one designed to be drunk while sitting in the sun, having just left the ocean or the beach. They also brew Cloud Catcher, a 5.0%-ABV Pacific Pale Ale brewed with Galaxy, Ella, and Enigma.

Fork Brewcorp Hyperlocal

Wellington, New Zealand
ABV: 5.9%

Fork Brewcorp, based at the Fork & Brewer brewpub in Wellington, won New Zealand's champion small brewery of the year in both 2018 and 2019, a show of their consistent brilliance, and an achievement made even more impressive when you see that they always have around 40 taps of their own beer. *Forty*. Few other brewpubs or breweries can compete with that many beers, or with their high quality across a complete mix of styles. Hyperlocal has become their core NZ Pale Ale. It's a lightly hazy amber brew made with all-New Zealand malts, which give the beer the kind of plump sweetness that makes the tropical-scented hops taste even more fruity and lush. The hops in this beer are Riwaka and Nelson Sauvin, and these bring passion fruit, gooseberry, mango, and grapefruit. As well as being brilliant brewers and great brewpub runners, the guys behind Fork are also top blokes. Go visit them if you're in Welly.

Gage Roads Single Fin

Palmyra, Australia
ABV: 4.5%

Summer Ale is an Australian style that deserves more attention worldwide. It's usually very pale in color, unfiltered, and dry-hopped with the most tropical Aussie hops, plus it's under 5.0% ABV. It works because it's the sort of beer to buy by the slab and keep in the fridge at all times, especially through the long, hot summer when you'll want to grab a cold can and crack it open while watching the cricket or playing in the yard. In Single Fin, Galaxy and Enigma hops give mango, soft stone fruit, passion fruit, and melon. The beer has a slightly honeyed body of malt and a really crisp, clean finish. It's great with fresh seafood or spicy Southeast Asian salads.

Garage Project Pernicious Weed

Wellington, New Zealand
ABV: 8.0%

Hops have been grown in New Zealand since the 1840s, specifically in the region of Nelson in the north of South Island, where they were planted by British and German settlers. By the end of the century there were also American Cluster hops, but a disease called black root rot wiped out many acres, forcing the New Zealand brewers to set up a Hop Research Committee. Cluster and English Fuggle were crossbred to give distinct new Kiwi varieties, which were then bred further to give the famous varieties we know around the world, including Nelson Sauvin, Motueka, and Riwaka. In Pernicious Weed, a golden Double IPA, Garage Project use Nelson Sauvin and Rakau, and these give lots of grapefruit, mango, orange, citrus peel, some roasted pineapple, and a lasting, gripping kind of bitterness.

Hill Farmstead Double Galaxy

Greensboro, Vermont, USA
ABV: 8.0%

Hill Farmstead's founder, Shaun Hill, makes annual trips to the southern hemisphere hop harvest to select the hops he wants to use in his brews. Back home, he and his team make a series of single-hopped beers with Australian and New Zealand hops (and American ones, too), including Riwaka, Motueka, Nelson Sauvin, and Galaxy. These beers are singular in their hop profiles and their unmatched ability to squeeze and saturate the hop flavor and aroma while also remaining elegant and complex. With Double Galaxy, an 8% ABV DIPA, you get an intense hit of Galaxy aromas with condensed tropical fruits, tangerine, over-ripe pineapple, stewed melon, then depths of resinous, pithy, and even grassy hops with a long, clean bitterness. The body has a slick fullness that helps to fatten the fruitiness, while the carbonation is light—together they give a mouthfeel that's become defining of a Hill Farmstead beer.

Brewlander & Co. Hope

Singapore, Singapore
ABV: 4.5%

In Chinatown Complex, a hawker center in Singapore, you've got over 200 food stalls cooking a delicious variety of dishes. Walk all through the center and, if you know where you're going, you'll also find a couple of beer bars. I was looking in the fridges of one of these bars, after something local, when I happened to meet John Wei, who owns Brewlander. They had one bottle of his beer left, a Saison called Pride. It was refreshingly fragrant with citrus peel and phenolic spice, plus a bright dryness, and I took the beer away and ordered a plate of steamed dumplings with a Szechuan chili oil—it was great to have such a good beer with good food, and the experience brought together the old and affordable traditions of the hawker center and the modern thirst for craft beer. I've since also had Brewlander's Hope, a gentle, refreshing, easy-going Summer Ale made with Kiwi hops for a lightly tropical, grape, and stone-fruit aroma and a crisp, lager-like finish. I'd order a spicy laksa with that one.

RED IPA

As IPAs came to dominate the American craft beer market, so brewers began looking for more variations on the style and that led to a spectrum of different-colored IPAs: White, Gold, Red, Brown, and Black. Red IPAs are similar to regular American IPAs, but they are made with more specialty and caramel malts, which gives the beer its different color and a range of nutty, toasty, and caramelized flavors. The hop varieties used are more commonly the older C-hops like Cascade, Centennial, and Chinook, plus Simcoe and Amarillo. Those hops interact with the darker malts in a different way to how they do with only pale base malts, giving less of the brighter, freshly squeezed citrus aromas and more of a tangy cooked citrus, plus pine and resinous herbs.

The Pacific Northwest Red is a style often seen in the Pacific Northwest, where the beers are made with all PNW ingredients and are hop-heavy with resinous, piney, and grapefruit-pithy hops. In California, the Reds tend to be lighter bodied and more bitter. Midwest Reds are deeply bitter and sticky with C-hops, while East Coast Reds often have more maltiness, showing that there's still some regionality in IPA brewing. It's in Australia that this style really dominates and it's a common beer for most breweries to make. Typically for this style, the beers are 6.0–7.5% ABV, and range in color from amber to mahogany.

Modus Operandi Former Tenant

Mona Vale, Australia
ABV: 7.8%

This beer looks red and smells green. The specialty malts used in Former Tenant give it some caramel, bread, and a lasting sweetness, while the hops—Mosaic and Galaxy—give you their expected tropical fruits and some caramelized citrus and pine, and they're turned a little funky and dank with all the malt in the brew. That funky dankness is also a wink toward the beer's name, because the previous occupier of the brewery's building was engaged in "illegal horticultural endeavors." The space is better used today, and it's a smart brewpub filled with fresh, cold beer, plus fresh hot pizzas, burgers, and wings. Modus Operandi brew a range of beers, with a Session Pale, Pale Ale, and IPA in their core range, but it's Former Tenant for which the brewery is best known.

Nova Runda Fireball

Zagreb, Croatia
ABV: 6.2%

Brewed with Comet hops, Fireball blasts out as a deep red brew with some rich caramelized malt, giving toffee apples, honeycomb (cinder) toffee, and bitter molasses (black treacle), which add a warming depth befitting this beer's end-of-year seasonal release. The hops are resinous, herbal, pithy, and grapefruit-y, and leave a lot of bitterness that combines with the malt bitterness. Nova Runda were one of Croatia's first craft breweries and, after years of gypsy brewing, opened their own brewery in 2019. Their main beer, an American Pale Ale brewed with Citra, Magnum, and Cascade, is a floral, piney, and grapefruit-y brew that's a classic version of the style. Zagreb has a lot of craft beer bars, and while you might not go there specifically for beer, if you are there, then you'll be happy with the variety.

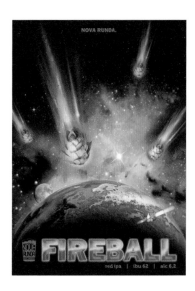

Maine Beer Co. Zoe

Freeport, Maine, USA
ABV: 7.2%

Zoe is an American Amber Ale and it's the sort of beer that's able to combine old-school maltiness—a mix of caramel malts that give a nuttiness, some hints of roasted malts and malt loaf, and lots of underlying toastiness—with the pithy, roasted citrus and resinous pine of Centennial, Simcoe, and Columbus hops. What's great about this beer is how those bigger malts are never heavy or sweet, allowing the hops to lift it up and then balance it with a deep bitterness. Maine Beer Co. have the motto "Do What's Right"—they support a lot of charities and are environmentally conscious, something you can see from their solar panel-clad brewery. Go to the large, bright taproom if you get the chance, as they brew many excellent beers.

Hop Federation Red IPA

Riwaka, New Zealand
ABV: 6.4%

Brewed in New Zealand's hop region, this Red IPA uses local Cascade, Motueka, and Southern Cross, plus American Simcoe hops. These hops would usually emit lush tropical fruits, but when combined with the darker caramelized malts—which give a slightly roasted, teacake, and toast sweetness—they turn more jammy than juicy, with marmalade, roasted grapefruit, baked lemon, and some fresher pithy pomelo flavors. This is a beer that's ideal paired with charred and roasted meats and vegetables, or try it with Korean wings or a barbecue.

Parallel 49 Ruby Tears

Vancouver, Canada
ABV: 6.0%

A classic C-hop combination of Cascade, Centennial, and Columbus gives Ruby Tears its dominant aroma of grapefruit, marmalade, and a dank, resinous pine. The malt base has some crystal malt sweetness, but it's gentle and soft in the body, balanced between the bready base malts and the honeyed and caramelized specialty malts. It comes together as a complex, hearty, yet easy-drinking Northwest Red Ale, and is a really good example of the style. Parallel 49's tasting room is a large space with shared benches and street food. It's a good place to get a flight of beers and some snacks—I always think hoppy reds are great with slow-cooked meats, smoked food, and mac 'n' cheese. Now, as a vegetarian, I had Ruby Tears with a spicy jackfruit taco, and it was very good.

Pivovar Clock Twist

Potštejn, Czech Republic
ABV: 6.2%

Clock has a smart, modern, beer hall-style taproom 120 miles (200km) east of Prague where you can sit next to the tanks if you're inside, or you can sit in the outside courtyard. They have a mix of classic Czech-style lagers, plus some regular IPAs and a rotating range of specials. It's this co-existence of lager and IPA that is coming to define Czech craft beer, where the beers stand out because of their excellent abilities to balance big flavors. Twist is a great example of a beer which achieves that balance. It's a deep amber color, hazy, with some caramelized citrus and caramelized malts, tangy orange, sweet berries, and a deep bitterness, but all in harmony.

Six String Brewing Double Dark Red IPA

Erina, Australia
ABV: 10.0%

Six String's headline brew is Dark Red IPA which, as the name suggests, is a dark red color. It rocks with toasty caramel, some dark unsweetened chocolate, and a really smooth texture, with hops that are loud and in-your-face, being citrusy and resinous, but without dominating the overall balance of flavor. In their Double Dark Red IPA, they've doubled the malts and trebled the hops and turned it up to 11 (that doesn't quite work when the ABV is 10.0% but, whatever, I'm sticking with it). It's rich, heavy, boozy; there's molasses (black treacle), dried fruit, some savory roast, booze, and tons of bitterness (literally: it's 100 IBU), and the hops are like grapefruit marmalade, caramelized grapefruit, orange liqueur, and sticky ginger cake. It's a big, intense, amplified smash hit of a Red IPA.

BLACK IPA

It was the oxymoronic name that initially made Black IPAs stand out: how could an India *Pale Ale* be *Black*? It led more brewers to attempt the style, and to attempt the trick of brewing beers that looked dark but tasted light. For a few years—2010–2015 were probably peak Black IPA years—they were popular, but, as other kinds of IPA have emerged, like Session IPAs and all the Hazies, the Black ones have been left behind. However, that seems to be changing and there are once again more Black IPAs being brewed. Anecdotally, many newer Black IPAs are quite strong and these are now moving toward being like a dark, Hazy-style IPA, where the smooth creaminess of malt gives the beers lots of texture and fills out the fruity hop flavors.

The best Black IPAs have a fullness and richness of body, with just the merest hint of dark grain flavor. Instead of roastiness, the malts are toasty, chewy almost, with the dark malts giving a hint of savoriness. It's not easy to make a Black IPA which smells like tropical fruits, and there's something in how the fruitiest hops interact with the darker malts that changes their aromas, but these beers can still produce very prominent citrus and pine qualities. They usually range from 6.0% ABV to 8.0% ABV, but you'll also see Session-strength and Imperial-strength versions.

Pivovar Raven Jet Black IPA

Pilsen, Czech Republic
ABV: 6.0%

This is one of the finest-looking Black IPAs you'll ever see, especially when it's poured properly from a Czech beer tap. It's the foam that makes it beautiful: creamy, smooth, and almost white against the near-black beer beneath it. Foam is one of the most under-appreciated parts of a beer pour, and I think it deserves more attention. It's also important here because a lot of the nicest hop aromas are hanging out in that foam. The hops are like citrus pith, roasted grapefruit, and some pine resin and lemon, and they are full and striking. The creamy foam leads into a creamy brew, with some full malts, some toasty sweetness, and some bitter roast at the end, all laced with the hop flavor. If you're in Pilsen, go to the Pilsner Urquell brewery, then make time to go to Raven, too. They have a taproom a few miles north of the city where you'll find classic Pilsner-style lagers, some zingy sours, good hoppy beers, and excellent dark brews, including a Double Black IPA.

Elusive Brewing Shadow of the Beast

Finchampstead, England, UK
ABV: 5.0%

Back when Andy Parker was working full-time in the tech industry and only homebrewing for fun, one of his beers—an American Red called Level Up—won a national homebrewing competition and was made at a commercial scale. That success, plus several other collaboration brews, helped Andy make the decision to quit his job and start Elusive Brewing. He sold his first beer in 2016 and then Shadow of the Beast came a few years later as a leading resurgent for the fading popularity of the Black IPA. It's near-black and has the best mix of piney, pithy hops and a hint of dark malt, all in a light-drinking beer. Andy still brews Level Up, a beer which changes hops each time, and it's a nutty, toasty beer with a resinous and citrusy hop profile. He is a busy bloke and, as well as brewing full-time, he has also written a book about homebrewing and opened a small taproom in the brewery.

Eleventh Fort Black India Pale Ale

Samutprakan, Thailand
ABV: 8.0%

I really like this line on Eleventh Fort's website describing their origins: "Before we jumped into the commercial beer scene, we were producing underground beer in small batches and distributed them through our trusted channels." It gives us an idea of some of the challenges faced by passionate Thai brewers in a country where small-batch brewing and even homebrewing were effectively illegal. The work-around was to make beer in someone else's brewery, which is how Eleventh Fort was able to grow professionally. They have a small range of beers, including an IPA made with some local honey, and a juniper-infused Pale Ale. Their Black IPA is a big, full-flavored brew and it's made with Thai coffee beans, roasted in Chiang Mai, and some sea salt. If you've ever put a pinch of salt in coffee, or added coffee to a savory dish, then you'll know that it can enrich flavor, rounding out roastiness and softening it. The beer is fruity and chocolatey from the coffee and there's malt sweetness and a lot of herbal, resinous hops. It's an impressive beer and that addition of salt is marvelous.

Cervejaria Maniba Black "Metal" IPA

São Leopoldo, Brazil
ABV: 7.4%

Black "Metal" IPA is Maniba's flagship beer—and not many breweries can say that about a Black IPA. It's a classic version of the style, top-heavy with American hops which combine with some roasted malts to give an impression of a wholesome breakfast with freshly roasted coffee and fresh fruit juice. It's a big beer, with a high level of bitterness, with that bitterness coming from both roasted malt and hops. In the middle it's got some sweeter malts and then it's got an oily citrus character from all the hops. Try this with smoked foods—smoked sausage, tofu, or turkey in a sandwich.

Deep Creek Dusty Gringo

Silverdale, New Zealand
ABV: 6.8%

This one's an India Brown Ale and from that we expect the base of a strong brown beer and then all the hops of an IPA on top. The malts are toasty and chocolatey with some caramelized sugar with roasted nuts, staying on the lighter side for a darker beer and giving a creamy, mocha-like depth. The hops are citrusy, peppery, and piney, with some roasted tropical fruits, and those hops are both aromatic and flavorsome, leading to a spicy, peppery bitterness. Deep Creek make some very good Pale Ales and some fun tiki-inspired sour beers, including the freshly squeezed, shaken, and suitably tropical Aloha, made with guava and passion fruit.

Fat Heads Midnight Moonlight

Middleburgh Heights, Ohio, USA
ABV: 8.0%

Midnight Moonlight pours a deep brown, and what makes it stand out is how citrusy this beer is—often in a Black IPA you don't get that fresh grapefruit, orange, or tropical fruit aroma, but Fat Heads manage to keep that here. It's got loads of citrus, some fruity berries, then just a little bit of roast right at the end, all in a smooth-textured, full-ish bodied beer with a bitter finish. Not many Black IPAs are better than this, as is evidenced by how it's consistently won big awards, including Great American Beer Festival medals every year from 2015 to 2018, plus World Beer Cup medals in 2016 and 2018. But then we expect fantastic beers from Fat Heads, especially heavily hopped ones, with their best-known IPA being Head Hunter, an old-school, pine and grapefruit C-hop bomb with a big bitterness.

KAIJU! Where Strides The Behemoth

Dandenong South, Australia
ABV: 10.0%

Kaiju is a genre of Japanese movies in which a massive fictional monster smashes up a city. In beer terms, KAIJU! Brewery have smashed up the Aussie brewing scene with their monstrously hoppy beers and boldly branded brews. Where Strides The Behemoth is the Godzilla of Black IPAs. It's 10.0% ABV, black, oily, thick, and molasses-like (treacly), with a rich and creamy foam. The hops are intense, piney, pithy, resinous, and powerful. There's dark chocolate, licorice, some boozy sweetness, orange liqueur, and a big bitterness at the end, with the hop flavor lasting for ages. It's become a cult Aussie craft beer. Kaiju Krush is their tropical Pale Ale and probably the brewery's best-known beer—it's like a mini-monster with a fun, fresh, and fruity aroma.

THE HISTORY AND EVOLUTION OF IPA

From 18th-century ales brewed in London and shipped to India, via 19th-century Burton-brewed beers, through to 21st-century hazy and juicy IPAs, which now dominate bars and beer stores, the history of India Pale Ale is a 300-year story of change.

The romance of history and beer styles is that we tend to look back into the past with a halcyon stare and a storyteller's desire for the most unusual or interesting moment, which, through the re-telling of it gets stuck as some kind of misunderstood folklore. That's what happened with IPA: it's become this mythologized old beer, a beer brewed to be very strong and very hoppy so that it could survive an arduous six months at sea, and arrive in India transformed into a bright, sparkling, remarkable new beer, drunk with empire-leading gusto by thirsty British dignitaries. Is that true? Not quite, but it's a good story, and regardless of what's fact or fiction in that story, IPA is the most popular craft-beer style today and it did ostensibly begin this way.

By the 18th century, India was a key trade route for Britain. The East India Company was a dominant force and they would bring exotic goods like spices and textiles home from India and sell them for great profits. The English merchants who were based in India buying and selling goods drank a potent spirit called arak, which is made from raw palm sugar, sometimes distilled, other times fermented by the hot sun. Thirsty Brits underestimated arak's potency, and many were killed drinking it. As traders were joined by troops, the deaths continued to rise and—while disease was also a factor—arak was a destructive drink. Beer would be a better choice.

The first Pale Ales were exported to India from around the 1780s. The captains on the East India Company saw potential to buy and sell beer (the captains were the ones who profited, not the East India Company), and they started loading barrels into their bows. Porter was always shipped in greater volumes than Pale Ales because Porter was drunk by the troops, whereas the paler beers were saved for the officers.

Porters, Pale Ales, and other "stock," meaning "stored" ales, were the standard beers of the day and they were high in alcohol (by 20th-century standards), heavily hopped, and aged in wooden barrels for a year or so—this was just how beer was made back then.

"Strong and hoppy" is today associated with IPA, and there is science to back that up because the natural preservative qualities in the hops and the alcohol helped to stop the beer going bad, which was especially important in warmer climates, although the first beers weren't deliberately brewed for the journey—they were just the normal beers.

The name India Pale Ale was first mentioned in 1829. By the 1830s, much of the India Pale Ale produced for export was being brewed in Burton-upon-Trent, in the English

An old India Pale Ale label.

Midlands, by breweries like Allsopps' and Bass. We can argue that the beers brewed in Burton were a more specific style of India Pale Ale deliberately made for export as they'd evolved into a new and important beer style.

These Burton India Pale Ales used only pale malts, were heavily hopped with Kent-grown hops, mostly Goldings, for bitterness and were also dry-hopped, and they were 6.0–7.5% ABV. They were very well attenuated, meaning very dry, so there was little residual sugar to continue fermenting in the barrel, though we can imagine some flavor development happening with wild yeast and oxidation. When the barrels arrived, the beer was transferred into bottles where it would have carbonated, becoming a bright, dry, and refreshing long drink—there's definitely romance in that idea.

Through the middle of the 19th century, Pale Ales become more common in British pubs. Synonymous with Bitter, these beers were pale and bitter, as their name suggests, and they were eventually stored for less time and drunk fresh, meaning that domestic recipes differed from export ones. Then, by the end of the 19th century, the export market for British brewers was being challenged by German brewers and Americans, and more people were looking for lighter lagers instead of heavier ales. India Pale Ale was no longer a big export beer, it was no longer stored in big barrels for months, and it was no longer strong or hoppy, but Pale Ale did remain in the pubs, albeit now a low-alcohol (around 4.0% ABV) brew.

India Pale Ale remained a low-ish alcohol ale and verged on extinction until craft brewers discovered the story. To those brewers, India Pale Ale was a new and evocative beer with a long, interesting history, and it came at a time when new American hop varieties were becoming available (like Cascade) and being used in beers like Sierra Nevada Pale Ale. Brewers started to make beers that were stronger and hoppier than Pale Ale, with attached romanticized stories of sea journeys, firmly wedging the IPA myths into the collective consciousness of generations of drinkers.

The India Pale Ales of the 1980s and onward were nothing like the beers of the early 1800s, and the new ones were designed to be drunk as fresh as possible to get the maximum bitter and aromatic impact from the citrusy, floral American hops. Those early craft brewers took India Pale Ale and they turned it into IPA.

As more drinkers turned away from bland mainstream lagers and toward flavorsome craft beers, brewers became more comfortable with making bolder and more bitter brews, ones that give a hollering high-five to the high-alpha American hops. By the mid-to-late 1990s IPA was becoming an important beer in craft breweries. And then it shifted again. A one-upmanship seemed to spur on more extreme examples through the 2000s, with super-bitter beers and stronger Double IPAs. And people loved it. It was challenging and thrilling and brilliant and new.

Societé The Pupil is a good example of a modern IPA.

From there, the excitement settled down and balance and flavor became a bit more important. The bitterness was reduced, there was a bit more malt, the hops shifted to be used for aroma and flavor, and they gave us more of the kinds of IPA that we're familiar with today. Once we had that foundation, the variations started to increase and the word "IPA" came to stand for a broader family of beers, where if you attached those letters to something it meant that it was going to be hoppy. Craft beer started its "IPAsation" which has given us Session, Double, and Triple IPAs; Black, White, and Red IPAs (with Imperial versions of all of them); Belgian IPAs; Sour IPAs; Fruit IPAs; Hazy IPAs; New England IPAs; and more. In the 2020s, it's hazy and very fruity IPAs, with low bitterness, which dominate for now. One thing is for certain: we love IPAs.

India Pale Ale is a beer from history. A near-mythical thing. A beer that was aged for a long time and sailed from Britain to India. *And it's a beer we'll never be able to taste.* It's got a brilliant story and great history, but it's not what we drink today; today, we drink IPA, a beer that's all about freshness and the impact of hop flavor and aroma. No beer style has evolved more than India Pale Ale and IPA, and it continues to change today.

OTHER PALES AND IPAS

If I can define the craft beer business in as few words as possible, then they are: IPA sells. Put those three capital letters in a beer's name and people will buy it. That's seen a huge evolution of the style into a whole family of different beers with sub-categories, diverse types, and a never-ending search for new innovations. I've given some of the more common ones their own chapters, like English (see page 72) and Pacific IPAs (see page 75), and here I've added a range of other IPAs.

There are IPAs brewed with hops grown in some of the world's other established hop-growing locations—Spanish IPAs and Patagonian IPAs. There are IPAs with fruit in them, a development from the end of the 2010s when brewers who were seeking to get as much citrus aroma into their beer as possible actually started to add citrus fruits. There are soured IPAs as well as ones sweetened with lactose and with added adjuncts (Culinary IPAs or Milkshake IPAs). There are IPAs made with Belgian yeast, wild yeast, and Kveik yeast (that's a Norwegian strain which has been domesticated for its fruity esters). If you lined up a West Coast IPA, a Hazy IPA, a Milkshake IPA, and a Sour IPA, you might not necessarily taste any similarities, and there's no simple way of defining the IPA category anymore (though they should at least have a hefty aromatic hop profile), but if it's got IPA on it, then people will buy it and that's continuing to bring experimentation and new styles onto the bar.

Brasserie La Malpolon French IPA

Lavérune, France
ABV: 6.0%

Brasserie La Malpolon are based just outside of Montpellier in the south of France and they use as many local ingredients as possible. They get barley from the Auverge, as well as some from their own region, and they brew with a mix of Alsatian and Catalan hops—they might not be as well known for hops as other countries, but France and Spain are in the top 10 of the world's hop-growing countries. In their Mediterranean Pale Ale, La Malpolon use Catalonian hops, while in their French IPA they brew with French-grown Cascade, Columbus, Aramis, and Barbe Rouge. It's a deep amber-colored beer, which gives it a caramel and bread-crust depth—this is a little sweet and old-school, and smothers the hops somewhat, but they do come through with a floral, peppery, herbal character, and give a robust bitterness (the French beer palate is a bitter one). The brewery's Bière de Blé is a refreshing Witbier that uses local malt and hops, plus fennel seeds, which add a nice aniseedy fragrance.

Brewski Passionfeber IPA

Helsingborg, Sweden
ABV: 7.0%

If you like fruity IPAs, then Brewski make your kinda brewskis. With a mango Double IPA, a passion-fruit, mango, and pineapple IPA, and a mango and raspberry Pale Ale, plus this passion-fruit IPA, they are some of the fruitiest hop-lovers in the beer world. All the fruited IPAs are hazy and yellow, with the raspberry one having a little blush to it. They are all full-bodied and have some residual sweetness which enhances the fruit flavors. These are, in turn, emphasized by the hops used. Passionfeber IPA is tropical, tangy, and exotic, though don't necessarily expect a glassful of ripe fresh-fruit flavor, as it's more subtle than that. It has sweetness, bitterness, and a little ping of tartness which makes it like a refreshing long cocktail.

Great Leap Brewing Pale Ale No.6

Beijing, China
ABV: 5.5%

Did you know that China is one of the world's largest hop-growing countries? Those hops typically go into the country's pale lagers, which combine to make up the largest beer market in the world, and in those beers the hops are indistinct, almost too delicate for you to even notice whether the brewers bothered to add them or not. If you want to know what Chinese hops can give to a beer, then you need something a little more punchy, such as Great Leap's No.6, which is brewed with only Chinese Qingdao hops. It's an old-school kind of pale ale base using only Chinese malts, being amber in color with some caramel and toast. The bitterness is light, but balanced, and the aroma is gently peppery and spicy in a German kind of way. Great Leap have expanded into a couple of cool brewpubs in Beijing, but the most fun place to visit is their original hutong location, which is a uniquely Beijing experience: a small bar which is hard to find down the city's backstreet hutongs.

Cerveza Patagonia Küné

Bariloche, Argentina
ABV: 5.0%

There's a little pocket of craft beer in Patagonia which is little known about. Focused on the Argentinian town of Bariloche, which is near a significant hop-growing region, you'll find dozens of small breweries, and, if you're in Bariloche itself, you can barely walk a block or two without passing a brewery or craft beer bar. Cerveza Patagonia's Küné is made with Patagonian malt and hops. It's a golden brew with some bready and toasty malts and a hint of caramelized sugar. The hops give a floral, peppery, lightly pithy, and fruity character with a long and refreshing bitterness. The beer is available in cans, so it's one that you can stuff in your backpack if you're hiking, then walk back to Bariloche to the brewery's spectacular brewpub, with an elevated view over the lake and mountains in the background. The brewery was part of Quilmes and is now part of AB InBev, but that doesn't change how good the view is.

LOS TABARNACOS
Milkshake IPA   6.5% ALC/VOL

Brasserie du Bas-Canada Los Tabarnacos

Gatineau, Canada
ABV: 6.5%

This is a Milkshake IPA and that's a term I've come to dread seeing in bars and bottle stores. Do I really want to drink an IPA that's juicy with citrusy fruits and then has lactose and vanilla added to make it creamy? The simple answer is: no. But (very) occasionally I'll have one that changes my mind, like Los Tabarnacos. This one is a very light hazy blonde. It's hopped with Citra and Mosaic, which you can tell as soon as you crack into the can and a blast of tropical fruits comes out. The additions of mango purée and lactose sweeten the beer and give it a lusher texture, but the thing which really makes this one good is that they add toasted coconut, which gives a savory depth at the end and stops it being sweet. My mind was happily changed by this beer. This is part of a trend of Culinary beers that are inspired by food, often sweet stuff like smoothies, pie, or cake.

Juguetes Perdidos Hop de Lis

Buenos Aires, Argentina
ABV: 6.6%

Belgian IPAs reached a peak of popularity in the early 2010s. Those beers were brewed like a typical American IPA—pale malts, American hops, dry, bitter, around 6.0% ABV—but, instead of using a neutral American ale yeast, they were fermented with a Belgian yeast more often used in Saisons or Belgian Blondes. Those yeasts vary from spicy and phenolic (think cloves) to fruity and peppery (think banana or stone fruit and pepper), and a transformation happened to the hop aromas when they combined with the yeast esters, giving us a whole new range of fruity characteristics. Only a few Belgian IPAs remain, and Hop de Lis is a great

example. It's the kind of golden color that glows in your glass. It's very dry and lean, which emphasizes the yeast's peppery and spicy finish, and the aromas are a mix of peach, clove-studded pineapple, banana, and citrus zest. It's a great combination of American and Belgian, brewed in Buenos Aires.

Pastore Brewing Playa de Agua

Waterbeach, England, UK
ABV: 6.0%

Releasing their first beers in 2019, Pastore Brewing and Blending make several different ranges of mixed-fermentation beers, including quick ones with fruity yeast and *Lactobacillus*, steel-aged ales, and barrel-aged brews. Playa de Agua is one of the quick ones and uses a fast-fermenting and fruity Kveik yeast alongside souring *Lactobacillus*. Here the yeast and a large dry-hop with El Dorado and Rakau give a beer with an unreal amount of fruity character, like over-ripe tropical fruit, fermenting and funky stone fruits, banana, tannic peach skin, passion fruit, ruby grapefruit—it reminded me exactly of a tropical juice I've had before and the texture is exactly that of good fruit juice, having the same body and acidity (but not strongly sour), with a dry, but not bitter, finish. It's an incredibly impressive beer.

Hudson Valley Amorphia

Beacon, New York, USA
ABV: 6.0%

Hudson Valley have become specialists in Sour IPAs. Their beers tend to start out with a base of raw wheat, malted oats, and lactose, then fruits, flavors, and acidity are built into that. Some examples of their Sour IPAs include lychee, chamomile, lavender, and Mosaic hops; wildflower honey and grapefruit purée; white chocolate, vanilla, and cardamom, and a Citra dry-hop; and molasses, pineapple, lime, and almonds. Amorphia is strawberry and vanilla plus Mosaic and El Dorado as a dry-hop. It's a thick pink beer, creamy like melted strawberry gelato; it's sweet and sour (actually, Sweet & Sour IPA might be a better name for some of these); the vanilla makes it extra fruity; and the acidity resembles that of an under-ripe berry, while the hops also have a berry-like character. It's unusual and quite remarkable. Hudson Valley have a taproom that you can visit to drink in or take away cans. They regularly release new beers and if this kind of sweet, sour, hoppy adjunct IPA is your thing, then they're peerless.

Monkish Brewing Co. Biggie, Biggie, Biggie

Torrance, California, USA
ABV: 10.1%

After IPA and Double IPA comes the Triple IPA. Most of the versions we see are in the Hazy style and Monkish have become one of the best at making them. They are dense, thick, sticky, sweet, and heavily juiced beers, with a fully saturated hop flavor which leaves you drunk, dozy, and seeing double (or triple), but they are supremely impactful beers. After the Triple IPA you'll also see Quadruple IPAs, which are often 12.0% and above. Many of these beers are like really boozy orange juice that warms you up on the way down. Approach with caution because they drink like juice but have the equivalent of about five shots of vodka in them. I'm sure there'll also be Quintuple IPAs by the time you're reading this.

Duvel Triple Hop Citra

Breendonk, Belgium
ABV: 9.5%

Duvel Triple Hop has the foundation of a Belgian Strong Golden Ale and is slightly stronger than the regular Duvel. It uses the same bittering hops—Saaz and Styrian Golding—and then it's dry-hopped with Citra in what the brewery calls a Belgian IPA. It's perfectly bright, has an uplifting and unrivaled carbonation, and a low malt profile, but still it has a robust body capable of gripping onto the hops. Those hops are not overdone and yet it's rich with hop aroma and flavor, with Duvel's yeast giving new characteristics to Citra's fruitiness. There are gooseberries, lime peel, fermented tropical fruits, white grape, white wine, and some tangy citrus, with the peppery and pomaceous yeast adding another dimension. It's bright, bold, snappy, exciting, enticing, elegant, and unrivaled in its clarity of hop flavor and drinkability for its strength. I don't think there's a Double IPA in the world that can rival Duvel Triple Hop's depth, drinkability, complexity, and balance.

AMERICAN WHEAT ALE AND WHITE IPA

Where Belgian Witbier is dry, citrusy, and spicy, and German Weissbier or Hefeweizen is smooth and banana-like, American Wheat Ales are closer to an American Pale Ale, and White IPAs are the hopped-up development of the Wheat Ale.

The base brew of an American Wheat remains similar to that of its European cousins (around 40–50 percent wheat), and the difference is a result of the yeast, which is typically a traditional ale yeast and not one used for its fruity or phenolic ester profile. American Wheat Ales are between 4.0% ABV and 6.0% ABV, usually unfiltered, and range from lightly hazy to opaque. The hops in these beers could be subtle European varieties, giving some spice and citrus peel, or they could be highly aromatic and fruity, making them more like a Pale Ale. It's a style that came early in the development of American craft beer and was a good gateway kind of beer for new drinkers. Since then—much like the whole industry—the style has got progressively hoppier.

White IPAs use 25–50 percent wheat in the brew, making them full-bodied and hazy, though not as full and hazy as a New England IPA (however, the space between White IPA and Hazy IPA is, quite literally, cloudy). They will be aromatically hoppy with American and Antipodean hops (with citrus, tropical fruit, melon, and stone fruit aromas), smooth-bodied, around 6.0% ABV, and with a neutral or lightly fruity yeast. They used to be more popular than they are today, having been overtaken by New England-style hazy beers.

Three Floyds Gumballhead

Munster, Indiana, USA
ABV: 5.5%

Gumballhead can lay claim to being one of the beers that created the hoppy American Wheat style. It's super-citrusy and tropical, with tangerine, apricot, peach, lemon, lime, pine, and pineapple in the aroma. Those hops are softened and almost sweetened by the residual yeast and the wheat in the beer, which gives a fuller body to the brew and gives a heightened hop flavor, before a characteristic (for Three Floyds, anyway) bitterness at the end. A few years ago, this beer stood out for its haze and hop combo, whereas today those kinds of beer are everywhere, so it's now held up (correctly) as a classic. Three Floyds have been brewing since 1996 and their Alpha King, Zombiedust, and Dark Lord are all also classic and much-loved examples of their styles.

Marz Community Brewing Co. Jungle Boogie

Chicago, Illinois, USA
ABV: 5.5%

Jungle Boogie is an atypical American Wheat Ale. It uses specialty wheat, which gives a hazy red beer with some sweeter, fruitier, lightly caramelly flavors. The brewery adds rooibos tea to this beer, and that creates a berry-like fruitiness, while a small addition of Mosaic hops pulls everything together, giving some of its own berry fruit, plus some light citrus. It's a clever beer and a nice counterpart to all the heavily hopped IPAs brewed elsewhere. Marz started out with a tiny little brewkit but have since grown into a smart and impressive warehouse in Bridgeport, south Chicago. That space has lots of beer, good sandwiches, arcade machines, leather sofas, a view over the brewhouse, and a gallery space. Marz also brew a line of non-alcoholic drinks, including kombuchas, shrubs, seltzers, sodas, and soft drinks spiked with CBD.

Zmajska Pivovara Hoppy Wheat

Zagreb, Croatia
ABV: 4.9%

Zmajska Pivovara's Hoppy Wheat is very pale yellow, almost like lemon cordial, with a light haze—just looking at it, you can tell it's going to be a lovely, refreshing brew. It's very light and very dry, but then manages to keep a nice creaminess to its texture. The hops bring elderflower and gooseberry, and are lemony and lightly citrusy, without being overwhelming, and it's the sort of beer that you want to drink in the Croatian sun with a big plate of fried fish or squid and a squeeze of lemon. The Dragon brewers started as homebrewers at a time when Croatia had no craft beer, and opened one of the first small breweries in the country, later adding a small taproom. Given their homebrewing backgrounds, they encourage anyone who makes their own beer to come along and drink it and share it there with others.

Cervejaria Octopus Zephyr

Rio de Janeiro, Brazil
ABV: 4.5%

Cervejaria Octopus are known for their Hazy IPAs and DIPA. Octopus' Garden is their main Hazy DIPA and it's a great brew, one that's characteristically smooth-bodied with lots of tropical fruits and a cut of passion fruit and citrus pith at the end. Zephyr is their American Wheat Ale. From a brewery that specializes in modern IPAs, it's hazier than most, but that's no bad thing because the extra haze is able to hang onto more of the hops in this beer, as well as give it a smoother, creamier texture which is really pleasing to drink. It's double dry-hopped, so the hops are bolder than in most Wheat Ales, and they give tropical fruits, passion fruit, some sweet red berries, strawberries, and stone-fruit esters, and a little pepper and dank resin at the end. It's fun and refreshing, and good with spicy roasted cassava fries.

Volta Bräu Follow the White Rabbit

Basel, Switzerland
ABV: 5.5%

Every year I go away for a weekend to drink beer with some mates. One year, we found a way in which we could drink beer in four countries in one day: we started with an early pint at the airport in London, then we flew to Switzerland's Basel Airport, which is actually in France, and had a beer in a local French café, before taking the train to Freiburg in Germany and visiting a few brewpubs, then we ended the night in Basel. The next day we fully explored the Swiss city and Volta Bräu was a favorite place—a hip brewpub with a good selection of beers. Follow the White Rabbit is their White IPA. The hops—Amarillo, Citra, and Cascade—give lemon, mandarin, and citrus pith, but it's not overly aromatic or bitter, and there's a suggestion of the yeast adding its own fruitiness. We also liked their Session IPA.

Brave Brewing Co. Stay Gold

Hastings, New Zealand
ABV: 4.5%

Brewed using NZ wheat and barley from Canterbury and adding Antipodean hops, this Pacific Wheat Ale is a golden color with just a little haze to it, suggestively telling us that this one is primarily designed for dealing with deep thirsts. It's a gently fruity brew with some aromas of passion fruit and sweet stone fruit, which immediately draws you in, then the malt is clean, crisp, and leads to a light, refreshing finish—it's the kind of beer I want with Vietnamese food or even with avocado on toast for brunch. Brave Brewing is run by husband and wife Matt and Gemma Smith who grew up in Hastings, moved to Auckland, then returned to their hometown to start making beer in 2014. Their tasting room is the kind that warmly welcomes you in and immediately makes you feel at home. Check out their Tiger Milk IPA, which is their main IPA, and a mix of citrus and tropical hop fruitiness.

My Beer Friend Chiang Mai Accent

Chiang Mai, Thailand
ABV: 5.5%

It's not easy being a brewer in Thailand. There are difficult rules, which means you either need to be a very big brewer or a brewpub that makes and sells at least 500 pints a day. Not everyone can achieve that, but there's an excited thirst for craft beer in Thailand and one way for brewers to get around the legislation is to brew overseas and import the beer back. This is what My Beer Friend do, then they sell their beer in their own bars. I walked into My Beer Friend, in Chiang Mai, and ordered Chiang Mai Accent, a beer that's brewed with Thai wheat. It was a hazy amber-yellow color with some bready malts, some fruity aromas from the yeast, some pithy hoppiness giving extra floral and citrus, and a clean bitterness, putting it somewhere between an American wheat and a European one. It's a really good, refreshing, and interesting beer, served in a cool bar.

BLONDE AND GOLDEN ALES

The earliest British-brewed Golden Ales were made with British malts and floral and lightly fruity English hops, and they came out in the 1980s, just as lager sales were overtaking ale sales for the first time. They were a counterattack, of sorts, and they became a new midpoint between the old-fashioned bitter ales and the brightly carbonated lagers. Today, they are still a crossover beer, with some versions moving between malty lagers, lager, and British ales, and others between the refreshment of a Pilsner and the citrusy hops of a Pale Ale. A recent trend has been for regional and national breweries to release subtle blonde and golden beers to compete with the dominance of light lagers and also to give the craft beer drinker something a little more subtle: not everyone wants a lager, but also some people want something less impactful than an IPA, and Golden Ales have become a go-to, everyday kind of beer.

The base beers are usually simple, with a bready, toasty flavor and not much sweetness, often only using pale malts, with the Blondes being lighter than the Golds. The bitterness is typically low to medium, and the aroma can range from gentle to strong, with any hop varieties being appropriate, though most brewers go for the citrus and tropical aromas of modern hops. They are usually between 4.0% ABV and 5.5% ABV, and the best versions have a good balance between malt and hop, as well as being clean and refreshing to drink. As the style continues to evolve, there are now more aromatic American Blondes, which are light-bodied and fruitily aromatic, like a gentle, low-malt, low-bitter Pale Ale.

St. Austell Brewery Tribute

St. Austell, England, UK
ABV: 4.2%

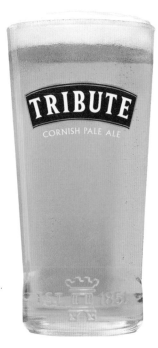

You're by the beach in Cornwall eating fish and chips and drinking a pint of St. Austell's Tribute. It's the best sea in the country, the kind of turquoise usually seen in Spain. The sea air is fresh, edged with that salinity of seaweed and sea spray. The chips are fat, a mix of soft and crispy, and they're hot and salty, while the fish is flaking inside its bubbly, crunchy batter. The sand in front of you is white, the sun is yellow, and your pint is golden. Tribute is toasty with Maris Otter malts and aromatic with fresh citrus from a mix of English, Slovenian, and American hops. That's my dream lunch. Tribute is a perfect example of how British cask ales modernized toward American hops, and it's one of the best-selling cask ales in the country. St. Austell brew some of my favorite ales and I love them for how they combine a base of English malt with bright American hops, with their Proper Job being a peachy and grapefruity Pale Ale, while Big Job is one of the best West Coast-style Double IPAs you can drink in Britain. But always start with a pint of Tribute. And watch out for seagulls flying in to steal your chips.

Platinum Golden Ale

Ho Chi Minh City, Vietnam
ABV: 5.0%

This is Vietnam's original craft beer. It was introduced as an alternative to the local lagers and started out as a light, filtered, crisp, lager-like beer, but, as the market has matured and as more Vietnamese drinkers shift from Saigon Lager to local Craft Bia, so Platinum have shifted their brew to be unfiltered and fruitier with hops, while focusing their message on "100% natural"—important in a growing market that values unprocessed products. It's the sort of easy-drinking, light-bodied beer that you want in the warm, humid climate of south Vietnam, while the hops add a little lemon and melon aroma. Platinum also make a few dry-hopped versions of this beer to appeal further to the growing numbers of craft-beer drinkers in the country.

Fallen Brewery New World Odyssey

Kippen, Scotland
ABV: 4.1%

With a base of lager malts—Pilsner, Munich, and Vienna—plus some Saaz hops, New World Odyssey takes some inspiration from easy-going lagers and then modernizes it by using an ale yeast and a late addition of Citra and Mosaic hops. Those hops give tangerine, peach, and passion fruit to go with the bready and toasted malts, which have a little bit of sweetness to bring out extra hop fruitiness. It's a really nice Blonde ale, one that's lively with hop flavor, but also still restrained by alcohol and malt. Fallen are based in rural Stirlingshire, to the south-east of the Highland mountains, and they brew in what was once Kippen railway station, first built in 1856—some of their core beers are named to reflect that heritage, with Local Motive Session IPA, Just the Ticket Pale, hoppy Sleeper Pils, and Chew Chew, a salted caramel Milk Stout.

Fox Farm Little Brook

Salem, Connecticut, USA
ABV: 4.6%

Little Brook is a hoppy Blonde Ale. It's a hazy yellow with a bright white foam and the hops come out right away: stone fruits, grapefruit, lemon, grape, and some light spice, with those hops staying elegantly all through the beer, which is light-bodied and has a tingly kind of carbonation that makes it even lighter—it's wonderful. Fox Farm are becoming well known for their excellent lagers, as well as their top-class hoppy beers, and they are all brewed in a converted old dairy barn surrounded by 30 acres (12 hectares) of land. Their tasting room has a mezzanine where you can watch over the brewing or, if the weather's good, you can sit outside and ground yourself in all the green space. It's a very handsome brewery and tasting room.

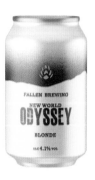

Burbrit Brewery Rangoon Blonde

Yangon, Myanmar
ABV: 5.0%

It wasn't easy for Burbrit to start brewing in Myanmar. Once they'd decided that they wanted to open a brewery, it took them two years and some legal appeals just to get the license to allow them to make beer, but finally, in 2016, they got approval to open the country's first craft brewery. But selling new kinds of beer into a market that's only known pale, cheap lager was always going to be a challenge—they were trying to teach the locals about new kinds of beer like Pale Ales and Wheat Beer (and explain why they cost a lot more). With persistence, good beer, some cool taprooms, and then canned beer, they've established themselves as Myanmar's local craft brewer. Their beers are fairly sweet and not heavily hopped, which suits the local palate, and Rangoon Blonde is their best-seller. It's described as a lager, but its malty, nutty, bready flavor, with a gentle hop character that offers some honey and floral notes, is more reminiscent of a Blonde Ale.

Devil's Peak First Light

Cape Town, South Africa
ABV: 4.5%

Devil's Peak were one of South Africa's first craft breweries, opening in 2012. They know what most people want to drink—crisp, refreshing lager—and they've made their own great versions to appeal to the masses. Next to those come their more interesting beers and King's Blockhouse is a very popular IPA which is heavily hopped but retains its balance, with a lacing of bright citrus and light tropical fruit all the way through it. With First Light they've got a beer right between the lager and the craftier beers. It's fresh, easy-drinking, and unchallenging for the lager lovers, but interesting enough for the hop heads—a great all-rounder.

Morada Cia Etílica Hop Arábica

Curitiba, Brazil
ABV: 5.0%

You might not expect to find coffee in a Blonde beer, but in Hop Arábica the combination of the toasty malts and the floral, fruity, and faintly cocoa-like coffee beans works really well. The beer is a collaboration between brewery Morada Cia Etílica and Lucca Cafés Especiais, Brazil's most-awarded coffee shop, who source all their own beans.

The base brewing of the beer and the coffee happen separately, and for the coffee they lightly roast the beans to extract the flavor so that it is low in bitterness and more prominently fruity. When the two base brews are mixed together, the resulting beer is a bright and clear American Blonde, and it's neither strong with hops nor with coffee. Instead, the hops harmonize with the top fruity notes in the coffee, giving some berries and stone fruit, before both the hops and the beans add their own different kinds of bitterness. It's a clever mix of two great drinks.

PALE AND HOPPY

Very pale, very light, very hoppy, low-alcohol ales are a very important contemporary craft-beer style in Britain, one that was introduced by brewers in the early 2000s. The beers in this category have proved their longevity by becoming core beers for most British breweries today (the style arguably also influenced the Session IPA). In a way, these pale and hoppy session-strength beers, brewed with American and Antipodean hops, have redefined traditional British brewing and pub-drinking by coming to replace older styles of brown English-hopped bitter on the bar. We're seeing them in all serving formats—cask, keg, bottle, can—and they can work equally well in each, though I think they gain a special kind of elegance when perfectly kept and poured from the cask: the hops sing in a subtle, expressive, and appealing way. Outside of Britain, the Australian categories of "Mids" and "XPA" have emerged as lower-alcohol Pale Ales where hop aroma joins a light drinkability and a firm bitterness.

These beers work so well because they combine that session-strength ale with the bursting citrus of modern hops. The best retain their overall balance, and are not overwhelmed by the hops, although they are still dominated by them. They differ from Pale Ales and Session IPAs by being lighter in body and crisper in bitterness at the end, though there is an obvious crossover between the other styles. I've collected these beers together here based on their lighter malt profiles and brighter hop aromas.

Marble Pint

Manchester, England, UK
ABV: 3.9%

This is a modern classic British ale and a defining example of the pale and hoppy session beer style, coming out of Manchester, which was one of the cities where this style first properly developed and grew in popularity. It's got a very light body of pale malt, just barely there in flavor, but absolutely there in structure, as if it's been built to hold hops. Those hops are a mix of American and Kiwi, and they give you grapefruit, gooseberry, lemon, and tropical fruits, with a dry and bracingly bitter finish. Go to the Marble Arch pub, where the brewery started, as it's the best place to drink this beer. This old Victorian boozer has a slanted floor that leads you right to the bar, where you'll always find a pint of Pint being poured. When they put their beer into 500ml cans, they got complaints that it wasn't a full pint, so they changed the name to Metric in response.

Colonial Brewing Small Ale

Margaret River, Australia
ABV: 3.5%

"Mids" have become an important category in Australian craft beer. They are around 3.5% ABV, pale and light-bodied, refreshing, and with a fruity hop aroma and flavor, where they combine a modern Australian vibe with a foundation of British-style sessionability. Australians drink a lot like the Brits, favoring long sessions and lower alcohol, only they have the benefits of more sunshine and space. One of the best places to experience the sun and space is Margaret River, where there are lots of breweries, almost all of them with their own lake, surrounded by land where people run around, play catch or cricket, or laze in the sun and relax—I've never been anywhere with better or bigger beer gardens. Go to Colonial's taproom and have a Small Ale with its light, biscuity malts beneath fresh citrus, pine, and tropical aromas.

Sawmill Brewery Extra Pale Ale

Matakana, New Zealand
ABV: 4.9%

In October 2019, Sawmill's brewery was extensively damaged in a fire. No one was hurt, but their brewery, taproom, and restaurant had to close. They set about rebuilding and other local brewers offered them tank space so they could continue to make their range of excellent beers, which includes a New Zealand Pilsner and a crisp IPA. I really like their XPA, and while I've put XPAs into other chapters, I'm going with Pale and Hoppy for this one because it's white-gold in appearance and very light to drink, almost lager-like in its snappy refreshment, which, for me, embodies the best of the pale and hoppies. Sawmill XPA is fresh and lively with tropical fruits like mango, grape, and passion fruit, and they make this into a beautiful, refreshing, easy-drinking beer. Happily, they've been able to reopen, and as a B Corp business they're adding great value to their local community with their commitment to social and environmental responsibility.

McLeod's Heathen

Waipu, New Zealand
ABV: 3.8%

This Session Pale Ale is a perfect mix of the maltiness of a low-alcohol English-style ale, with its soft, biscuity depth and smooth mouthfeel, and the juicy freshness of modern hops, which give peaches, grapes, and some sweet citrus. That malt has enough of a plumpness that it's able to enhance the fruitiness in the hops without creating a sweet beer. McLeod's Pizza Barn is the place to visit to drink this. It's one of those bars that is central to a small community and has its own local warmth and character. There you can try all the McLeod's beers, which include a great Brown Porter, a hoppy and crisp Lager, seasonal unfiltered IPAs, and stronger bottled brews, like their hoppy Barley Wine. Their pizzas are handmade and piled high with toppings—ideal to go with a Heathen.

Oskar Blues One-y IPA

Longmont, Colorado, USA
ABV: 4.0%

Two trends combine here into one small but mightily tasty beer. It's a Hazy IPA, juiced with lots of fresh tropical fruit and citrus, plus a little pine, and it's only 100 calories per can. Most of the world doesn't care about beer calories (does it really matter if it's 100 calories or 150 calories? That's, like, half a banana, one cookie, a handful of potato chips, or a couple of star jumps difference), but the Americans do care and 100 has became a bullseye number for brewers to aim for. For craft brewers, low-calorie doesn't mean low-flavor and One-y's success lies in being an intensely aromatic and fun beer which is dry and refreshing. To some, this might be a light beer, but to me it's a great pale and hoppy, low-ABV beer that's the sort of thing I want to slam after a long run or on a hot day. And I'll probably have two or three because I don't give a damn about the calories.

Beak Brewery Lulla

Lewes, England, UK
ABV: 3.5%

Beak began life as a cuckoo brewer, moving between other breweries before opening their own place in the summer of 2020. The venture has been an immediate success and every new release of cans has their fans stocking up, while many of us make the journey to Lewes to drink their beer from the brewery taproom. Their Parade IPA is one of my favorite British Hazy IPAs. It's got the ideal balance of extra-fruity hops with a dry bitterness. Lulla is their Table Beer, which has emerged as a popular style and one that's low in alcohol and high in hop flavor. This version is like a typical Hazy IPA, only refined to 3.5% ABV, and it's light, bright with lemony, pithy, passion fruit-like hops. Now that I live by the sea in East Sussex, not far from Lewes, it's exactly the kind of beer I have in the fridge to take to the beach.

Balter Brewing Captain Sensible

Currumbin, Australia
ABV: 3.5%

Captain Sensible is another great example of the Aussie "Mid" ale, which joins the XPA and Pacific or Summer Ale as important Australian beer styles that are core beers for most breweries. What connects those styles is an easy drinkability, a balance of refreshment and fresh hop flavor, and usually a moderate to low alcohol content, something that suits the temperature and drinking temperament of the country. Captain Sensible is a copper-colored beer, which tells you that there's some specialty malts in there giving it texture and body and a touch of toffee, but it's really clean and light, then bursting with mango, passion fruit, and mandarin hops in the aroma—it's ideal for a beer brewed on the Gold Coast. The brewery was started in 2016 by some pro-surfers and their mates, and they had great success thanks to the quality of the beer. At the end of 2019, they became part of Carlton & United.

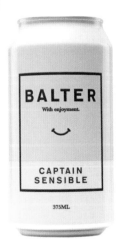

AMBER AND RED ALE

Before Pale Ales and IPAs came to dominate craft beer in America, Amber Ales and Amber Lagers were among the most popular kinds of beer. They were stronger and more flavorsome than a light lager, and they arrived long before the bold hoppiness of IPA which would come to define a maturing of the American beer palate (before, arguably, it immatured toward sweet novelty beers). Those early amber beers took inspiration from British ales and (perhaps with a retro-fitted story) from old, pre-Prohibition American lagers, which have a more defined malt flavor, a fuller body, greater bitterness, and some extra alcohol compared to the light lagers that created a mono beer culture in America until the 1980s. There are many examples of these kinds of beers that most drinkers will know well: Brooklyn Lager, New Belgium Fat Tire, Sam Adams Boston Lager, and Alaskan Amber. The malt-forward early ambers remain, but the style has generally become more aromatically hoppy, though balance still prevails.

Contemporary Ambers and Reds are like Pale Ales to IPAs (I've included a separate chapter for Red IPAs; see page 78), but weaker, less malty, and less hoppy overall. Most range from 5.0% ABV to 6.0% ABV. The malt is usually toasty and veers toward toffee, but will rarely be sweet. Bitterness is crisp, but not often high. And the hop profile could be subtle, or it could be noticeably citrusy and fruity. You might also see some beers described as Irish-style Red, somewhat of an anomaly of a beer that probably evolved out of English-style Bitters.

Pizza Port Chronic Ale

Bressi Ranch, California, USA
ABV: 4.9%

Pizza Port's Ocean Beach brewpub is one of my favorite places to drink beer. It's a few blocks back from the Pacific Ocean and they always have great house-brewed beers, brilliant Pizza Port core brews made at their Bressi Ranch brewery, and big pizza pies. Chronic Ale is Pizza Port's straightforward Amber. The malt is toasty, gentle, and old-school in its mix of caramelly and bready flavor. It's a little sweet to begin with, but then dry to finish, with a low bitterness, and it's one of those beers that is unremarkable yet also wonderful in its familiar simplicity—it's a perfect beer to go with a pizza. You might see Pizza Port's Shark Bite on tap, which is a 6.0%-ABV Red Ale that's more malt than hop, with lots of caramel malts and a deep bitterness. And if you're at the Ocean Beach brewpub in summer through fall, you should see Jetty, their grapefruity and bitter San Diego-style IPA.

Effet Papillon Rye Amber Ale

6.8% ABV

Mérignac, France
ABV: 6.8%

I've never had a beer that tastes more like biscuits than this one (that's the British biscuit, by the way, not the American one covered in that strange gravy...). It's wonderful. The malt character is deeply interesting. It's nutty, creamy, and a little chocolatey. The malt is soft, layered, richly moreish, and almost chewy, with some extra fruitiness coming through at the end in the form of raisins, berries, and some rye spice. There's a little sweetness which cuts through to a dry, refreshing finish and a lift of bubbles. The brewery also makes an exceptional Wheat Ale brewed with a yeast which produces some clove phenols that spike the beer with a zesty, tropical, tangy, racy spice. It's very refreshing and quite unusual in a very good way. The subtle additions of rye in the Amber Ale, and the use of a phenolic yeast in the Wheat Ale, change and lift these beers and create something way more powerful than you'd expect. Like a beery butterfly effect, if you like.

Cervecería Austral Patagonia

Punta Arenas, Chile
ABV: 5.0%

What's now known as Cervecería Austral is Chile's oldest brewery, which was founded in 1896 by a German brewmaster called José Fischer. This relatively large brewery is one of the southernmost in the world. They make a pale lager, a pale Bock, a dark ale, and a beer using the local calafate berry. Patagonia is their dark amber-colored ale (it's called a Pale Ale, but there's nothing pale about this beer). It's rich with malts in the middle with some caramel, nuts, toffee, and toast, giving it a comforting, filling kind of richness (which is good in the cold weather), then the hops are spicy and herbal at the end. It might be too malty or sweet for some, but it's a taste enjoyed by the locals and it'd be a great match for spit-roast lamb, which is a popular local dish.

Tröegs HopBack Amber Ale

Hershey, Pennsylvania, USA
ABV: 6.0%

This is a classic American Amber Ale. Its balance is what makes HopBack so good: it has a lot of malt and a lot of hops, yet when they're together they both feel and taste restrained and refined, and it's the sort of depth that only comes from brewing (and drinking) the same beer thousands of times. The name refers to the hop back, a vessel between the kettle and fermenter which can be filled with hops to give the beer extra aroma. For HopBack, Tröegs use whole-flower Crystal and Nugget hops and these give a subtle citrus aroma, some grapefruit and lemon pith, some stone fruit, spice, and pine, and a general evergreen hoppy quality. The malty base of the beer gives it an amber-orange color and a background of toasty malt and bread. Tröegs make some excellent hoppy beers, including Nugget Nectar, an Imperial Amber Ale.

Turtle Lake Brewing Company Ho Tay VPA

Hanoi, Vietnam
ABV: 5.6%

Turtle Lake is an impressive brewpub on the bank of Hanoi's Ho Tay, or West Lake (though the brewery's named after Hoan Kiem lake, south of the city). It's smart and modern, with windows looking into the brewhouse where they make a range of American-inspired beers, often with a local twist: Helmet Boy Saison is 8.1% ABV and uses local spices, while Big Boy Pants is an Imperial Stout with macadamia, cacao, and vanilla. VPA is their Vietnamese Pale Ale. It's an amber color with some sweeter, caramelly malts and some mild aromatic hops giving grapefruit peel, pepper, and roasted lemon. It's balanced and refreshing, and a good match for the mostly Western-inspired bar menu.

Nail Brewing Red

Bassendean, Australia
ABV: 6.0%

Nail have been brewing since 2000, making them one of the longest-lasting craft brewers in Australia. That longevity hasn't seen them age badly and, instead, their position as one of the mature, trustworthy, go-to brewers is assured through their reliability, availability, and quality. They are also smart and see the beer trends coming, which has led them to release their Mid, a super-fruity, highly bitter, low-strength beer called MVP, and VPA, their Very Pale Ale. Nail Red has a rich backbone of malts, which makes it relatively full-bodied but not at all caramelly or sweet. Instead, the beer has a textured, complex depth (Nail always nail their malt bases). It's heavily hopped with Citra, which comes out very orangey and zesty, with a pithy bitterness that clings around, and the combo of malt, citrus hops, bitterness, and booze all come together perfectly. If you're in Australia, you'll be hammering some Nails.

Galway Bay Bay Ale

Galway Bay, Ireland
ABV: 4.4%

Galway Bay started as a brewpub in Galway in 2009 and have since grown both the brewing and the pub side of things, opening numerous sites in Dublin. Their bars feature long and excellent beer ranges, including everything in the Galway Bay range, from a good Helles-style Lager to a smooth Milk Stout to one of Ireland's best Double IPAs, Of Foam and Fury. Bay Ale is their take on the Irish Red Ale, a style that's mostly like a reddish British-style bitter. It's got nutty, toasty, slightly caramelly malts, then a firm bitterness and a little freshness from minty and spicy hops, which is their update on the traditional style.

TRADITIONAL BRITISH-STYLE ALE

This is not the kind of beer you take home and drink from a bottle or can; it's the kind of beer that you should be drinking in the pub, by the pint, ideally handpulled from a cask. They are beers that are impeccably balanced between malt and hops, though they may be more prominent in one or the other. They are beers with subtlety and depth. They call for you, but don't shout at you. They are moderate in alcohol, so you can drink a few of them—indeed, you should drink a few because these are the kinds of beer that seem to improve from the first pint to the third, their depths being revealed as you spend time in the beer's company. No Double IPA or Fruit Sour is able to do that.

In this section, we bring together Bitters, where the color may range from gold through to brown, and the hop character ranges from spicy and herbal to fruity. There are Milds, which are notable for a lighter hop profile in most examples and a richness of malts. Scottish Ales are usually malt-forward. Then there are Strong Bitters which are higher in alcohol, with American-influenced Strong Bitters often hoppier (and you might not want three pints of those...). What links these beers is typically a low-ish alcohol content, the use of English malts, which give toast, cookies, dried fruit, and cocoa, plus the flavors and aromas of English hops. Some of these styles could be going out of fashion, stuck behind the citrusy hops of craft beer, but several notable craft brewers are rejuvenating this category for younger drinkers. Likewise, several old-school Best Bitters have gained a kind of cult following—not the hyped-up cult following that sees people queue up for a four-pack of limited-release cans, but the kind where you crave something simpler, something almost restorative, and grandfatherly.

Skebo Bruksbryggeri Höstlöv Bitter

Skebobruk, Sweden
ABV: 4.6%

Stockholm's Akkurat is one of the world's great beer bars. They have an incredible selection of draft Swedish beers, rare Belgian beers, and others from around the world, covering every beer style you could hope for. While I was thinking about what kind of hoppy Swedish craft beer I fancied, I asked for a taster of Höstlöv Bitter, a beer brewed for the bar and served from the cask. I took one sniff and a sip, and I ordered a pint of the Bitter right away. It was one of the tastiest glassfuls of English malts and hops that I'd had in a long time. The malt was biscuity and nutty, while the hops were tangy and pungent, oily and orangey, flavorsome and deeply bitter, but not prominently aromatic. I love it when a beer surprises me and surpasses all my expectations. It was so good I had a second, forgetting all about the Swedish IPAs.

The Five Points Brewing Co. Best

London, England, UK
ABV: 4.1%

Five Points Best is one of the very best beers brewed in Britain. That's a big statement, I know, but it's a perfect beer in many ways. It's a beer that appeals to both a traditional ale-drinker and a modern drinker, and it's brewed by people who really know, understand, and love a classic Bitter and its importance in the pub. It's only available in cask and it pours a bright amber color. The malt is deeply layered into the beer and gives Graham crackers (digestive biscuits), toast, and a nuttiness that together are evocative of tea and cookies. The modest 4.1% ABV means that while it's deeply malty, it's never sweet or chewy, and it's also balanced by Fuggle hops which give a deeply interesting bitterness and a spicy freshness. It's a world-class beer, best drunk by the pint, preferably several in a spicy, minty row.

Magnolia Brewing Co. Blue Bell Bitter

San Francisco, California, USA
ABV: 4.7%

Magnolia is a brewpub in Haight Street that started out brewing English-style ales and serving them next to good pub grub. It has the cozy, worn-in feel of a classic boozer, and, sitting there with a pint of Blue Bell Bitter, made me feel at home while drinking on the other side of the world. Blue Bell Bitter is brewed with Maris Otter malt, Goldings hops, and English ale yeast to give this classic copper-colored ale a chewy, toasty, bread-and-toffee malt depth with lots of floral, woody, lemon- and orange-peel hops. Across town, Magnolia have a large brewery and restaurant in the Dogpatch, plus owner Dave McLean is also part of Admiral Maltings, where they floor-malt American barley. The maltings has a taproom so you can drink beers brewed with their own malts, and, unlike most beer menus that list the hops used, this one tells you about the malt.

Harvey's Brewery Sussex Best Bitter

Lewes, England, UK
ABV: 4.0%

Harvey's Best is a classic British ale, and a favorite of many drinkers (in the south of England, anyway; there are regional divides in real ale preferences in the UK—I'm from the south, so this is my pick). Harvey's is a red-brown color. It has a stewed-tea and tea-loaf kind of malt flavor. There's a spiky, peppery, earthy hop depth and a yeast that presents itself with a peppery zing and something fruity that's hard to describe—you just know it's distinctively a flavor of Harvey's beer. When served from the cask it is vibrant and elegant, and it is the perfect example of a beer that evolves as you drink it and can present new qualities and depths from pint to pint. To me, nothing can beat a great Bitter that's served perfectly.

Boxcar Dark Mild

London, England, UK
ABV: 3.6%

This is a low-alcohol Dark Mild made in Hackney, East London. Alongside Boxcar's many hop-forward ales, a Dark Mild is an anomaly, but it's a great anomaly and a malty alternative to all those tropical hops. It's dark brown and surprisingly full in body given the low ABV. There's a lot of dark malt flavor, some brown bread, caramel, and dark fruits, and a gentle bitterness. It's equally brilliant on a cold day or a hot one, capable of being comfortingly malty and refreshingly light. It also distantly reminds me of the cans of Dark Mild that I liked when I first started drinking beer. It would seem that Boxcar's Sam Dickison had a similar relationship with Milds, and he makes this beer as a happy memory of those early malt-sweet pints. Go and visit the brewery in the taproom near Bethnal Green.

Sarah Hughes Dark Ruby

Sedgley, England, UK
ABV: 6.0%

The Sarah Hughes beers are brewed in the Beacon Hotel in Sedgley. In 1921, Sarah Hughes became the landlady of this pub-hotel, which had a Victorian-style tower brewery dating from the 1860s. She continued to homebrew beers until her death in 1951, when her son took over, but only for six more years before brewing stopped. After a 30-year hiatus, Sarah's grandson John Hughes brought the brewery back to life, using Sarah's recipe for Dark Ruby. It's a remarkable strong Dark Mild: malty and smooth, almost creamy and chocolatey; there's vanilla, dried cherries, plums, sweet vinous fruits, and so much more. I had three pints of it and each mouthful gave me something new and exciting. Mild is a misunderstood style, so if you think Milds are boring, then you obviously haven't drunk Sarah Hughes's Dark Ruby. The Beacon Hotel is a must-visit pub (just watch out as they close mid-afternoon), and it's also worth traveling around the West Midlands to explore the malty Bitters and Milds uniquely still found in the region.

Stewart Brewing 80/-

Edinburgh, Scotland
ABV: 4.4%

From the 1880s, a new taxation was put on Scottish beer based on its strength, with lower-strength beers taxed 60 shillings (60/-), going up in increments of 10 shillings: 70/-, 80/-, and sometimes 90/-. Into the 20th century, these beers came to be known as Light, Heavy, and Export, ranging from roughly 3.0% ABV to 5.0% ABV. Since then, Scotch Ale has somehow become synonymous with stronger malty ales, with the idea of the "Wee Heavy" or "Scotch Ale" category developing with craft brewing's Americanization, but the reality is that most Scottish Ales were, and still are, low in alcohol. Stewart's 80/- (spoken 80 shilling or just 80) started out as a beer brewed for a famous Edinburgh pub, The Athletic Arms (colloquially known as the Diggers because it's opposite a cemetery), but is now sold elsewhere. It's a dark amber-brown and the malt is wonderful in this beer: chewy, with raisins, tea bread, caramel, chocolate, strong tea, and toast, with a light bitterness to finish.

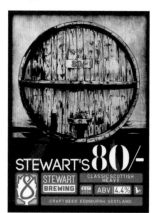

Cerevisia Craft Brewhouse Rattanak

Phnom Penh, Cambodia
ABV: 5.7%

Several countries in Southeast Asia are developing and emerging with their own small breweries, but there is still very little craft beer in Cambodia. Little, but not none, and if you're in Phnom Penh and want something more than the local lager, then you have a few options: Himawari Microbrewery is in a fancy hotel with views over the converging Tonle Sap and Mekong rivers; there's Hops Craft Beer Garden, a cool, smart spot with homebrewed beers; or there's Cerevisia, who have two taprooms in town. They brew an American Pale Ale, Irish Red, English Porter, and German Wheat beer, and their Rattanak is a strong English Pale Ale brewed with Cambodian honey. It has a floral and honeysuckle aroma; there's some honey sweetness, biscuit malts, and a spicy hop finish. Their light and fruity Blonde Ale is a good refresher on a hot day.

Conshohocken Brewing Puddlers Row ESB

Conshohocken, Pennsylvania, USA
ABV: 5.4%

ESB means Extra Special Bitter, and in the categories of British-style Bitter, this is the strongest and richest in malt. There aren't that many ESBs brewed in Britain and, in many ways, ESB has become an Americanized update of the old English Ale, where the slightly stronger and hoppier beer suits US tastes better than UK tastes—perhaps this is because most American examples are served cold and fizzy, dulling the subtleties of a classic Bitter when compared to the cask-conditioned British brews. Conshohocken's Puddlers Row is a true-tasting, British-styled ESB. It's pale amber in color, almost toward English IPA in appearance. It's toasty and bready with malts; there's some caramel, then a deep bitterness with a spicy, tangy, stewed-citrus hop depth. It tastes very English and it's great with a grilled Cheddar sandwich.

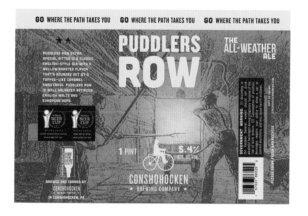

Pike Brewing Co. Kilt Lifter

Seattle, Washington, USA
ABV: 6.5%

Not many breweries make a beer like Kilt Lifter anymore. It's one of those old-style ales that leads us all the way back to the beginnings of craft beer, which is specifically true in the Pacific Northwest where a Scotsman named Bert Grant was very influential in craft beer's emerging years. Kilt Lifter is a wonderful beer, somewhat inspired by the idea of a malty Scotch Ale, which has become an American construct more than a Scottish one. It's a deep red beer that's toasty with some dark caramel, caramelized dark fruits, and maple syrup, but it's not sweet. The hops give an earthy kind of bitterness, which works with a hint of roast and smoke way in the background. I was really taken aback by this beer when I drank it in the brewpub in Seattle's Pike Place Market. I was also taken aback by the bar, which is filled with incredible breweriana—you'll want to add plenty of time to your visit just to look at everything in this wonderful pub.

MODERN BRITISH-STYLE ALE

This is where the old conventions of classic British cask ale meet with citrus-scented hops, giving a new and modern emphasis to British beer. These beers take the foundation and structure of traditional pale brews and change the decoration with the use of aromatic hops. The early beginnings of these beers started with Golden Ales (ostensibly introduced to rival growing lager sales) and evolved toward American-hopped Pale Ales with a base of British malts, while alongside them came very pale and very hoppy, lower-alcohol ales. They've settled somewhere between classic British Pale Ales and modern American ones, and the best are served from the cask where the barrel brings a softness to the citrusy hops, emphasizing some of the more subtle flavors and aromas, and giving the malts a nice, toasty roundness.

The beers in this category vary from under 4.0% ABV to around 6.0% ABV. They are usually just pale malts, and have a rich malt flavor, but it's the hops which are usually the prominent flavor, being enticing, exciting, and fruity, while the bitterness can be anywhere from subtle to strong. These beers sit separately from Pale and Hoppy, Session IPA, and Pale Ale because they have a fuller malt character and a gentler hop aroma than the other styles—and because I think this kind of modern beer deserves its own space.

Oakham Citra

Peterborough, England, UK
ABV: 4.2%

In 2009, Oakham got a delivery of a new American hop variety called Citra. It hadn't been used in England before, and was only just reaching American brewers, but there was a lot of excitement about this greatly aromatic hop. Oakham used the hop exclusively in a golden-colored ale (they call it a Session IPA now, but that's a recent name change, probably reflecting that style's popularity) with some toasty, chewy Maris Otter malts, which provided just the right amount of sweetness to be able to push forward the hops. And what a hop profile it was—and still is. Loads of citrus, tangy tropical fruits, fermenting mango, lychee, grapefruit, gooseberries, white grape, and more. It's the sort of beer that if you see it on cask, you order it, no matter what else is on—the elegance it gains from being cask-conditioned is a perfect example of just how well American hops work with English malts in pale cask ales. They make a version called Green Devil, which is a bigger version of Citra at 6.0% ABV, and this is also excellent—Oakham are very good at making modern, pale, well-hopped pale beers.

Boundary American Pale Ale

Belfast, Northern Ireland
ABV: 3.5%

This one might be a mere 3.5% ABV, but where it's restrained in booze, it's assertive in flavor. It's an amber-ish color and the base malts are a little chewy and toasty, giving it the body that a low-alcohol beer needs to ensure it still has texture and balance. The hops are West Coast American, with floral, pine, lemon, and grapefruit jumping out, and a pithy, herbal bitterness underneath. Boundary is a cooperative, and over 1,000 people have invested in the brewery, which enabled them to build and grow in their hometown of Belfast—they were only the city's second small brewery to open, and emerged into a challenging market dominated by big beer. They brew a few Hazy IPAs, plus an ever-changing range of varied and interesting seasonals, including barrel-aged brews, big Stouts, and Sours.

Northern Monk Eternal IPA

Leeds, England, UK
ABV: 4.1%

Way before anyone else used the words Session and IPA together, British brewers were making low-alcohol pale beers that were heavily hopped with American varieties, creating a popular category of beers. Lots of those beers are now called Session IPA to reflect the linguistic changes and the importance of the word IPA on a beer today. Northern Monk's Eternal IPA is a hazy yellow (it'll be clearer on cask); it's brightly citrusy and pithy, the malt is gently biscuity, the beer has a lasting bitterness at the end, and it's all beautifully balanced—it's the epitome of a modern British ale. If 4.1% ABV sounds a little strong, then Northern Monk also brew Striding Edge, a 2.8%-ABV "Light IPA," which is really great, or their Faith is an excellent Hazy Pale that you can find from the cask, keg, and can.

Thornbridge Jaipur IPA

Bakewell, England, UK
ABV: 5.9%

One of the first modern-style British Ales, and one of the first to get widespread appreciation from beer-drinkers, Thornbridge's Jaipur can be considered a classic craft beer. It's one malt—the mighty Maris Otter—and a mix of six different American hops which combine in this punchy pale beer, which is brilliant gold in color with a thick, creamy white foam on top, especially if it is served properly from the cask (I think this beer is best on cask). The malt is lush and quite full with Maris Otter's characteristic toastiness, while the hops are oily with orange peel and grapefruit, and lush with stone fruit, peaches, apricots, and pineapple—it's not the intense, juicy kinds of fruit that we taste in modern IPAs, and it's that subtlety which makes this a quintessentially British brew despite its strong American accent.

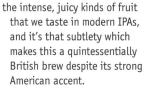

BROWN ALE

Brown Ale has become somewhat forgotten amid the fast-moving parts of modern craft beer. Neither excitingly full-on hoppy nor richly malt-sweet or roasted, it's a middling kind of beer that few people properly cheer for. Brown Ales pre-date Porters, the style that emerged with the industrialization of brewing. At that time, as beers began to reach a wider commercial audience, styles and brand names became more defined, but there was no "Brown Ale." It took until the early 20th century for the Brown style to evolve into its own shapes in Britain, with dry northern browns (think Newcastle Brown Ale) being the best known—though that's had little impact on modern craft beer.

Today, there are two main types of Brown Ale: British Brown Ale and American Brown Ale. British Brown Ale is more malt-forward. It's nutty and toasty, and perhaps a little roasty, with a richness to the body, a firm bitterness, and low hop aroma (Newcastle-style Brown is much lighter in body). American Brown Ale tends to give a lighter body (perhaps perceptibly different because it is served cold and carbonated instead of cask-conditioned). It's nutty and malty, but not sweet, then American-hopped for bitterness and aroma, being like Brown IPAs or India Brown Ales. There's a prevalence of Brown Ales brewed with coffee, especially in North America, and we also see Imperial Browns, which are stronger in alcohol and fuller bodied, usually with a robust quantity of hops. Will drinkers start rooting for Brown Ales or are they disappearing behind the bright tropical tastes of pale hoppy beers?

Theakston Old Peculier

Masham, England, UK
ABV: 5.6%

This probably doesn't count as a Brown Ale, but it is brown and it is an ale, and I want to put it in the book because, while working on these pages, I had a pint of Old Peculier in a pub in Oxford and it was glorious. It's also one of the first beers I specifically remember drinking when I was beginning to get interested in different ales. That was probably in 2005 and I didn't really like hoppy beers at that time, but I did love malty ales, and this was a beer that changed my drinking. It's soft-textured and gentle, yet it has a lot of underlying malt. It's not roasted, but has some dark flavors, some biscuit malts, perfectly cooked toast, some dried cherries, even a little banana, and some teacake, and a long English hop bitterness to finish. It's a brown-colored ale that's a glass of tasty malt flavor and a firm bitterness. It's a classic British beer, and if you drink near the brewery you might be lucky enough to find it served from wooden casks.

Braukollectiv Horst

Freiburg, Germany
ABV: 6.2%

Braukollectiv call this beer a California Brown Ale, but you could also call it a Brown IPA, as the Cascade and Centennial hops give it a big aroma of roasted citrus, burned pineapple, grapefruit, and dried lemon. The dark amber body of the beer is a little caramelly and roasted, but with a good balance of malt and enough toasty sweetness to tame the bitter hops. Braukollectiv is made up of four friends—two Germans, an American, and an Australian—who each independently started homebrewing, then all found themselves in Freiburg, inevitably meeting over a few beers. One beer led to another and their hobby-brewing turned into pro-brewing in 2014, when they released Dolly IPA. With a black sheep on the logo, the beer was celebrated as being the black sheep in a world of Helles, Dunkel, and Weissbier.

Full Moon Brewworks Andaman Phuket Dark Ale

Phuket, Thailand
ABV: 4.7%

One of the few brewpubs in Thailand, Full Moon opened in 2010 and Andaman was their first beer (since updated a little with a new recipe and the addition of Phuket to its name). It's a Dark Ale in the British tradition, brewed with floor-malted Maris Otter, and it's somewhere between red and brown in color, with a sand-colored foam. It's gently caramelly, raisiny, chocolatey, and nutty, with a distinctive flavor of British malt and a smooth body, but it's all restrained and dry with a clean bitterness at the end, almost like a Dunkel lager. If you're in Phuket, then their taproom is a smart Westernized place to sit and enjoy some beers, with the food being more American brewpub than Thai food cart, although there are some local dishes. They will also be pouring small-batch beers, some using local fruits and other ingredients, and Chalawan Pale Ale, a popular and well-distributed Thai craft beer that you'll likely see if you're visiting and in search of something hoppier than a Chang.

Cervecería Insurgente Brown

Tijuana, Mexico
ABV: 5.5%

Go to Tijuana to drink beer because it's great fun. There's a whole complex of brewery bars, and there are also taprooms and cool places to eat and drink. Insurgente's taproom has a good rooftop space where you can sit and drink a range of different beers—a refreshing Witbier, an American IPA, and Xocoveza, which is inspired by Mexican hot chocolate and brewed with cocoa, coffee, pasilla chili pepper, vanilla, cinnamon, and nutmeg. It's spicy, fragrant, and warming with pepper and alcohol. Their Brown is on the hoppier side of the style, but not full Brown IPA. You get the roasted malts with some sweetness in the middle, and a long hop bitterness, plus some piney, grapefruit-y hop aromas. It's a good beer to have with roasted and fatty meats, smoked or grilled pumpkin, or strong, nutty cheeses.

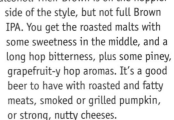

Anspach & Hobday The Smoked Brown

London, England, UK
ABV: 5.5%

Anspach & Hobday's core range of beers features modernized versions of classic British beer styles, which is represented by their labels showing a Victorian and a contemporary equivalent. It was a Porter which inspired Paul Anspach and Jack Hobday to start the brewery in the first place, and their excellent version is a 6.7%-ABV beer that's deeply roasted but not coffee-bitter, with a great depth of malt and then a firm bitterness at the end—kind of old-London Porter served fresh. Their Smoked Brown remembers the time when malt was kilned over fire, giving all beers an inherent smokiness. In this beer, the smoke is subtle, mixing with the aromas of roasted nuts, distant bonfires, cacao, and coffee, then some toffee and dried fruit in the middle, and a strong bitterness. It's the perfect kind of beer for grilled and smoked food, giving some additional smoke like an extra bit of seasoning—it's with food that Brown Ales can really be elevated and become more exciting.

Behemoth Brewing Brave Bikkie

Napier, New Zealand
ABV: 6.0%

The toasty, nutty, biscuity malt flavors in a Brown Ale make it a good style of beer to add adjuncts to, and that's what Behemoth have done here with Brave Bikkie, brewing a Brown with cocoa nibs and coconut. I'm a sucker for coconut and this one is really good, getting that richly creamy, coconutty flavor which combines with roasted malts to be like a lamington or a Bounty, but it's not sweet, with the cocoa and coconut both being almost savory in their depths. Brave Bikkie is an irregular brew, made only occasionally, so those with a sweeter tooth might want to look out for Behemoth's Triple Milk Stout, made with chocolate malt, cocoa powder, cocoa nibs, and vanilla, while those who prefer Pale Ales should have their Kiwi-hopped Chur.

Tempest Brewing All The Leaves Are Brown

Galashiels, Scotland
ABV: 10.5%

This is an Imperial Brown Ale brewed with maple syrup. It's a rich dark brown with a large tan foam. The maple comes through right away, along with some vanilla, cake, and cocoa. The body is soft and smooth with more of the distinctive depth of nutty, caramelly maple syrup running right through it, bulked out with lots of bready and toasty malts and some roastiness. It reminds me of pancakes and maple syrup, which is no bad thing, and I imagine that breakfast would be a great pairing for it, perhaps with some roasted bananas and pecans on the side (assuming you like 10.5%-ABV beers in the morning...). If All the Leaves sounds too much for you, then Tempest's Long White Cloud is a great New Zealand-hopped Pale Ale which is tropical and peachy with a powerful bitterness at the end.

PORTER

Porter was the world's first industrialized beer style, made in London's ever-growing breweries from the middle of the 18th century. As the breweries grew larger, and generally sought to improve the overall qualities of their brown beer, they moved into a new brewing era, one which used new technology and needed to sell more beer and have recognizable brewing brands, and that aligned to give us the more defined style of Porter. It was heavily hopped and stored in really large wooden tuns for a long time. By "really large," I mean *really* large, as some held millions of pints, while by "a long time" I mean many months, perhaps up to a year, with that aging evolving and maturing the flavor—some of it was drunk "stale," meaning aged, while some was drunk "mild," meaning that it was not aged for so long. This new and improved kind of beer was, in many ways, the starting point for modern beer production and it allowed Porter to become London's beer. But that was a long, long time ago, and the constant evolution of beer styles and brewing processes means that today there's nothing analogous to those old, dark ales.

Porter was important to the emergence and growth of craft beer and was one of the first styles to be brewed in America in the 1980s, coming to define how different dark ales were to light lagers, and that timing coincided with its resurrection in Britain (brewers had stopped making it around the time of the Second World War). Today, you might see Robust Porter, Brown Porter, or London Porter, and they are all essentially similar, with the Robust version perhaps being stronger, roastier, and more hopped. Most regular Porters are 4.5–6.0% ABV. They are dark and smooth, often having a more chocolatey and caramelized flavor than the roasted and coffee character in a Stout, and Porters are also usually lighter-bodied but stronger in alcohol than a Stout.

Five Points Railway Porter

London, England, UK
ABV: 4.8%

Of all London's beers, a handpulled pint of Railway Porter is the one I come to crave more than any other (often when I'm hungover, actually...). First, it looks so good: very dark brown with a creamy tan foam. Then you get the aroma of freshly milled dark malt, which is bready and burned at the same time. Those malts are more bitter and roasted than most Porters and they sit in a body that's full and smooth for the beer's relatively low 4.8% ABV. It's a beer that is both hearty and restorative, comforting and exciting, and a joy to drink. Five Point's Brick Field Brown is also one of the great dark cask ales brewed in Britain, and it's a pint of pure, delicious, toasty malt. If it's cold outside (and I'm hungover), then I'm usually on my way to find some Five Points beers on cask.

Second Chance Tabula Rasa

San Diego, California, USA
ABV: 6.2%

Not many breweries win gold at the Great American Beer Festival in the same category on more than one occasion. But Second Chance won gold in the Robust Porter category in 2016, 2017, 2019, *and* 2020, a remarkable run (who knows what happened in 2018). I judged in 2019 (but not the Robust Porter category) and then flew straight from Denver to San Diego where I was visiting friends, so, when I saw the results, I had to stop at Second Chance's taproom in North Park. Tabula Rasa is worthy of its awards. It's a Robust Porter. It has the dark chocolate, cocoa, and coffee that you expect, plus some nutty coconut and salted licorice, but what makes it so good is the density and complexity of flavor, a real richness but one that isn't heavy or sweet, ending with a deep bitterness. It's exceptional.

Magpie Brewing Co. Porter

Jeju, South Korea
ABV: 5.6%

For superstitious Brits, seeing a single magpie could be an omen of bad luck. Not so in Korea, where the magpie is a symbol of good luck or a herald bringing good news (seeing a crow, however, is bad luck to Koreans). Magpie Brewing Co. started in 2011 with the goal of bringing good beer to Korea. They've certainly succeeded and have led the growing craft-beer scene since their arrival. They now have a brewery, taproom, and restaurant on the island of Jeju, plus two taprooms in Seoul, serving a Pale Ale, IPA, Porter, and Kölsch in their core range. The Porter was my favorite beer when I visited. It has dark chocolate, dark malts, some sweeter caramels, and a fullness of flavor where other Porters can become watery. Magpie brewed Korea's first sour beer and their classically brewed Gose, called The Ghost, was awarded Champion Beer of Asia in the 2019 Asia Beer Championships. That's not just good luck, that's good brewing.

Hogshead Brewery Gilpin Black Gold

Denver, Colorado, USA
ABV: 5.6%

There are very few American breweries who do cask beer well. Much of the cask ale is an approximation, or it's just taken from the tank, put into a cask, and that's then rolled onto the bar as some kind of novelty. Not so at Hogshead in Denver. They fill the casks with beer that is still in need of some extra conditioning and time, then they leave it until it's ready before putting it on the bar. That extra time and care produce something exponentially better, fresher, livelier, and more special—they pour it properly, too, and it comes through a sparkler on the tap to create a creamier foam. Gilpin Black Gold is appropriately named for its 24-carat

quality. It's everything you expect and want in a Porter, and it's made better by being on cask, where the smoothness and roastiness of the malt are made fuller and emphasized, rather than flattened, by being fizzed from the keg. Go to the brewery in Denver and drink proper American cask ales.

Alexander Brewing Black

Netanya, Israel
ABV: 7.0%

The Alexander Brewery is one of Israel's largest craft breweries, based north of Tel Aviv. They brew a wide range of styles, including an excellent Belgian Blonde, and they routinely win significant awards at the best beer competitions. They make a considered effort to be good to the environment, as well as producing some beers with profits going to local causes, and they're all brewed by a former Israeli air force pilot. The Black is a Robust Porter at 7.0% ABV. It's all malt in the middle, both roasted and caramelized, with some dried-fruit sweetness, dark chocolate, and plenty of grain richness and weight, and there's a bittersweet finish that gives it a balance between flavor and easy drinkability. Snack on some grilled halloumi drizzled with Israeli date honey on the side.

Cerveza Fauna Penélope Coffee Porter

Mexicali, Mexico
ABV: 6.2%

Coffee is a common ingredient to add to Porter and Stout, and that makes sense as the roasted coffee flavor can also bring notes of nuts, chocolate, and fruits, while working really well with the flavors of roasted grain and fermentation. Cerveza Fauna's Penélope pours dark brown with a mocha foam, and the coffee comes through first with its roast and a light fruitiness. It's quite light and refreshing for a stronger dark beer and it ends with an espresso-like fruitiness. Fauna are well known for making great dark beers, with a Milk Stout made with cocoa and cinnamon, while their highly regarded and annually released Señor Matanza Russian Imperial Stout is a big, boozy, barrel-aged brew.

Emerson's London Porter

Dunedin, New Zealand
ABV: 5.0%

Emerson's have been brewing since 1992, making them one of New Zealand's oldest craft brewers. Richard Emerson's eponymous brewery is important for many reasons in Kiwi brewing: for being one of the earliest brewers (the Hopfather is the title of his autobiography); for effectively inventing the NZ Pilsner style; for the number of brewers who have worked there and moved on to start their own breweries (or at least been inspired by the high-quality processes they have in place); for having one of the best taprooms in New Zealand; and, finally, for the exceptional beers they brew. London Porter was the first beer that Emerson brewed, inspired by a European trip that steered him toward his life of beer-making. Today, it's a robustly malty beer, one that's creamy and smooth and chocolatey, with some berry fruitiness and a refreshing dryness at the end.

DRY STOUT

Stout's initial entry in beer's dictionary would've come with the definition of "strong Porter." Stout was a word that denoted a higher strength rather than a specific beer style. In London breweries, there was a divergence between Porter and Stout in the later years of the 19th century, with recipes remaining similar as the strengths leveled. Both beer types were typically aged, and they overlapped with the rising popularity of Mild, Bitters, and Pale Ales, which were unaged (hence they tasted milder and more bitter). As Mild's popularity grew, Porter in particular become less fashionable and would eventually disappear for several decades in the middle of the 20th century. By then, Stout had evolved into its own defined style. Stout and Porter have weaved in and out of each other's histories, and have been constantly fluid in their ever-evolving recipes, so there's no "authentic" version of either.

The most famous Stout in the world today is brewed in Dublin, and it's that beer which is seen as an archetypal Dry Stout. This roasted, dry, dark, and smooth-textured beer would come to define the style—that texture is produced by nitrogen and creates the characteristic creamy foam. Today, Dry Stout is a sessionable style with strengths in the 4.0% ABV range. It'll likely have a notable roastiness and bitterness and a smooth body, often because it's served with nitrogen. Here we also have some Export Stout, a more robust and stronger version of a Dry Stout, and American Stout, which is usually stronger, more bitter, and hoppier than an Irish-style Dry Stout.

Carlow Brewing O'Hara's Irish Stout

County Carlow, Ireland
ABV: 4.3%

This is the Irish Stout that you want to order if you're in Dublin—or anywhere else you see it. It'll give you the quintessential Stout experience, just with a greater volume of flavor to its better-known counterpart: creamy tan foam, rich malt body, cocoa and coffee, a crisp snap of roasted bitterness, some anise, and a dark berry fruitiness from the hops. I think it's the texture that makes this kind of beer so appealing, and it's a joy to drink. If you see Carlow's Leann Folláin, then it's a 6.0%-ABV "wholesome stout" that's rich, chocolatey, vinous, and super-smooth. Wonderful stuff. They also brew a caramelly Irish Red and an Irish Pale Ale. Chase them all with an Irish whiskey, as they share a smooth, sweet maltiness—my favorite is Redbreast.

Anastasiou Alceme

Athens, Greece
ABV: 5.3%

The first time I went to Athens I got really drunk in The Local Pub, a brilliant Irish bar with a soundtrack of rock music that's run by Fotis Anastasiou. You can probably picture the pub: Guinness, Kilkenny, and Murphy's fonts on the bar (plus lots of craft beer—Fotis was pioneering for good beer in Greece), British pint glasses, Irish whiskey behind the bar, a Premier League game on TV, old beer signs, dark wood—a place loved by locals with a brilliant atmosphere. When I went back for my second visit a few years later, Fotis had taken over the two buildings either side of his pub and put a brewery in them. The Anastasiou beers include a great Pilsner and Kölsch, some bitter Pale Ales and IPAs, but it was their Irish-style Stout that impressed me the most—it felt right drinking that beer there. It's roasted, not rich but deep with the flavors of dark malt; it's bitter with hops, not nitro'd but still smooth, and with a great depth. A great beer served in a great pub.

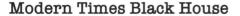

Modern Times Black House

San Diego, California, USA
ABV: 5.8%

Modern Times is a brewery that also roasts its own coffee beans, which are well sourced and either packaged as single-origin or blended, and, alongside their colorful cans of beer, they also sell cans of cold brew. Black House combines beer and coffee. It's built on a base of pale two-row malt, then loaded with tasty darker malts that sound as if they're from the local bakery, including kiln coffee malt, chocolate malt, biscuit malt, and oats. The beer has a deep roastiness, although it isn't astringent. It's quite light in body, letting the house blend of beans give some dark fruitiness, berries, cacao, and a kick of caffeine, with a balancing hint of umami. It's a great mix of dark beer and coffee.

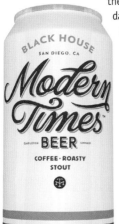

Bell's Brewery Kalamazoo Stout

Comstock, Michigan, USA
ABV: 6.0%

This is a classic American Stout. If you see Stout prefixed with American, it could mean a number of different things (often all together): stronger than usual, hoppier than usual, or with some added ingredients, usually coffee. Kalamazoo Stout is 6.0% ABV and made with lots of hops and some licorice. It has some fresh coffee aroma, some cherries or berries, a hint of that aniseedy licorice, and some resinous hops. The body is comfortingly smooth and carries a mix of fruit and chocolate before a firm bitterness at the end, which meets with a dryness. It's definitely worth visiting the brewery's Eccentric Café in Kalamazoo, if you can. You'll most likely be drawn there by their excellent

IPAs, such as Two Hearted and Hopslam, but don't overlook their dark brews. They make a Double Cream Stout, a Cherry Stout with tart local Montmorency cherries, and Expedition is their excellent Imperial Stout.

McSorley's Old Ale House Dark

New York, USA
ABV: 5.0%

There's a refreshing lack of beer choice at McSorley's Old Ale House: a dark beer or a pale one. Whatever you order, you get two small, chunky glass mugs of beer, served with lots of foam. Nothing is distinctive about the beers, in all honesty, and it's hard to know if the dark one is a Dry Stout or a Schwarzbier (and it doesn't really matter, to be honest—it's dark, tastes of licorice, and is a little treacly and well carbonated). What does matter is the experience of drinking in McSorley's. It's a bar that's been open since 1854 and is New York's oldest surviving Irish pub. Walking in today, over sawdust-covered floorboards, you'd swear that you'd just jumped through a time warp. The main bar still has the old taps, though these are no longer in use. There's some old memorabilia—photos, tankards, ornaments, the coal stove—all around. It's a storied place and a proper old boozer of a pub. Women were only allowed in from 1970; they didn't install a female toilet until 1986; and it was only in 1994 that the first female worked behind the bar.It's a rare taste and experience of old New York.

Strange Brew Mandy Black

Athens, Greece
ABV: 7.0%

Most people associate Greece with golden sunshine, golden sand, and golden lager, so it's perhaps a little surprising to have two Stout entries in the same chapter, but I drank a lot of really good dark beers while I was visiting Athens—and Mandy Black was the best beer that I drank there. It's an Export Stout, so a stronger-than-usual version of a Dry Stout. It smells like a sack of dark malt, like cacao and coffee beans. It's rich with malt flavor and it has a fullness in the mouth, but not a heaviness. It's bitter, not sweet. There's dark chocolate and the pure flavor of dark malts, and it ends with a little vanilla and dark fruits. It's a world-class Stout. In Strange Brew's taproom I also loved drinking their Jasmine IPA, a hazy, 7.2%-ABV IPA that's very light for its strength and super-juicy with melon and tropical fruits.

Cervejaria Garimpero Tucano

Campinas, Brazil
ABV: 4.2%

Tucano is a textbook Dry Stout, and that sort of dark beer which drinks like a light one—a good thing in the sultry Brazilian climate. You get lots of roasted barley flavor, cacao, espresso, malt, and then a fruitiness in the background with some berries or the tartness of dark chocolate. It's clean, bitter, and balanced, but still with a lot of depth, and it's a perfect example of the style. Their main beer is a West Coast Double IPA called Irineu. It has a deep orange color which gives a jamminess to the malts and makes the Mosaic and Ekuanot hops taste juicier and plumper, with citrus and stone fruit before a long-lasting bitterness.

SWEET STOUT

Where Dry Stouts are bitter with roasted dark malts and end with the dryness that their name tells us to expect, Sweet Stouts are fuller-bodied, smoother, and less bitter. A few things can provide the sweetness (or at least the perception of a sweeter Stout): Oats used in the brew will create a richer mouthfeel and a fuller-bodied finish, instead of a bitter dryness, with Oatmeal Stout being a popular beer style; milk sugar (or lactose) will go into a Milk Stout or Cream Stout, with brewers using less roasted barley and hops to enhance the smooth creaminess of the texture; or chocolate, vanilla, coffee, and other flavorings can be added to enhance the sweeter flavors of this kind of beer, often alongside oats or lactose.

Most of these styles are around 5.0–6.0% ABV for the standard beers, but there are Imperial and stronger versions of all of them, including some with a heavy hand in the adjuncts/candy drawer. Most keep the classic dark malt qualities of a Stout, with more mocha than espresso, though the style is generally getting sweeter as the collective craft beer-drinking palate shifts. The smoother qualities of these beers can make them work really well with spicy foods, roasted and barbecued meats, and some lighter desserts. One warning: vegans and those who are lactose-intolerant might want to take a closer look at the labels before automatically opening beers like this.

Samuel Smith's Oatmeal Stout

Tadcaster, England, UK
ABV: 5.0%

Samuel Smith is a curious brewery who are known in Britain for having an estate of old-world pubs (with some happily old-world beer prices) with oddball rules, like no phones allowed. In the US they are better known for their old-world bottle labels and beer selection, which is well distributed and much loved, meaning the beers have come to be seen as defining examples of many styles, and rightly so. The Oatmeal Stout is creamy, nutty, smooth, and a touch savory from the oats, with a bittersweet dark-chocolate finish; their Nut Brown Ale is a traditional, old-style, nutty Brown; their Imperial Stout is a moderate 7.0% ABV with a great body of cacao and dried fruits; and Stingo is a wood-matured Strong Ale. If you're in a pub and they have Old Brewery Bitter on handpull, then order this classic Yorkshire ale which is served from a wooden barrel—just don't be tempted to take a photo of it on your phone or you might get into trouble.

Tree House Brewing That's What She Said

Charlton, Massachusetts, USA
ABV: 5.6%

Better known for their IPAs, Tree House also make this very good and much sought-after Milk Stout. That's What She Said contains lactose to produce a sweet creaminess, which is enhanced by the malts being big on the caramel and chocolate and low on the bitter roast, giving it the qualities of a chocolate malt smoothie, helped by the brewery's characteristic lush mouthfeel. Tree House is a hugely impressive brewery that's grown very big, very quickly, on their foundation of (mostly) heavily hopped and hazy beers, and they are a great example of a brewery that's become a destination, with people driving across the country to visit the brewery's taproom and campus (it feels big enough to be a campus, anyway) and stand in line to buy a case of their Double IPA. When you taste it, it's easy to see why: it is saturated with hops in a way that's almost impossible to comprehend, while also creating the soft mouthfeel that's come to be expected with the style.

Playground Brewery Witch Chocolate Stout

Seoul, South Korea
ABV: 5.7%

The founding idea behind Playground, which opened in 2015, was that drinkers could find a simple pleasure in drinking beer, the kind of simple, joyful, childlike pleasure that comes from playing in the park. The Witch Chocolate Stout is brewed with some oats for added smoothness and that combines with lots of dark grain to give a full-bodied and smooth beer with layers of toffee, sweet coffee, and cocoa. Their taproom is American-inspired, and it's a simple set-up with bare brick, graffiti, an open kitchen serving beer snacks, and a long beer line-up, including styles like a Session IPA, Saison, and cherry Wheat beer. It's the kind of adult playground where you can jump from beer to beer and have a brilliant time.

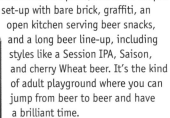

McAuslan St-Ambroise Oatmeal Stout

Montreal, Canada
ABV: 5.0%

Oatmeal Stout is one of my favorite types of beer, and within two deep gulps of this beer in a bar in Montreal, St-Ambroise became one of my favorite versions of the style. It came as a near-black beer with a thick, tan-colored foam; it looked beautiful and it tasted beautiful. It was creamy, smooth with the oats, a lush depth of dark chocolate but not sweet, and with a deft lightness and lasting bitterness which nicely combined dark malt and hops. I went back later that day and drank several more glasses, then I had a bottle next to a plate of poutine, which was a great match—the savory gravy and cheese curds were really good with the soft roastiness in the beer. The brewery has been making beer since 1989, and their Pale Ale is a reflection of the old style of beer, mixing Cascade and Willamette hops with some European varieties, giving a more floral, subtle Pale compared to the West Coast wallops we're more used to today.

Dois Corvos Galáxia

Lisbon, Portugal
ABV: 6.0%

Dois Corvos, meaning "Two Crows," was one of Portugal's first craft breweries, opening in 2015 and later adding the country's first taproom. That taproom is long and narrow, leading to the brewery at the back. On tap they'll have their dry and bitter Session IPA, aromatic with Citra and Mosaic hops, plus their IPA, which is fuller-bodied and more malty, but still with loads of American hops. Galáxia is their Milk Stout, brewed with lactose and oats for a creamy sweetness to go with the roasted dark malts, which gives a nice overall impression of dark chocolate. When I was there, I'd spent the morning eating my way around Lisbon's *pastel de nata* bakeries and I had a box of them in my bag. I couldn't resist eating one while drinking Dois Corvos's Finisterra, an 8.5%-ABV Imperial Porter. It was a good match.

Seven Bro7hers Brewery Sling It Out Stout

Manchester, England, UK
ABV: 5.5%

This one has a couple of great stories. First, the brewery: the name is literal, as it's run by seven brothers. With that many little lads running around, their dad sought some solace in the cellar of their house, where he homebrewed. One by one, as the boys turned 18, they drank dad's homebrew and eventually, via other careers, decided to all come together and start their own brewery in Salford, Manchester. The second story involves Kellogg's, who have a factory in Manchester. Like any food production, there's some stuff that can't be sold, but is still perfectly edible, so Seven Bro7hers and Kellogg's partnered up, with the brewery making three beers out of otherwise wasted cereal. There's an IPA with Cornflakes, a Pale Ale with Rice Crispies, and this Chocolate Stout with Coco Pops, which smells nostalgically like the cereal, with cocoa and vanilla, while the body has a lightness to it for a Stout. The seven brothers have four sisters and they make gin at Sis4ers Distillery. I bet parties at their house are good fun.

Thirsty Crow Vanilla Milk Stout

Wagga Wagga, Australia
ABV: 5.2%

Thirsty Crow is a brewpub in Wagga, sort of midway between Melbourne and Sydney (in the same way that Manhattan is midway between Portland, Maine, and Richmond, Virginia). Their core range is mostly a crowd-pleasing mix of hoppy easy-drinkers: a crisp, Kiwi-hopped Pilsner; a peachy and passion-fruity Summer Ale; and a bitter golden IPA. It's this Vanilla Milk Stout for which they're best known. It's brewed with lactose, with lots of Heilala vanilla from Tonga added later. You immediately get vanilla and it's reminiscent of cookies, chocolate cake, and mocha. The beer is smooth and creamy, generous but not overly sweet, and with the vanilla adding a luxurious depth. Have it with a Tim Tam, a famous Aussie chocolate bar.

THE STORY OF CRAFT BEER

It was, of course, a slow start. Craft beer would create a fundamental shift in drinking habits in America, and then all around the world, but it wouldn't be an immediate change.

Anchor Brewing, in San Francisco, were the important pioneers in American small-scale brewing, and they were on their own for many years before others joined them (helped by the legalization of homebrewing in 1978). It's from 1980 that we see more and more breweries and brewpubs beginning to open. This came at a trough of brewery numbers—just around 90 in North America—and a monoculture of mainstream lager. The first microbrewery beers were in bold contrast to those lagers: there were Amber Ales, Pale Ales, Red Ales, Porters, and Stouts. Most of these beers began as European recipes, which were Americanized with local ingredients, the most important being the use of new varieties of American hop to give beers with a strong bitterness and a citrusy, floral aroma.

I think two words defined, and continue to define, craft beer: local and flavor. The idea of being able to visit a local brewery—and support a small local company—resonated with a new generation of people, while the beers they were now looking to buy were way tastier than macro lagers. Together they made a statement: "I choose something different."

As well as flavor, the entrepreneurship of craft beer offered variety. It was free from boards of directors who were only interested in maximizing profits; it was able to brew new things regularly and to experiment; and it was free from rules. It created a new drinking culture and one with more choice than ever before.

Through the 1990s, the number of breweries steadily increased. Hops came to be the characteristic that was associated with craft beer, and Pale Ales and Amber Ales increased in popularity. Beers were typically moderate in alcohol and only some very special or seasonal releases ever got above around 8.0% ABV. In the 2000s the growth continued, and the variety of beers began to increase. IPAs started to get more and more popular. There were now more Imperial Stouts, and some of these were aged in bourbon barrels. Breweries started to grow and expand.

There were around 2,000 craft breweries in America by 2010. By now, strong, bitter, and aromatic IPA had become craft beer's chief style. Then came the stronger and hoppier Double IPAs. Next came waves of popularity for other beer types: more barrel-aged Stouts, Saisons, Sour Beers, Session Beers. But mostly just lots of IPAs.

Brewery numbers boomed, starting from around 2013, and this is increasing year on year. IPAs have become an extended family of beers now, with Hazy IPAs the must-brew and must-drink style. Once-small breweries are now very large national and international brands. That local brewpub now has several brewing facilities and a couple of bars. They're in every major grocery store. They're on airplanes and in movie theaters.

The Whittiker Hotel was one of many bars across North America to serve Anchor Tivoli Lager Beer (left). An old beer label for Anchor Steam Beer, brewed in San Francisco, California (above).

A Beer Bar in Bangkok, Thailand.

Judging beer at the China Craft Beer Awards 2016.

Into the 2020s, there are 8,000 craft breweries in America. The market is now vast and varied, reaching all parts of the country, and is responsible for inspiring the whole world when it comes to beer. Much of that inspiration takes in the spaces (like the brewpubs and bars) as well as the beer styles. And there are small breweries in almost every country in the world, with certain markets growing rapidly and excitingly, like Southeast Asia, Eastern Europe, and South America.

There's also now the ongoing co-existence of craft beer and large global brewing companies, with an increasing number of craft breweries owned by big ones, and this is changing the landscape of beer around the world. For many, that's created a renewed focus toward independence, while others show an ambivalence to what's become a new normal for the industry. It remains to be seen what will happen with this, but my feeling is that a lot of consumers just don't know or care who ultimately owns a brewery—if you know, then you make informed choices; if you don't, then you're happy buying the beers you're buying. It's a recent challenge that many drinkers are still trying to reconcile with (especially if a favorite local brewer is no longer independent).

In Britain, where cask ales have long given a localized beer culture, the important moments of change came in a couple of different waves. A shift began in the 1950s with the introduction of cold, kegged ales, coupled with a greater availability of bottled beers and with people drinking beer at home (those carbonated kegged beers tasted more like the bottled beer, so were more familiar when sitting on the sofa drinking beer and watching television). Then came kegged lagers and sales began to catch up with the antiquating brown and bitter cask ales. The reaction from the traditional brewers was to start making lighter Golden Ales. Many microbreweries opened in the 1980s and onward. Ales got lighter. Classic styles like Porter returned to pubs after a long hiatus. Beer styles evolved. Lager sales overtook those of ale

for the first time in 1989 (Britain was the last market in the world to become lager-drinkers). In the late 1990s and into the 2000s, British ales got aromatically hoppier as American hop varieties began to be combined with British pale-colored ales. Through these changes, small and local breweries remained important thanks to the pub culture.

The first shift toward a more focused British "craft" brewing industry came in around 2007 with more inspiration taken from American breweries. Then came an even greater leap forward, from around 2010 onward. This was when more small breweries were opening; there were more American Pale Ales and IPAs; there was more good kegged beer and then canned beer; and there was also more excitement about beer variety, which has continued exponentially ever since. Today, there's a small resurgence of breweries making traditional and modern cask beer, the older regional brewers remain, and there is all of the progressive hoppiness of contemporary craft beer.

All around the world, modern small breweries are now opening, and this is changing drinking cultures and creating new ones. Many of these new brewers are in countries that don't grow the ingredients needed for beer, so the grain and hops are all imported, as is the inspiration, which mostly comes from American breweries. Gradually, these faraway breweries are evolving to suit their local markets and making beers with a more localized culture and appeal. It demonstrates the maturing of the industry.

The history of craft beer is an ongoing story of small businesses trying to make a difference and do something new. There's a never-ending search for newness, or for celebrating traditions in new ways, which has defined craft beer through the past five decades, and that's not going to change any time soon.

BALTIC PORTER

As Porter brewing developed in London and the breweries increased in scale, many of them started shipping larger volumes of beer overseas, with the Pale Ales that arrived in India being the best known (though overall much more Porter was drunk in India than Pale Ale). A lot of Porters docked in the ports of Eastern Europe, where it became a popular kind of beer, providing warmth and sweet sustenance with its high alcohol content. When local breweries began opening in the region, they continued to brew the dark beers, but combined the brewing process with that of lager brewing from Germany, meaning that many of these Baltic-brewed Porters used a lager yeast and/or underwent an extended cold maturation.

Today, a Baltic Porter could be brewed using an ale or a lager yeast, though more important than the fermentation is the maturation and a long cold-conditioning, which should define these beers. The best are rich with dark malts, but without any harsh, burned, or acrid roastiness, and they are often surprisingly light for their high strengths (usually 7.0–11.0% ABV). Baltic Porter has become Poland's beer style and it's the kind of beer by which each craft brewery can be judged. On Polish Baltic Porters you'll see a number with a degree symbol next to it, usually 19°–24°. That's a reference to the original gravity of the beer, meaning the amount of fermentable sugars before fermentation; and the higher that number, the richer, fuller-bodied, and more premium the beer will be.

Browar Kormoran Imperium Prunum

Olsztyn, Poland
ABV: 11.0%

Imperium Prunum is made using *Suska sechlońska*, which are smoke-dried plums. Smoking was an old way of preserving a bountiful fruit harvest a few hundred years ago in the very south of Poland, and the smoky, chewy, sticky sweetness became something unique to the local palate, a flavor reminiscent of grandmother's kitchen. In this beer they add a definite smokiness, a dark fruitiness like charred dried fruit. There's a port-like texture and vinous flavor, lots of dark chocolate but very little roastiness, with the smoke remaining all the way through to the end. It's a whopping 26° Plato, giving us the 11.0% ABV, and that creates a thick, luxurious, complex beer, lifted at the end with the smoke. It's a special and rare beer with a unique flavor from the plums.

Jack's Abby Framinghammer

Framingham, Massachusetts, USA
ABV: 10.0%

Released every January, Framinghammer is a big Baltic Porter, brewed long and slow by a lager-focused brewery. It's made sweeter and chewier than most by using oats and brown sugar, and these combine with the dark grains and the alcohol to give the beer a great complexity of sweet dough, dried cherries, vanilla, molasses (black treacle), a nice creaminess, and some warmth. Jack's Abby put the base brew into a bunch of different barrels and add various ingredients to bring out a broad series of barrel-aged versions of Framinghammer, which might include a straight-up bourbon-aged brew, some in brandy barrels, some with coffee, and ones with Graham crackers (digestive biscuits), gingerbread, and even PB&J. The flavored ones are good dessert beers.

Thisted Bryghus Limfjordsporter

Thisted, Denmark
ABV: 7.9%

A distinctively Danish-tasting Baltic Porter, this beer is brewed with black licorice and a little beechwood-smoked malt. It's almost black, and there's mocha and woody aromas and a fudgy softness in the middle. The licorice definitely comes through, but it's not overwhelmingly aniseedy or strong; instead, it combines with the smoked malt to give the savory kind of licorice that's popular in Scandinavia. The finish on the beer is long and dry, keeping this big, dark beer nice and light. For the licorice-lovers out there, Thisted make a special edition that contains *17 times* more of the sweet-spicy root. Thisted Bryghus was founded in 1902, and today it's independent and run by its shareholders, most of whom are local to the brewery.

Põhjala Öö

Tallinn, Estonia
ABV: 10.5%

Baltic Porter is popular in Estonia, and Põhjala are masters at making the style. *Öö* means "night," and the beer is darker than the darkest of nights. It has the kind of chewy texture that is immediately hearty and comforting. It's opulent with dark malts, with cacao, caramel, coffee, and chocolate, plus some plummy dried fruits. For such a big beer it ends really light, a skillful trick of the brewers that makes this the kind of beer you'll open and drink without really noticing the strength. Põhjala have a taproom in Estonia and there they pour their full range of beers—you'll want to try as many as you can since they are one of Europe's top brewers. I haven't actually been to their new taproom (but it looks great!). I have, however, been to their old one, where me and some mates got really drunk on very strong beer and then went to a Russian club nearby and drank loads of vodka. Tallinn's a fun place (as far as I can remember).

IMPERIAL STOUTS AND BARREL-AGED STOUTS

Empress Catherine the Great of Russia, who ruled from the middle to the end of the 18th century, supposedly ordered and drank large volumes of Extra Stout Porter, meaning an extra-strong version of London's famous beer style—the beer was said to be so strong that it'd last for seven years. Whether true, mythologized, or just made up, over time the style acquired the name Imperial, which became synonymous with high strength (so today's prefix of Imperial, to mean stronger than normal for any style, actually dates back to the 1830s). Like a lot of old British styles, it took the emergence of American craft beer to bring this type of beer to a new prominence. In this case, Imperial Stout became a flagship strong beer that demonstrated just how different craft ales could be to macro lagers.

Imperial Stout (sometimes called Russian Imperial Stout) is made by breweries all around the world, and it continues to be one of the strongest and most impactful beers in their ranges. They are typically over 10.0% ABV, reaching 15.0% ABV or higher. They are usually bitter-sweet, roasted and rich, and loaded with chocolate and coffee flavors, and typically have a full body, with some finishing dry and bitter and others being sweeter. These beers often include adjuncts and flavorings, such as vanilla, chocolate, coffee, coconut, maple syrup, and spices, and might also be brewed with oats or lactose for more sweetness and texture. Being so strong, and so flavorsome, they've become the main style of beer aged in barrels, most typically old bourbon or whiskey barrels. This means that the beer sucks flavors such as toffee, vanilla, coconut, and bourbon from the wood.

The Kernel Imperial Brown Stout 1856

London, England, UK
ABV: 10.0%

If you want a suggestion of what Imperial Stouts were like in the 19th century, then this beer is a good place to start. It's based on a recipe from 1856 and, although it uses modern ingredients and equipment, and is not stored for a year before serving, the base brew remains close to the old London brewing traditions. It's a deep brown beer that's full-bodied and almost creamy, with layers of malt flavor which unravel as you drink: there's wholegrain toast, caramel, some light coffee, chocolate biscuits, brown malts, and some roasted grain, then there's dried plums, tobacco, wafts of distant wood smoke, and maybe some vanilla or cocoa. The Kernel also make Export Stout 1890 based on another old recipe, which is deeply malty and roasted, and there's a modern-inflected Export India Porter that is robust with dark malt and hopped almost like a Black IPA.

Dieu du Ciel Péché Mortel

Montreal, Canada
ABV: 9.5%

Dieu du Ciel's Péché Mortel is one of the world's great Imperial Stouts. Brewed with coffee, the beans percolate with roasted bitterness, kicking out some caffeine along with the chocolatey flavors of malt. It's become the brewery's flagship beer and they've developed a line of variants, including some barrel-aged, some with coconut or chocolate, another with lactose to make it a latte, and some with fruit. Try whatever you can, but the best I've had is the one they serve from a nitro tap in their wonderful brewpub in Montreal, where the nitro makes the beer creamy and smooth. If you're in the brewpub—and it should be high on your must-visit list—then it's a block away from Fairmont Bagel. Montreal bagels are sweeter than their New York counterparts, and one of those with a little cream cheese is a great match for Péché Mortel.

Pasteur Street Brewing Cyclo Imperial Chocolate Stout

Ho Chi Minh City, Vietnam
ABV: 13.0%

Like all the Pasteur Street beers, this one uses a selection of delicious and exotic Vietnamese ingredients. In Cyclo, they add Saigon cinnamon, vanilla beans from Mui Ne, and cacao nibs sourced by Maison Marou, who gather amazing chocolate from around the country and have a series of single-origin bars (they have a store in Saigon that's a chocolate-lover's dream). Those ingredients combine to produce a luscious, luxurious, incredible beer that's rich with chocolate, subtly spiced, a little fruity and roasted from the cacao, and deep with an intense complexity. If you go to one of Pasteur Street's taprooms—they have them in Ho Chi Minh City, Hoi An, and Hanoi—then I suggest ordering a flight of their beers to try their full range of Vietnamese craft beers, and hopefully they'll have Cyclo on tap.

Borg Brugghús Nr.19 Garún

Reykjavik, Iceland
ABV: 11.5%

A brooding, dark brew, this is the sort of thing to drink when it's cold outside. The beer pours ink-like with a thick, tan foam. It rolls heavy, leaving legs down the side of the glass. It's deeply roasted, very clean from the soft Icelandic water, and bitter with coffee and chocolate. There's some aniseed, licorice, molasses (black treacle), and stewed fruits, and it gets more vinous as it ages. Borg Brugghús make just about every beer style you can think of, plus a few that you've never heard of before, including a couple that use malt smoked over a fire of dried sheep dung—smoking this way is traditional in Iceland.

Great Lakes Blackout Stout

Cleveland, Ohio, USA
ABV: 9.9%

There's an over-abundance of barrel-aged, flavored, or 12.0%-plus ABV Imperial Stouts on the market right now, but I often just crave a straight-up big Stout, one that's a joyful glass of strong malt and alcohol, unfussed by other stuff. There are several classic American-brewed Stouts that fit the bill, such as Bell's Expedition, Brooklyn Black Chocolate, Old Rasputin by North Coast, and Great Lakes's Blackout Stout. This beer is released toward the end of every year and it's everything I want in an Imperial Stout: hearty, bitter from hops and malt, chocolatey, and coffee-roasted; there's some dried fruits, and a hint of savory smoke and pine resin. It's not sweet, just wonderful to drink. Their regular Porter, Edmund Fitzgerald, is a classic dark beer that everyone should try.

Galway Bay Two Hundred Fathoms

Galway Bay, Ireland
ABV: 10.0%

Galway Bay's annually released Imperial Stout is aged in Teeling Small Batch Irish whiskey barrels. That blended whiskey is soft with ginger, sweet rum, vanilla, oak, and toffee, and the richly chocolatey Stout that goes into the barrels is infused with the wood, the spirit, and some spice, with molasses (black treacle) and the softness of the whiskey making this a subtle and wonderful collaboration. To take the project through another life cycle, the brewery also occasionally returns the barrels to the distillery, who then put more whiskey in them. Try and drink the beer and whiskey side by side to see how the flavors overlap.

Fierce Very Big Moose

Aberdeen, Scotland
ABV: 12.0%

Brewed with lots of oats, plus cocoa husks, coconut, cinnamon, and vanilla, Very Big Moose started out as a collaboration beer with BrewDog's Aberdeen bar before becoming a regular brew. It's a chewy kind of Stout that's big on malt, but low on roast, being chocolatey, a little fruity like dried cherries, and a little spicy from the cinnamon, plus it's not overly sweet, nor is it overpowered by the adjuncts. Fierce have also made some barrel-aged versions of VBM, some with maple syrup, others with extra coconut or coffee, meaning it's become a fun plaything for additional ingredients and variants. Whichever one you get you'll be happy with your choice. A good food match for VBM would be cranachan, a mush-up of oats, cream, honey, whisky, and raspberries. Fierce also brew a beer version of that dessert, which is an oatmeal Pale Ale with tart raspberries.

Toppling Goliath Kentucky Brunch Brand Stout

Decorah, Iowa, USA
ABV: 13.0%

Perpetually one of the world's highest-rated and most sought-after beers, Toppling Goliath's KBBS, brewed with coffee and aged in bourbon barrels, is a behemoth of a brew, though you'll probably never get to taste it. It has an extremely limited release that you have to get from the brewpub, but even to do that you have to win a ticket in an online lottery beforehand. In 2019, under 1,000 12oz (355ml) bottles were available, just one per person, and it was $100 per bottle (several days after the launch, they were selling for ten times that on the black market). That kind of rarity and hype naturally enhances people's perceptions, but it's an exceptional and impactful beer, one that's decadent like dark chocolate, unctuous with maple syrup, and boozy like an espresso martini. If you can't get KBBS, the brewery makes several other big Imperial Stouts that are *slightly* easier to find.

De Struise Black Albert

Oostvleteren, Belgium
ABV: 13%

Brewed in East Vleteren, not far from the Trappist monks on the west side of town, De Struise are known for their strong beers, their Belgian Quads, their barrel-aging program, and for making very high-quality beers. Black Albert is one of the best. It's molasses-like (treacly), black, and rich, yet the Belgian-style carbonation keeps it from being heavy. There's dark chocolate, hints of bourbon, some berry fruits, plums, dried cherries, some creamy mocha, sometimes a little peppery funk from the yeast, and a really deep bitterness from both roast malt and hops. It's a majestic and complex beer that'll evolve as you drink it (and evolve if you choose to cellar it for a year or two). Given that it's a big Belgian Stout, you should probably pair this one with some good chocolate truffles—it's so strong that it can handle white chocolate or go with some nutty truffles. If you see Cuvée Delphine, then this beer has been aged in Four Roses bourbon barrels for a year; it's more luxurious and richer with molasses, vanilla, toffee, and oak.

Kane Brewing Co. Morning Bell

Ocean, New Jersey, USA
ABV: 9.2%

Released once a year, in February, this is an Imperial Milk Porter aged with coffee beans roasted by Rook Coffee. The coffee is a big flavor in this beer, bringing roast, a bit of fruitiness, and some sweetly fermented aromas. The addition of lactose gives this a richer and creamier, latte-like mouthfeel and some caramel, and it balances all the darker malt and coffee character really well. They usually make a few variants, which might include cacao or vanilla, cinnamon, and maple syrup, and if you're lucky you'll find a bourbon barrel-aged version.

Bottle Logic Fundamental Observation

Anaheim, California, USA
ABV: 13.5%

Released annually to a lot of excitement, Fundamental Observation is a Madagascar vanilla-infused Imperial Stout aged in a mix of different bourbon barrels—the barrels vary each year, as does the ABV. What's great about this beer is how the barrels and vanilla come to enhance each other's characteristics, which in turn makes the malt depth of the beer richer (vanilla has that trick of being able to enhance flavor in sweet things in the way salt does in savory things). The vanilla is dominant, as is the barrel, so there's little subtlety in this beer and it's all bourbon, booze, vanilla fudge, maple syrup, chocolate, and a thick body. However, there's some restraint in the beer and some kind of massive balancing act happens between sweetness, bitterness, barrel, and booze.

Boatrocker Brewers & Distillers Ramjet

Braeside, Australia
ABV: 11.5%

For Aussie beer geeks, the annual release of Ramjet is something to circle in the diary. Since 2013, Boatrocker have been brewing a big Imperial Stout and they succeeded in their aim of aging it in uniquely Australian barrels. When you drink a Ramjet, the beer is at least the third different drink to be matured in the wood. The barrels begin with Australian red wine or fortified wines; then they go to the Starward Distillery in Port Melbourne, who make whiskey using Australian barley, with the whiskey picking up a vinous flavor from the wines; then, finally, once the whiskey is ready, the barrels are emptied and passed on to Boatrocker, who fill them with Stout. The mix of Australian wine, whiskey, and beer creates an ever-changing palate in Ramjet, with the base brew giving its chocolate, caramel, and coffee, the wine some jammy and dried fruits, and the whiskey some booze, toffee, and spice, plus the background of oak and vanilla.

5 Elementos Abyssal

Fortaleza, Brazil
ABV: 12%

Abyssal is one of Brazil's highest-rated beers. It's made with barley, rye, oats, cocoa, and molasses (black treacle), which give it a full body and an oily kind of texture. The molasses adds some deeper flavors of caramelized sugars, without leaving the beer sweet, while the cocoa gives some milk-chocolate flavors. It ends with a good amount of espresso-like bitterness from the roasted malts and a lot of hops. If Abyssal doesn't sound sweet enough for you, then 5 Elementos brew a Brunch Stout called Coffee & Pancakes with lactose, maple syrup, and coffee, though the 12.0% ABV might suggest supper rather than breakfast.

PASTRY STOUTS

"Sundaes and smoothies, cupcakes and cookies, tiramisus and truffles, milkshakes and marshmallows; there's ice cream, cheesecake, cornflakes, and donuts; cacao, coconut, nut syrups, maple syrup, milk sugar, always some vanilla, usually shitloads of coffee, all freakshaked into a Fat Imperial Stout that's over-adjuncted and under-attenuated. Most taste like American gas stations: flavored hazelnut coffee, vanilla in everything, cinnamon donuts, and fusel fumes." That's something I wrote for *Ferment* magazine in 2018 and, for me, it still describes Pastry Stouts perfectly. These are immature and obscenely strong beers that are overloaded with the sort of sweet ingredients you'd normally find in pastries. Flavored Stouts have been popular for years, but what takes them up to Pastry level is how stodgy and sickly sweet they are from the combination of a high final gravity (residual sweetness) and the heavy adjuncts that are added—often flavorings, gallons of espresso or syrup, actual cakes and chocolate bars, and usually lots of lactose. This isn't my favorite kind of beer, but lots of drinkers go crazy for them. The worst aspect of this category is how some are served with sprinkles or donuts on the rim of the glass, like an actual dessert. Feel free to order that while I'll be gulping down delicious lagers at the other end of the bar.

Salvador Brewing Co. Cookie de Chocolate

Caxias do Sul, Brazil
ABV: 11.0%

Coffee with a chocolate cookie was the inspiration for this beer, which uses cocoa, vanilla, and hazelnut to approximate the cookie, then adds loads of coffee for extra roastiness. It smells just like a cookie in a way which'll make you say "wow!" Sweet baked cookies, toasty nuts, and the heady luxury of vanilla, then baking chocolate and sweetened espresso; it's thick, lush, and good fun—these beers have to be fun. If Salvador haven't got Cookie de Chocolate, then they'll have another dessert-like drink, perhaps based on chocolate donuts, affogato, or cherry chocolate cake. They have a great taproom and large outdoor space, serving pizzas, burgers, and beer snacks—probably best to start on one of their Pale Ales and save the Pastry Stouts for pudding.

Amundsen Dessert in a Can Pecan & Maple Pie

Oslo, Norway
ABV: 11.5%

Amundsen have become one of Norway's largest craft breweries, and their core range is a typical mix of IPAs and Fast Sours with a Hoppy Lager for some refreshment. But they're becoming known around the world for their flavor-packed brews like Glazed & Confused, a 13.5%-ABV, super-sweet, loaded donut of a Stout brewed with biscotti, marshmallow, strawberry, caramel, coconut, vanilla, and pecan. They also have a barrel-aged Marshmallow Imperial Stout, a coconut chocolate chip cookie Imperial Stout, and a Neapolitan Ice Cream Imperial Stout, as well as a range of beers called Dessert in a Can, featuring Chocolate Mud Cake and Mint Chocolate Crisp. The Pecan & Maple Pie is like a liquid slice of pie. Nutty with both pecan and maple, it's syrupy, sweet, and chewy, with a heavy spoonful of booze at the end. They also make barrel-aged versions of the Dessert brews.

Brouwerij de Moersleutel Coconut Milkshake Smeerolie

Alkmaar, Netherlands
ABV: 10.0%

Started by four brothers—Pim, Tom, Rob, and Max—Brouwerij de Moersleutel call themselves Beer Engineers and their name translates as "The Wrench." They are known for their rotating range of beers with lots of hazy IPAs and strong Stouts. Smeerolie (the name means "lubricating oil") is their main Imperial Stout and The Coconut Milkshake version—which I bought mostly because of the can as it reminded me of Crash Bandicoot—contains coconut, vanilla, and lactose, and sweetens the Stout into something that's pudding-like, luscious, and sweetly coconutty. It's the sort of beer that makes you smile as you crack open the can and smell all the chocolate. It's decadent and will definitely leave you feeling well lubricated.

Wylam Brewing Imperial Macchiato

Newcastle, England, UK
ABV: 10.0%

Wylam's brewery in Newcastle is in the Palace of Arts, a dramatic and impressive old building, while the team behind Wylam are also responsible for the equally impressive By The River Brew Co. in the center of the city and beneath the iconic Tyne Bridge—having a pint of their hazy Heedbanger IPA, while looking out at the bridge, is one of the top beer experiences in Britain right now. Imperial Macchiato is a double hazelnut praline coffee Imperial Porter. It's a monster of a beer. Intense, rich, warming, and sweet, bonkers and boozy, this is reminiscent of hazelnut coffee—only at 10.0%.

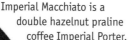

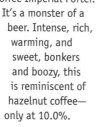

Angry Chair Brewing Imperial German Chocolate Cupcake Stout

Tampa, Florida, USA
ABV: 11.0%

If you want to know what a Pastry Stout really tastes like, then Angry Chair should be your go-to dessert brewers, just know that you really need a sweet tooth to chew through these ones. The beer's name gives you a clue as to what to expect: it's an Imperial Sweet Stout brewed with coconut, Madagascar vanilla, and cacao. Made in Tampa, this is a Disney-sweet sip of liquid cake, one that's like chocolate milk, chocolate syrup, and coconut chocolate bars with a lip-sticking finish. They brew a non-Imperial version at 7.5% ABV, which is kinda like the light beer version of a Pastry Stout. If you want more and not less, then there's a bourbon barrel-aged version of the bigger one.

Horus Aged Ales Hazelnut Crown

Oceanside, California, USA
ABV: 14.2%

If you're going to do something, do it properly; if you're going to make a Pastry Stout, then really pack that thing with as much sweet stuff and booze as you possibly can. That seems to be the vibe at Horus Aged Ales, a brewery where everything is barrel-aged and most things are irresponsibly strong and sweet. The brewery has a different story to most: it's run by Kyle Harrop, who has a day job in accounting and does the beer stuff by night. He doesn't own a brewhouse, so others make the beer for him and then he trucks it back to a storage facility filled with oak barrels, where the beer matures. He's a serial (cereal?) collaborator, and many of the maddest and most ridiculously strong beers come from the collabs. Hazelnut Crown is brewed with (*takes a deep breath*): hazelnuts, Geisha coffee, coconut candy, coconut syrup, coconut water, desiccated coconut, shredded coconut, and toasted coconut, and that's all added to a beer that's over 14.0% ABV. It's a supersized freakshake that's syrupy, sticky, fudgy, candy-like, and crazily coconutty. I don't know if this particular beer will be brewed again, but you can expect Horus to have a range of big fat Pastry Stouts.

BARLEY WINE AND STRONG ALE

Originating in Britain, Barley Wine's name came from its vinous taste and high alcohol content, often being the strongest ale that a brewery produced. The big booze in these brews was originally produced with the first runnings of wort in a parti-gyle brew, which involved getting a couple of different beers out of one mash, with the stronger first runnings of wort going into one kettle and the weaker second runnings (weaker because more water was added, thus diluting the sugar) going into another, and then these were boiled and hopped differently as two distinct beers, one strong and one weak. Few brewers make it like that anymore, and the style became unfashionable until a few decades ago, when craft brewers in America reinvented Barley Wine.

Now, two main types exist: English Barley Wines have sweet malts and a strong bitterness from berry-like English hops, while American Barley Wine is closer to a more malty Double IPA, being strongly bittered and usually flavorsome with citrusy American hops. Both are around 10.0% ABV and they share a generous and full body of malts that could give sweet vinous fruits, some caramel or rich malt flavors, and a potent strength of alcohol.

Here, we're also collecting together a general selection of Strong Ales, styles that aren't quite Imperial Stouts or Barley Wines, and nor are they spicy Belgian Quads or smooth Bocks, but can fit anywhere in between. They are all the sort of sipping beers that you want to sit and contemplate rather than stand and quaff.

Coniston Brewing Co. No.9 Barley Wine

Coniston, England, UK

ABV: 8.5%

Brewed annually, then matured for almost a year before one half is put into casks and the other half into bottles, No.9 is a classic golden British Barley Wine. It's won numerous awards, including Champion Beer of Britain a couple of times. The brewery is behind the Black Bull pub, which sits quite literally at the foot of the Old Man of Coniston, a 2,600-ft (800-m) fell in the Lake District. Book a table at the pub (and a room if you want to sleep), hike to the top of the Old Man, then return half a day later to a refreshing pint of Coniston's Bluebird Bitter before settling into a glass of No.9, a superlative golden Barley Wine. It's all pale malt, plus lots of Challenger and Goldings hops. It's sherried from age, the nutty kind of dry sherry that's bitter like almonds, or even a little reminiscent of aged champagne. There are golden raisins, roasted apples, dried apricots, and a madeleine-cake sweetness. What makes it so good is the full body and the intense bitterness that really lasts a long time. Order a half pint or open a bottle, sit back, and enjoy this with a cheeseboard or a piece of almond cake.

Sierra Nevada Bigfoot

Chico, California, USA
ABV: 9.6%

Sierra Nevada started out with three beers: Pale Ale, Porter, and Stout. With each they were able to take old English brews and make them American. They did the same thing when they Americanized old British Barley Wine and, alongside Anchor's Old Foghorn, they can claim to have introduced the style to Americans. This was a big beast of a beer back in the early 1980s, a fearsomely strong brew made more intense by the huge amounts of American hops that were added, creating a richly malty and caramelized beer with a deep bitterness like citrus peel and herbal spirit, and a booming aroma of piney, orangey hops. Sierra Nevada release a new vintage each year, and some people like to store and mature them because they evolve over time. I'd have one fresh, where it's on the edge of being an Imperial IPA, then try one the following year to see how it's softened, becoming more honeyed and marmalade-y and less bitter. It's an American classic and a textbook example of an American Barley Wine.

Jackie O's Wood Ya Honey

Athens, Ohio, USA
ABV: 13.0%

This is a dark Wheat Wine, which is like a Barley Wine but brewed with more wheat and usually fewer hops. Wood Ya Honey adds lots of local wildflower honey to the wheat base and then it's aged in bourbon barrels. It's a big, strong, dark brown, and hazy brew. The honey and bourbon are very evident, both sweet like vanilla and honeycomb. It's full, smooth, and creamy, then there's raisins and caramel, some roasted nuts, and, thankfully, a little dryness at the end to stop it becoming cloying. Jackie O's has grown from a brewpub, adding a large production facility a 15-minute walk away. They've built their fanbase on a mix of quality everyday drinking ales and some big-hitting, barrel-aged brews, all while having a particular focus on sustainability, which means they have a farm and grow produce. They also have a bakeshop where they use their spent grain in various delicious fermented and baked things. If you have a Wood Ya Honey, then you'll probably want some bread, perhaps with some aged cheese as well.

Varvar Brew Golden Ale

Kiev, Ukraine
ABV: 6.9%

This isn't a Golden Ale as most people know it. It's neither the English kind nor the Belgian one, and it's what could be considered a uniquely Ukrainian beer style that defies easy categorization. What you should expect in a Ukrainian Golden Ale is a sweet and strong malt-forward beer, sometimes with added aromatic hops, but not much hop bitterness. Varvar Brew's version is perhaps responsible for the emergence of this style, and it's a beer that's almost bright gold, malty, honeyed, and smooth, with the sort of sweetness that's pleasing but also balanced. There's some coriander seed in this, adding a nice orange accent and spice which mirror a similar fruitiness in the subtle addition of American hops.

Cervejaria Augustinus Hordeum

São Paulo, Brazil
ABV: 11.5%

The brewery is named after St. Augustine, the patron saint of brewing, while *Hordeum* is the Latin name for perennial grasses, the most important of which (for us reading this book anyway) is barley. Cervejaria Augustinus are homebrewers turned pro-brewers, who gypsy-brew in São Paulo and are known for their big beers—no watery session brews over here—including a 19.0%-ABV coffee and vanilla Imperial Stout. Hordeum is a ruby-red Barley Wine that's aged with bourbon-soaked oak chips. It's layered with the flavors of barley, from bread to toast to toffee and into dried fruits. The oak chips add some of their own sweetness, almost root beer-like, and the boozy vanillas of the wood add some good depth (they also make a version with extra vanilla that's more intense). The beer ends with a lot of malt sweetness, so this is one to pour with dessert—perhaps a *queijadinha* (a little coconut cake).

Haandbryggeriet Bestefar

Drammen, Norway
ABV: 9.0%

There's a nice way in which seasonal drinking can punctuate our year: the blooming and bright hops of a fresh IPA of spring, the softer Summer Ales or a snappy Pilsner in summer, the browning ales of fall, and then the dark brews of winter. For Norwegians, the Juløl tradition—Christmas beers—is an important one and annually almost every brewery will have a special dark, malty, festive ale ready for December. Haandbryggeriet, one of Norway's best and most interesting brewers, take their Juløl seriously and annually release lots of different festive brews, including a Pils, a dark ale, a bourbon barrel-aged Stout, and a spiced sour Julegløgg, which is like a beery mulled wine. Bestefar is a strong dark ale. It's layered with spice, dark fruits, dark malt, licorice, chocolate, cinnamon, and dried herbs, then vanilla and oak from a subtle barrel-aging. They also make a version aged in aquavit barrels. Enjoy either with gingerbread cookies.

Panhead Custom Ales Black Sabbath

Wellington, New Zealand
ABV: 11.0%

This beer was originally brewed as a festival special in 2014 and has been irregularly returning since then, but always coming back to much excitement. It's a big, oaked, black barley and rye wine, which means that it's brewed with both barley and rye and uses some dark malts. The oak is subtle, giving a suggestion of bourbon and cola. There's some rye spice, some toasty malts, lots of dried fruits, and some light coffee, and all together it's a smooth, sweet, bitter, and powerful brew. Panhead's other popular beers are mostly pale and hoppy, leading with their Supercharger APA, which is all-American-hopped with a sweetish body of malt.

CLASSIC PILSNER

When asked to picture a glass of beer I can almost guarantee that you'll imagine a golden glass topped with brilliant white foam. To most people, "beer" means lager—cold, pale, refreshing, crisply carbonated. The classic beer image is of a Pilsner, which was the first beer style to become truly global, and is now brewed and drunk in more places than any other alcohol. For many, these unchallenging, light-tasting lagers were the beers we gave up when we started ordering IPAs, and that rejection has come to diminish the greatness of lager and undermine its real diversity, especially that of maligned pale Pilsners. But that's all changing now with a resurgence of interest in great lager.

When we look at classic Pilsners, there are two primary types: Czech and German. Both typically use ingredients local to their homeland, both are around 5.0% ABV, and both are regular, everyday drinking kinds of beer—these aren't fancy or expensive brews; they're just normal beers. Czech-style Pilsners are usually rounded and sweet in their malt profile; they have a fullness of malt that often comes from using a decoction mash, which gives them a caramelized character. Czech Saaz hops are commonly used to give a floral, zesty, peppery aroma and a strong bitterness that balances some of the residual malt sweetness. German-style Pilsner is lighter in color and body, drier, crisper, and more carbonated. The German hops give it a zesty, spicy, floral, citrusy aroma and a sharp bitterness. Pilsner was invented in the Czech city of Pilsen, but it's more accurate to say that the ersatz Pilsners around the world are closer to the German versions.

Plzeňský Prazdroj Pilsner Urquell

Pilsen, Czech Republic
ABV: 4.4%

Pilsner Urquell is the beer that gave us the name Pilsner. The inciting incident in this beer's blockbuster story came in 1838, when 36 barrels of bad Pilsen-brewed brown ale were poured into the city's gutters, an event that led the townsfolk to build a big new brewery for themselves, which opened at the end of 1842. The Citizens' Brewery hired a Bavarian brewmaster and did something that few other Czechs were doing at the time: they brewed lager. And this lager, thanks to new English malting techniques, was gold in color. A beer born from revolt became a revelation, and today it's still the classic Czech-style Pilsner. It's caramel-like and sweet on first taste, rich from a triple decoction in the brewing process, and bitter from Saaz hops, which give a herbal and grassy aroma, and also help to balance out the sweetness. Go to the brewery for one of the world's greatest beer experiences: in the old lagering cellars you can drink the unfiltered version of this beer direct from a 4,000-liter wooden barrel.

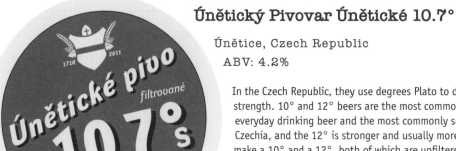

Únětický Pivovar Únětické 10.7°

Únětice, Czech Republic
ABV: 4.2%

In the Czech Republic, they use degrees Plato to distinguish a beer's strength. 10° and 12° beers are the most common, where the 10° is the everyday drinking beer and the most commonly sold strength of beer in Czechia, and the 12° is stronger and usually more premium. Únětický make a 10° and a 12°, both of which are unfiltered (though their long-lagering leaves them almost bright), and a filtered 10.7°, which I really like as it's a lager with a crispness and dryness that are rarely found in malty Czech beer. The malt flavor here is light, there's a brisk carbonation, and the bitterness grips and gives a tonic-like depth that really cuts at the end—the Czechs even have a word to describe that cut: *říz* (good luck pronouncing it). The brewery, which originated in the early 1700s but was resurrected in its current form in 2010, has a restaurant attached, and is an easy journey out of Prague. If you do go, look out for the brewery's two cats, named Deset and Dvanáct ("Ten" and "Twelve").

Budweiser Budvar Original

České Budějovice, Czech Republic
ABV: 5.0%

Budvar (Czechvar in the USA) and Pilsner Urquell are the two best-known Czech lagers around the world. They are often spoken of as if they are similar beers, and examples of the Czech Pilsner, but they are quite different in flavor profile and I'd argue that Budvar shouldn't be considered a Pilsner—it's a *Světlý Ležák*, a premium-strength, pale, Czech-style lager (Pilsner Urquell is also a *Světlý Ležák*, but it's easier here to classify that as *the* Pilsner). Budvar has some toasty Czech malts and a characteristic grain depth from a double decoction mash, but it keeps a crisp bitterness with a snap of Saaz hops, and a layered oily and floral Saaz character all through it. It is brewed in a very traditional way, similar to how it would've been made when it was first brewed in 1895: it includes whole-flower Saaz hops and is fermented and then lagered—or cold-stored—for 90 days, far longer than any other lager.

Dva Kohouti Místní Pivo 12°

Prague, Czech Republic
ABV: 4.9%

Opened at the end of 2018, *Dva Kohouti*—meaning "Two Roosters/Cocks"—is a collaboration brewpub between Ambiente, a restaurant group responsible for some of Prague's best places to eat and drink, and Pivovar Matuška, one of the top Czech craft brewers. They focus on one lager: their Místní Pivo 12° (or "Local Lager"), which is a classic-tasting Czech lager. It's deep gold in color, unfiltered and hazy. It has a richness of malt, an assertive bitterness, and a fresh Czech hop aroma. It is always served, as every Czech beer will be, with a thick head of white foam—Dva Kohouti are as focused on the serving as they are on the brewing, with their tap system specifically designed for the brewpub. There's a Czech saying that perfectly embodies their focus: "The brewmaster brews the beer, the server makes it." In other words, no matter how delicious the beer is, it's only as good as how it is served. Almost nowhere in the world has this kind of joint focus on quality beer and service, and that should be celebrated.

Notch Brewing The Standard

Salem, Massachusetts, USA
ABV: 4.4%

Notch brew the best Czech-style lagers I've tasted outside the Czech Republic, and some of the best lagers—*period*. It's Notch's focus on traditional processes and ingredients which defines the quality and character of their beers, which are brewed properly, slowly, and with respect and love for the classics. When you drink Notch lagers, you know that they can only have been made by someone who has sat and drunk dozens and dozens of mugs of that style of lager in the place where it tastes best, and that dedicated perfection is what Chris Lohring at Notch has achieved so brilliantly. The Standard is a faithful love letter to Czech Pilsner: it's brewed with Czech malt, it's double-decocted, open-fermented and lagered, and naturally carbonated until it's ready to drink. This process takes many weeks, at which point it's poured through Czech taps, giving the beer its essential thick foam.

Bierstadt Lagerhaus Slow Pour Pils

Denver, Colorado, USA
ABV: 5.1%

It takes Bierstadt Lagerhaus over 24 hours to fill one fermenter with a batch of Pils, a couple of weeks to ferment it, and then six weeks or more to lager it. Then, when you do order a glass of it, you're going to have to wait a further five minutes—the clue being in the name: Slow Pour Pils. The pour involves crashing the beer into a tall, thin glass and letting the foam settle, then repeating this until the glass is gradually topped up. This helps to create a full foam, which holds lots of German hop aromas, and also knocks back some of the carbonation, allowing the malt and hop flavors to push forward. The hops are pithy and grapefruit-like, and they grip all the way through the beer, leading to a deep and long finish. Bierstadt Lagerhaus is one of the world's great modern lager breweries. Their Pils, Helles, and Dunkel are world-class beers, brewed properly in a handsome old Bavarian brewhouse by lager-lovers, to be drunk deep. This lager is definitely worth the wait.

Rothaus Pils

Grafenhausen, Germany
ABV: 5.1%

Rothaus Pils is bright gold and lean in body, and yet rich with the flavor of Pilsner malt. The leanness—by which I mean a lack of sweetness but still with structure—combines with dryness and lots of peppery, fragrant, lemony German hops and their clinging, thirst-bringing bitterness. That combo of lean malt, carbonation, and deep bitterness defines German Pilsner, and Rothaus is a quintessential example. Three facts for you about this wonderful beer: when on draft or in 17oz (500ml) bottles, it's known as Pils, but if it's in 11oz (330ml) bottles, then it's called Tannenzäple Pils, although the beer is always the same; the brewery is, according to their website, the highest-altitude brewery in Germany; and the "Black Forest Girl" on the label is called Biergit.

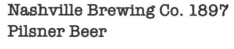

Nashville Brewing Co. 1897 Pilsner Beer

Nashville, Tennessee, USA
ABV: 5.0%

Nashville Brewing Co. opened in 1859 to brew German-style lagers and it changed ownership a couple of times, eventually becoming the William Gerst Brewing Company, which brewed until 1954. In 2016, Scott Mertie resurrected the brewery and brought lager-brewing back to Nashville. 1897 Pilsner is bright yellow in color from the Pilsner malt. It's got the distinctive aroma and flavor of floral, orangey, bitter Saaz hops, and it's a crisply refreshing beer. The image on this beer's label is Nashville's Parthenon, a replica of the one in Athens and opened for the Tennessee Centennial Exposition of 1897 to mark a century of statehood, where they would've likely drunk Pilsner beer from Gerst's Brewery. The Parthenon is still there today and makes a nice contrast amid all the live music bars in the downtown historic district.

Schönramer Pils

Petting, Germany
ABV: 5.0%

Brewed using German barley, a decoction mash, and a selection of aromatic German hops from Bavaria, and open-fermented like lager used to be, this Pils is then given a long, cold maturation for around six weeks. It's floral and herbal—even a bit grapefruit-y—from the hops, then deeply, crisply bitter, with the long conditioning time creating a natural spritzy carbonation. It's a perfect Pils, but then everything that Schönramer brews is excellent, including a superb Hell and Dunkel, and, unusually for a Bavarian brewery, a line of non-traditional German beers, including a German-hopped Pale Ale and IPA, a green-hopped Pils, and an Imperial Stout. They have a Bräustüberl next to the brewery where you can sample the beer if you wish. If you do and decide you love it so much that you want to move nearby, then the brewery offers a home beer-delivery service for locals.

Trumer Pils

Salzburg, Austria
ABV: 4.9%

Founded as a brewery in 1610, Salzburg's Trumer Brauerei has been in the Sigl family since 1775 and is now into its eighth generation. If you drink Trumer Pils in Austria, it'll hopefully be served in their bespoke Schlanke Stange glass (which translates rather prosaically as "slim stick"), a tall, straight, thin glass that shows off the beer's brilliant-yellow color and lets the pure-white foam sit on top throughout. The beer is really dry, which makes it crisply refreshing, and it's aromatically and enticingly hopped with whole-leaf flowers for a fresh, grassy, zesty aroma—it's glorious. Trumer make several other excellent lagers, including Hopfenspiel, a 2.9%-ABV Session Pils that's dry-hopped with Triskel and Cascade. There's also a Trumer brewery in Berkeley, California, where they make the Pils for the US—it's deservedly a beer with a cult appreciation Stateside.

MODERN PILSNER

The bitter crispness of a classic German-style Pilsner is a simple base from which brewers can evolve the style in modern ways. What I mean by modern is a new expression of hops, whether this involves using more of them, using them as a dry-hop, or using non-European varieties to create different aroma profiles, all while maintaining the fundamental qualities of a Pilsner: moderate alcohol strength, a simplicity of malt, and a firm bitterness. Lagers that are stronger and closer to IPAs fall under the Hoppy Lager style of beer (see page 154).

The two most established modern sub-categories of Pilsner are the Italian Pilsner and the New Zealand Pilsner. The Italian Pilsner uses lots of German hops late in the brew as a dry-hop, and it's a style that's become increasingly popular with American breweries who are proving that hops from Hallertau and Tettnang, in Germany, can be just as appealing as those from Yakima, in Washington state, in the USA. In Italian Pilsner we expect citrus pith, herbs, fresh grass, and floral aromas and flavor in a beer that's usually a little over 5.0% ABV, with a taut structure of malt, hops, and alcohol. The New Zealand Pilsner uses New Zealand hop varieties, which give a tropical and grape-like aroma, while the body is often fuller and maltier than a German-style lager and closer to a Golden Ale—some are also brewed with ale yeast, blurring the line between Lager and Ale.

Birrificio Italiano Tipopils

Lurago Marinone, Italy
ABV: 5.2%

There are several beers that will feature in every beer book I write, and Birrificio Italiano's Tipopils is one of them. It's a modern classic: it was one of Italy's first craft beers, and it inspired a unique Italian beer style—a style that has been adopted internationally. What makes Tipopils unique is the fact that it is a German-inspired "type of Pilsner," hence the name (the inspiration was Jever, the very bitter north German Pils), which combines lager-brewing techniques and ingredients with the British tradition of dry-hopping. Tipopils uses German hops—Spalter Select and Saphir— for an evocative, pastoral, floral kind of aroma, which leads to a bitter and complex lager—and one of the world's greatest lagers, in my opinion. Birrificio Italiano also make Extra Hop, a lower-alcohol and extra-hopped Italian Pilsner.

Lost and Grounded Keller Pils

Bristol, England, UK
ABV: 4.8%

Keller Pils is a refined beer that purrs with power and restraint. Its body is built on biscuity German malts and its personality sings with floral, peppery, grassy, and lemony German hops, which are more prominent than in most Pilsners. But it's the heart of this beer that really matters and that comes from the people who make it. Annie Clements and Alex Troncoso founded and run Lost and Grounded. Together they have started something special, something that brings people together, which is what makes this lager so great—not the malt, nor the hops, nor how long it's lagered (though Lost and Grounded have perfected this process over hundreds of brews and thousands of pints drunk). It's rightly celebrated by British beer geeks as one of the best lagers around.

Hop Federation Pilsner

Riwaka, New Zealand
ABV: 5.5%

Hop Federation are right in the middle of the hop-growing region of New Zealand and their Pilsner uses Riwaka, Nelson Sauvin, and Motueka hops to give characteristics of passion fruit, grape, and elderflower, with the aromas edging closer to Pale Ale than a classic Pils—a distinctive quality of a New Zealand Pilsner. Often, the malts in these New Zealand Pilsners are fuller than the German versions, and they aren't necessarily all *technically* lagers (but let's not get too pedantic or semantic), but this is a style of beer that's brilliant for being super-fruity in the aroma and very clean to drink, combining the best qualities of lager and aromatic hops.

Suarez Family Brewery Palatine Pils

Hudson, New York, USA
ABV: 5.2%

Palatine Pils has an ethereal kind of lightness that's almost impossible to describe. It's as though it has bubbles that are half the size of other Pilsners and a foam twice as tight. It has a kind of luminous lemon-yellow color. The hops are right there in the middle of it all, not calling for attention, but elegantly fruity, zesty, and peppery. I asked Dan Suarez, who started the brewery with his wife, Taylor, whether this was a classic or modern beer. He told me that it's striving for something classic, inspired by classic German lagers, but on reflection it isn't like those German beers at all, and neither is it modern in the sense of big hops or adjunct. To me, however, it is modern in how it tastes, how it presents, and how it's capable of being the kind of beer that gets drinkers excited about lager.

Pyynikin Mosaic Lager

Tampere, Finland
ABV: 4.7%

Pilsner malt, Mosaic hops, a lager yeast, and pure soft local water are all the ingredients in this recipe. This simplicity results in a beer that's gentle underneath, with some light bready malts and a soft, clean body, allowing the hops to blast through and dominate the aroma. Mosaic brings lemon, grapefruit, tangerine, and some tangy mango, and it's a fresh, enticing, lush kind of hop character, which works so perfectly with the simple malt base. For me, American hops used in a clean lager is one of the finest combinations of ingredients. Sure, I love mega-hopped IPAs, but when those hops are used in lighter amounts, they reveal some more interesting flavors. Pyynikin have grown to become one of Finland's top craft brewers and they have an impressive brewhouse restaurant by the river in Tampere.

pFriem Pilsner

Hood River, Oregon, USA
ABV: 4.9%

In the German style, but more heavily hopped, pFriem's Pilsner is immediately exciting for its abundance of German hops. We're all familiar with the intensity of citrusy American hops, but it's rarer that we get to experience German hops like Tettnang, Spalt Select, and Saphir in this way, and in pFriem's Pilsner they give citrus pith, dried grapefruit zest, pepper, lemon, fresh grass, and the warmth of a florist's store. These bold hops sit above a complex depth of malt that's richer than many German Pilsners, something which this trio of hops can grip on to. At the end, as the malt sweetness disappears, you'll be left with a lot of oily, pithy hop flavor and a dry bitterness, which is the ideal combination to make you want to drink more. pFriem also brew a Czech-style Pilsner, which is a celebration of Pilsner malts and wonderful Czech Saaz hops. All pFriem's lagers are very good.

Enegren Brewing Co. Lagertha

Moorpark, California, USA
ABV: 5.0%

Lagertha is a Mosaic-hopped Pilsner. Whenever I visit a brewery, the first style I'm looking for is a Pilsner or Pale Lager, and then I'll inevitably be unable to resist ordering any beer with Mosaic in it, so this is my ideal kind of brew. The base malts give some pleasing honeyed sweetness which helps to amplify the fruitiness in the Mosaic hops, giving gooseberry, grape, lemon, and stone fruit, with a floral and oily hop flavor running through the beer to a lasting bitterness. Enegren specialize in German styles, with a Helles, Hefeweizen, a strong Altbier, dark lagers, and a lot more.

THE IMPORTANCE OF CLASSICS

I've become increasingly interested in classic beers: those beers that define a style, a place, or a period of time. By drinking more classic beers we can get a better and deeper understanding of the wider world of beer—and that's about more than just their taste. It's about history, culture, people, and how we drink differently around the world.

The classic beers are often closely linked to an experience: a liter glass of Munich Helles sitting in a beer garden; a tall, hazy glass of Hefeweizen for a Bavarian breakfast; a foam-topped Czech Pilsner in a Prague bar; a glass of Lambic poured from a stone pitcher in a small Brussels bar; a pint of Bitter in a British pub, or a pint of Stout in Ireland; an American Pale Ale in a long-standing brewpub; an Australian Summer Ale by the beach. Or they are linked to a place: the Saisons of Wallonia; the Kellerbiers of Franconia; Polish Baltic Porters; drinking West Coast IPAs in San Diego; Scandinavian Jul beers at Christmas. Each of these beers reveals a different taste but also a different way of drinking.

Classics help us to understand beer. They give us a base knowledge of the flavors and the varieties of beer, and they allow us to see where evolutions come from. They enable us to analyze and critique beers, too (is that dry-hopped, unfiltered, 5.5%-ABV Kölsch really a Kölsch?). I think classics also give us the ability to taste variation within a traditional style. Take Belgian Tripel, for example. If you've only ever had Westmalle's Tripel, then you might think you have a good understanding of the style, but Tripel Karmeliet is very different (more spicy). As is St. Bernardus Tripel (malt and banana). And Unibroue's La Fin du Monde is different again (richer malt, less fizz). This knowledge enables us to make a more informed choice.

Craft beer is always modernizing. It's always looking for new, for different, for better, and that could be styles, ingredients, processes, or just pure "what if" experimentation. As we drink our way into the 2020s, crazy and creative experimentation in craft beer has come to define the current period of brewing. Beer has never been less beer-like. It's tropical fruit smoothies and chocolate coconut milkshakes. Beers are sweet and sour at the same time. They're using an unlimited breakfast buffet of adjuncts: cakes, nuts, fruits, sugars and syrups, vanilla, coffee, cacao. These supersized, super-juicy, and super-sweet beers are the zeitgeist, but I don't think many will ascend to classic status.

Many young or new drinkers today are brought into craft beer through these modern flavor-forward styles, meaning a lot of beer drinkers haven't had a traditional Belgian Dubbel or an English Mild or a Czech Dark Lager. Many aren't even interested, as if those beers come from a different era of drinking, and that's fascinating to see. It's creating an arrested development of beer appreciation in many beer drinkers.

Next time you're in the beer store scanning the colorful cans, don't forget to look more closely at those beers that you know (or think you know), or those classic beers, the old ones, the ones you always overlook because they're less interesting. Drink more classic beers.

Munich Helles (far left); Pivovar U Fleků produce a classic Czech Dark Lager.

PALE LAGER

Not all Pale Lagers are as bitter and dry as Pilsner. The best example of a lager that's golden and more malt-forward is the Munich Helles, which is the main type in Bavaria. This is a beer with a significant, though not sweet, malt middle, a light bitterness, and a softness of body that makes it eminently drinkable. It's a style that's been brewed since the 1890s and came about when Munich's dark-lager brewers conceded to the popularity of Pilsner and realized it was about time they made a paler lager of their own (a decision that led some of the prominent brewers at the time to revolt in anger). This new Munich Hell or Helles (which translates as pale or light in color) retained some of the characteristic maltiness of a Munich Dunkel and wasn't as bitter as the Czech or North German equivalents.

Today's Helles is a beer that's the epitome of balance and, like most beers, it is best drunk fresh and local, where some of the more delicate characteristics become more evident—the toastiness of malt, a little hint of yeast, the gentle carbonation, and the bite of the hops. Alongside Helles there are a lot of general Pale Lagers brewed that aren't quite Pilsners nor Helles, and these are discussed here. These lagers share an easy-going balance, one that's neither too sweet, nor too bitter, nor too strong in alcohol.

Utopian Brewing British Lager

Crediton, England, UK
ABV: 4.7%

Inspired by classic Munich Helles, but brewed using only British ingredients, Utopian's British Lager pours a brilliant golden color. The grain is a little sweet and chewy to begin with thanks to a decoction mash used in the brewing process. The English hops give a dry, spicy bitterness, but it's all restrained and refined and wonderfully reminiscent of what you'd drink in Bavaria. Utopian also brew a British Pilsner, which uses English Jester hops to give gentle stone fruit, funky tropical fruits, and a deep bitterness, while their Dark Lagers are also superb. Utopian is situated on a farm in the middle of Devon, in the south-west of England, and they are focused on sustainability, hence their sole use of British ingredients, including their own naturally soft well water. They are masters of lager.

Wayfinder Hell

Portland, Oregon, USA
ABV: 4.7%

Portland, Oregon, is an American epicenter of great lager. Perhaps it's the proximity to hops and a profusion of IPAs that has conversely created a desire for something different every now and then. It might be the weather, which makes pub-going one of Portland's great indoor sports, one that comes to value the all-day drinkability of a lager over a strong IPA. It might just be that they really understand great beer in Portland—and when you understand beer, you understand the joy of great lager. At Wayfinder they understand lager better than almost anyone else and their Hell is a stunning Pale Lager. The malts remind you of Munich, Germany, as does the complexity of the grain in the flavor, then come some American influences in the form of brisk bubbles and an enhanced floral Noble hop character. It's a simple beer and that's what makes it so good: it's classic and brewed by people who really know and love great lager.

Augustiner Lagerbier Hell

Munich, Germany
ABV: 5.2%

One of the great lagers of the world. Munich's Augustine monastery's brewery was first mentioned in 1328, making it the city's longest-running brewery. It's now privately owned and situated a short walk west of the center of Munich. Augustiner Hell is their main beer and it's the archetype of a German Helles. What makes it so good—and so popular— is its toasty malt flavor (they make their own malt in the brewery); the low carbonation, meaning you can drink a few; its pleasing, gentle bitterness; and the hint of fresh sulfur in the aroma, almost like a spritz of lemon. It's not a beer that stands out in any particular way, but that's why it's so good; Helles is an everyday beer for deep drinking, one that has been perfected over decades to create an unrivaled balance of flavor. The best place to drink this beer is in Augustiner-Keller, one of Munich's biggest beer gardens, or in one of the brewery's taverns in the city, like the Bräustuben which is attached to the brewery, or Groß Gestätten in the center of town—just a short walk from where the original monastery once was.

Tegernsee Spezial

Tegernsee, Germany
ABV: 5.6%

Alongside Augustiner, Tegernsee is one of Bavaria's most popular breweries. It's around an hour south of Munich, next to what was an old monastery, and situated beside Lake Tegernsee. Go visit it if you can—it's worth spending a few hours there, or even better, a few days. Go hiking, hire some bikes or a boat, and chill out by the lake, or, if you like running, then time your visit for the annual Tegernsee half marathon, which is one lap around the lake (there's beer at the end, of course). If you can't make it to the brewery, they have a beer hall in the center of Munich where you can drink their excellent Hell, plus this Spezial, which is a stronger and more bitter version of that Pale Lager with a greater malt complexity and richer body, plus a characteristic lemony-floral aroma. Spezial can be described as an export-strength lager, though that's an old categorization.

Cerveja Coruja Cerveja Viva

Forquilhinha, Brazil
ABV: 4.5%

Cerveja Coruja—Owl Beer—is based in the southeast of Brazil. Their Cerveja Viva is a pale lager with hints of honey, malt, and some lightly aromatic hops, but not with a strong bitterness, making it pleasingly easy-drinking. The brewery also makes Extra Viva, a 6.5%-ABV lager that bulks the body up with Pilsner and Vienna malts, and adds way more hops to it, making it closer to a Bock. This extra richness of malt and alcohol gives it much more oomph. Alongside these, Cerveja Coruja have some simpler lagers that appeal to the mainstream Brazilian drinkers and hopefully convert them to the more flavorsome lagers they produce.

Austin Beer Garden Brewery Hell Yes

Austin, Texas, USA
ABV: 4.5%

ABGB—that's what everyone calls this local institution—is a large beer hall and garden in Austin, Texas, where they've become known for great lagers, great pizzas, great music, and doing great stuff for their community. Hell Yes is their helluva good Helles, and one which is certainly more hop-forward than others, creating a floral and herbal aroma, while fuller-bodied malts give it some softness and balance. Their Pilsner is assertive in its hoppiness and bitterness at the end, while their Rocket 100, a pre-Prohibition-styled American Pilsner, is one of the great examples of this resurrected beer type. All these beers are best drunk in the brewery's beer garden, sitting on long shared benches beneath the cool shade of the trees. ABGB has adopted Hell Yes as their philosophy, donating 5 percent of profits to their Hell Yes Project, which partners with local charities and communities.

Brauerei Zehendner Mönchsambacher Lagerbier

Burgebrach, Germany
ABV: 5.5%

Some lagers are hard to categorize, especially those from around Franconia, in Upper Bavaria. The beers there are made to old traditions, following processes that have worked for decades and been passed on from brewmaster to brewmaster. The result is a region of Germany with more lager diversity than anywhere else, and what you'll typically find from the everyday lagerbiers is that they are golden amber in color (a richer color than a Munich Helles); unfiltered (though rarely hazy); maltier with a little more toasty sweetness; and low in carbonation. You can expect all these things from Mönchsambacher Lagerbier. Brauerei Zehendner is some 12 miles (20km) south-west of Bamberg, and it's a local favorite in an area that's spoiled for choice when it comes to great beer.

Young Henry's Natural Lager

Sydney, Australia
ABV: 4.2%

Down graffitied back alleys in Sydney's Newtown, you get to Young Henry's—the best combination of brewery, dive bar, and garage that you've ever seen. There's cool art, great music, a bar, brewery, distillery, lots of people, and the beer is served straight from the tanks behind the bar. Their Natural Lager is brewed with three Australian hop varieties—Summer, Sylva, and Helga— and these hops aren't there to make it taste like a Pacific Pale Ale; instead, they add a gentle fruitiness, some lemon, lime, peach, and pepper. This light hop character is enhanced by the beer being unfiltered and hazy, giving a refreshing yet fulsome lager with some grain complexity. They also brew Stayer, a "mid lager" with an ABV of just 3.5% and a tropical aroma from the hops, and Newtowner, their flagship Aussie Pale Ale, which is fresh and tropical. Out of their small distillery, they make a gin, which uses Australian hops as part of the botanical mix.

Alder Beer Co. Lewis

Seregno, Italy
ABV: 4.8%

This Keller Lager—Keller meaning cellar and used to denote an unfiltered beer, historically one served direct from the cellars—is on the hoppier side of the style, as we can often expect from Italian beer, thanks to their preference for higher levels of bitterness. This one is brewed with Hallertau Tradition, Mittelfrüh, Select, and Saphir, and they are characteristically citrus pithy, floral, herbal, and peppery, but there's enough malt to give the beer the structure we expect in a Helles-ish Lager. Keller is one of many German-style lagers brewed by Alder. There's also a Franconian-style Landbier (the Italians are big fans of Franconian lager), a Pils, Schwarz, and a Bock. Their Rockfield American IPA is also very good.

Newbarns Brewery Oat Lager Beer

Leith, Scotland, UK
ABV: 4.8%

Newbarns was started by four friends in the summer of 2020, focusing on the sort of beers you want to sit in the pub and drink a few of. It wasn't the best timing, given no pubs were open because of the pandemic, but the beers are just as great drunk at home. They have an excellent hoppy Table Beer, an ever-changing Pale Ale which is fresh and fruity, and a few superb lagers, like this Oat Lager Beer. Where a lot of lagers have a fine precision, this one was intended to be a little more rustic, a bit spiky and edged with character. It's lightly unfiltered; the use of Scottish oats and some wheat gives it some texture; pale malts add some classic bready flavors and a little sweetness; and English hops add a bracing, herbal, lemon-peel-type bitterness. It's a really good beer and now I've had a few cans of it at home, I want a few pints of it in the pub.

AMBER LAGER

Lagers began to modernize with the arrival of new brewing techniques and technology in the 1840s. This led to distinct styles such as dark Munich Lager (often known as Bavarian), golden Pilsner, and amber Vienna Lager. Vienna Lager was the first to gain notoriety outside of Bavaria and the Austro-Hungarian Empire, though Pilsner was close behind and soon overtook it, leading to the effective disappearance of the Vienna style. Yet amber-colored lagers have remained. Some of these are actually traditional, such as the lagers of Franconia. Others are semi-inspired by traditions, such as the Amber Lagers brewed in the early years of American craft beer, including Samuel Adams Boston Lager and Brooklyn Lager.

Vienna Lager is a common style today, and you'll see examples of it brewed all around the world. This lager style is expected to be amber-colored, nutty, and malty from the use of Vienna malt (or Munich malt), then bitter at the end from German hops. It's the kind of lager that is different enough from the ubiquitous Pale Lagers to be interesting, but not so different that it's alien. I also believe that, despite its history, Vienna Lager is a modern construct of a style which isn't necessarily related to the earlier Vienna brews (in the same way that IPA isn't India Pale Ale). You might see Märzen as another amber-colored lager, which was effectively an original Munich-style, paler lager pre-Helles—a style that was unique but also bridged different eras of brewing.

Schwechater Original Wiener Lager

Vienna, Austria
ABV: 5.5%

Brewer Anton Dreher developed the Vienna Lager style in the 1840s at his Klein-Schwechater Brauerei, which became world-famous and would grow to be one of continental Europe's largest breweries. They invented the style but didn't brew it for that long, replacing it with the more popular Pilsner. For the brewery's 175th anniversary (it is now part of BrauUnion, which is part of Heineken), they released a new version of Original Wiener Lager, so I wanted to try the "original" example of the style. And you know what? I didn't leave feeling like I'd drunk a few half-liters of beer informed by actual local history. I left feeling like I'd drunk a modern Vienna Lager, something more informed by an American beer-style guide than an old brewing log. My research suggests that Vienna Lager was not strong, was pale amber, and was quite sweet, whereas this beer was robust, bitter, dark amber, and strong—as US craft brewers tell us to expect. Regardless of that, Schwechater's lager is still a really good beer.

Eppig Brewing Vienna Lager

San Diego, California, USA
ABV: 4.6%

Eppig's taproom in Point Loma overlooks the dock, and as I sat there drinking through their range of great lagers, the sunset shone off the downtown skyscrapers across the bay and seals swam in the water in front of us. It was one of those unforgettable drinking experiences. I loved their Vienna Lager, which was deliciously malty—the kind that's all bread crusts and toast and a little toffee without the sweetness—plus it had a hint of something savory which balanced it really well alongside the peppery, spicy hop finish. I really liked their other lagers, too, especially the Special Lager, a strong, Japanese-style dry lager, which had a great bitterness at the end and a full structure of pale malts in the middle. Eppig also have a production brewery in Vista, which is large and smart, but it doesn't have seals swimming out the back.

Augustiner Bräu Märzen

Salzburg, Austria
ABV: 4.6%

To drink this beer, you have to go to the world's greatest beer hall. It's in a monastery in Salzburg. Go inside and there are several large halls, plus a beer garden outside that's big enough to seat 1,000 people beneath the shade of chestnut trees. There's food sold from "delicacy stalls" (like a canteen on the side of the beer hall) and this includes roasted meats, sausages, cheeses, radishes, breads, and baked goods, or you can bring your own cold food with you. When it comes to the beer, they still serve it as all Bavarian beer halls would've done in the late 19th century: there's a large cabinet of stone beer mugs, either a half-liter or full liter, and you grab one. Then you rinse it in a water fountain. You go to the cashier and pay for your beer. They give you a voucher and you hand your beer mug to the server, usually a burly bloke standing in front of a large wooden barrel. He'll fill your mug for you. The beer is one of the closest examples we might find today of old Vienna Lager. It's sweetly malty, nutty, low in carbonation, nice and bitter, low alcohol, and really excellent. It's a special place to drink a special beer.

Bohemia Obscura Vienna

Mexico City, Mexico
ABV: 4.9%

I've heard and read many times about how Vienna Lager went to Mexico and that the style remained popular there, but I think this is nonsense—and it's not even anecdotal nonsense that *might* be true, it's categorically false. There *was* a link between Austria and Mexico in the 1860s, with Austria's Maximilian I being the Emperor of Mexico from 1864 until 1867. That, however, ended badly, and it is also way too early in lager's timeline to suggest that Max made Amber Lager popular in Mexico—the earliest serious mention of lager-brewing in Mexico is from the 1890s. But what we can say for sure is that amber-colored lagers are popular in Mexico today and this is most likely because they work so well with the local food. Bohemia Obscura Vienna is a great example of a beer brewed by a large company (it's part of Heineken). It's pretty dark for a Vienna-style lager, it's a little nutty and slightly sweet, with some toasty malts, and finishes with lager's characteristic clean refreshment—it's at its best next to a plate of tacos.

Klášterni Pivovar Strahov Svatý Norbert Polotmavý

Prague, Czech Republic
ABV: 5.3%

Polotmavý is a Czech-style lager whose name means "semi-dark." This Polotmavý is made at the Klášterni Pivovar in Prague's Strahov Monastery. There's a small outdoor space as you approach and then, once you're inside, the first thing you see is the small, copper-clad brewhouse on your right. They make several beers, including a decent IPA, but it's the Polotmavý that I always want to drink. Darker and fuller-bodied than a Pilsner-style beer, it's more bitter and more deeply hopped, it's richer in malt, but not sweet, and the grain is biscuity and bready. It's not at all like any other lagers I've tasted around the world, but then this is a style that's unique to the Czechs and very few other breweries produce a Czech-style Amber Lager.

Braybrooke Keller Lager

Market Harborough, England, UK
ABV: 4.8%

Braybrooke brew on a farm in the Leicestershire countryside. They are directly influenced by Franconian lagers, with the brewery having a link to Bamberg's Mahrs Bräu. Keller Lager uses only Pilsner malt and Munich malt, which gives a rich amber color and a flavor of Graham crackers (digestive biscuits). It has a decoction in the brew process, which adds some chewiness to the body, and that's refreshed by German hops which give background balance and some structure to allow those malts to come forward. The beer is lagered for around six weeks, which helps to develop its final, beautiful flavor. There's something wonderfully moreish about this beer, with its completely satisfying malt flavor and the bitter balance of Bavarian hops.

Mahrs Bräu aU

Bamberg, Germany
ABV: 5.2%

Germany is my favorite place to drink lager. Bamberg is my favorite place to drink lager in Germany. And Mahrs is my favorite place in Bamberg. On tap at the brewery's tavern they'll have their very good Helles, a fragrant Pils, and their cult-like aU, or *Ungespundet*. The name means "unbunged" and comes from the time when matured beer was moved into small serving barrels; some were bunged, allowing carbonation to build up inside, while others were not, keeping them softer in carbonation. Mahrs aU, pronounced "aah ooh," is a deep amber color. It's nutty and biscuity, almost chewy with malt, but it's not sweet—this base is characteristic of lagers from this part of Germany—and it has a lasting peppery bitterness. Mahrs have achieved something rare: they are a traditional Bamberg brewery, making excellent versions of classic and local beer styles, and they've combined that with a craft-beer outlook, crossing over to the hop-loving beer geeks and adding cans to their range. Being present at some of the world's biggest beer festivals has helped, as has their rock 'n' roll boss, Stephan Michel, who is modernizing his family's long brewing history.

DARK LAGER

The earliest lagers were dark in color, relatively weak (around 3.0%–4.0% ABV), probably smoky from being made with barley that was roasted over open fires, and relatively sweet. Over time, the beer became drier and less smoky, improved with scientific developments, then expanded with industrialization, and by the mid-19th century "Bavarian Lager" meant a brown lager beer. As Pilsner's popularity increased, lager generally went from dark to light, but the old traditions of Dark Lagers remain in Bavaria and central Europe, where several important old styles are still common.

Munich-style Dunkels are classically brown-amber in color. While they may look dark, they tend not to have a strong, roasted malt flavor, being more toasted than roasted. Schwarzbier, which means "black beer," is another German lager style, but one that is perhaps now more common outside of Germany. The extra darkness of Schwarzbiers comes from using darker malts. They tend to be more roasted than toasted, though rarely will they go as far as being coffee-like and bitter. The Czechs brew Tmavý, and these Dark Lagers are fuller-bodied and smoother than the German versions—and perhaps sweeter, too. All are usually in the 5.0% ABV range, and, if you're looking for a great all-rounder of a beer style to go with food, then a Dark Lager is one of the best options—the toasty malt and balanced refreshment make Dark Lagers work with most cuisines.

Hofbräu Dunkel

Munich, Germany
ABV: 5.5%

At the end of the 16th century, the Bavarian royal family decided to build a brewery in the royal residence, mostly brewing only brown beer for the house's personal consumption. A few years later, they added a second brewery around the corner at Platzl No. 9, which just made white beer, or Weissbier. By 1808, the royal family brought all production together into the Platzl brewery and focused on making just Braunbier. Eventually, the brewery outgrew the space, by which time the royal family had outgrown owning a brewery, so they passed ownership to the Bavarian State, and the brewhouse was moved to the edge of town. The old brewery building was turned into a large beer palace, now known as the Hofbräuhaus. Their Dunkel is a classic. It's a clear copper-brown, and the grain is nutty and ever-so-slightly caramelized and roasted, but not bitter. Go to the Hofbräuhaus to drink this beer, as it's one of the most famous and most remarkable taverns in the world.

Dovetail Dunkel

Chicago, Illinois, USA
ABV: 4.8%

Dovetail say all the right things to me: decoction mash, old Bavarian brewing kit, open fermenters, horizontal lagering tanks to store the beer for at least four weeks, and beers brewed to classic recipes. All the lagers at Dovetail are excellent, but it was the Dunkel that really excited me while I was there: all bread crusts and toast, and there's a celebration of malt that's moreish and almost savory and chewy, without ever being sweet, while peppery hops and a little liveliness from the yeast keep everything fresh. The brewery's founders, Hagen Dost and Bill Wesselink, met while studying brewing in Germany, so it makes sense that German lagers and ales would be a significant part of their line-up, but they also admired Belgian brewing traditions and that influenced another side of their brewery: a coolship for spontaneously fermented beers, which are then stored for months or years until they're ready. Whether it's a Czech-style Pilsner, a Munich Dunkel, a Kölsch, or a Kriek, everything is brewed long and slow to old traditions, and everything is very good.

König Ludwig Dunkel

Kaltenberg, Germany
ABV: 5.1%

This is a beer brewed in an actual castle by an actual Prince. Prince Luitpold, who has run the brewery in Kaltenberg Castle since the 1970s, is a descendent of the Bavarian royal family, the Wittelsbachs, who are central figures in Bavaria's beer history: they wrote and signed the Reinheitsgebot (the Bavarian beer purity law); they started the royal brewery that became the Hofbräuhaus; and Prince Luitpold's great-great-great-grandfather's wedding was the event that created Oktoberfest. The König Ludwig Dunkel is a classic German Dunkel that has some caramel and bready depth, some dried-fruit sweetness, a fullness of body, and a light bitterness. Every summer Kaltenberg Castle hosts a medieval festival which centers on a two-hour jousting show. It's brilliant and bonkers, and sitting in the arena drinking a liter of Dark Lager from a stone mug is a great experience. The Wittelsbach family has influenced Bavarian beer for over 500 years—and they continue to play an active role today.

Pivovar U Fleků Flekovský Ležák 13°

Prague, Czech Republic
ABV: 5.0%

If the Hofbräu Dunkel is the classic German Dark Lager, then U Fleků's is the classic Czech version—U Fleků is also another essential beer hall that you should visit. They have been brewing beer since 1499, and until 2020 they only made one beer: a 13° near-black lager (they also now brew a 13° Pale Lager). It comes in chunky little glasses with a thick foam on top, and you'll almost certainly want a second before you're even halfway through your first because the smooth sweetness in the beer is a joy to drink. It's full-bodied, rich, and lightly roasty, with some dark berries, cocoa, and licorice. The experience of drinking in the old tavern is also great—they serve the dark beer next to classic beer-hall food.

33 Acres of Darkness

Vancouver, Canada
ABV: 5.0%

This is a cool brewpub-meets-Scandinavian coffee shop in the Pacific Northwest, with a pizza truck parked out front. The vibe is chilled out, helped by good music and shared tables, which you can sit at with a laptop during the day and a flight of beers by night. I went straight for the flight, and picked a round-the-world mix of a California Common, West Coast Pale, Belgian Tripel, and this Schwarzbier, the last beer so good that I finished it and ordered another to go with a pizza. Roasted but not bitter, there's some cacao and vanilla if you go looking for it, though it's mostly just an elegant, crisp, and dry Dark Lager that defies its black appearance with a brilliant lightness. I also loved the Tripel, 33 Acres of Euphoria, which was honeyed and spicy, with some banana and almond aroma.

Mack Bryggeri Bayer

Tromsø, Norway
ABV: 4.7%

Mack was founded in 1877 and long held the title of northernmost brewery in the world from its location in Tromsø, a fishing port inside the Arctic Circle that was once somewhere Arctic adventurers used as a pit stop or launch point. Today, visitors to Tromsø go for the northern lights and orca whales, and while they're there they will almost certainly go for a beer in Ølhallen, which has 67 taps and a microbrewery on the side. This used to be where the Mack brewery was before they grew into a larger site. Bayer was, and is, a taste of history, related to the earliest Mack beer and based on Bavarian dark lagers (hence the name—Bayer means Bavarian). It's light and simple to taste, with just a hint of darker malt flavor, which makes it refreshing and interesting without being challenging. Drink Bayer in Ølhallen, next to a huge stuffed polar bear, and pretend you're an old Arctic adventurer.

Heater Allen Schwarz

McMinnville, Oregon, USA
ABV: 4.6%

There's a misconception that Black Lager is going to be heavy and roasted, when in fact the very best ones are surprisingly light and absent of harsh roast, and that's the case with Heater Allen's Schwarz. It's a lager that pours almost black with a tan foam. The body is smooth in the Czech style, it has some body and richness, which is almost chewy and gives a suggestion of sweetness tempered by a hint of roasted malt, while a little waft of savoriness sneaks in at the edges in a really nice way. Go to the brewery, and if they haven't got Schwarz on tap, then they'll have the Munich-styled Dunkel (and if you're lucky, they'll have both). You'll also definitely see their flagship Pils, a Czech-inspired lager that's golden, bready, biscuity, and properly bitter at the end. Heater Allen are lager masters.

Round Corner Gunmetal

Melton Mowbray, England, UK
ABV: 4.8%

This Black Lager is a great all-weather dark beer. In winter, it has enough roastiness and depth of dark grain to make it satisfying and wholesome, while in summer, thanks to the fizz, it's a refreshing lager with a background savory quality. The hops are herbal and grassy, and give a freshness that lifts the palate in a really good way—drinkers are often wary of dark beers, but this can persuade them otherwise. I think it's a great style of beer to go with a wide range of dishes, from barbecued pork or fish to Southeast Asian salads, though the local pairing of their hometown's famous pork pies or Stilton cheese would also work, showing the diversity of this beer at the dinner table.

Eisenbahn Dunkel

Blumenau, Brazil
ABV: 4.8%

I went to Blumenau once and I can still barely believe what I saw there. It was October. It was hot. The city felt Amazonian, with the rainforest and a thick brown river running through it. Yet, all around me the buildings looked like fairy-tale Bavarian castles. There were German flags, pretzels, and oompah music (albeit with a samba beat), and people were wearing lederhosen and dirndls. It was remarkable and a reminder of the town's German heritage, which is always present but celebrated properly with their annual Oktoberfest. For a couple of weeks, the whole town dresses up in German outfits and they party—they really party. You'll find lots of regular Pilsner beer on sale, but you'll also find local beers at the party, including those from Eisenbahn, one of Brazil's oldest craft brewers. Their Dunkel is between brown and black, and more toward the roast flavor profile of a Schwarzbier. It's got coffee and chocolate flavors, but it's light-drinking and very refreshing, exactly what you want in the sultry warmth of Blumenau.

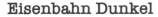

Von Trapp Brewing Dunkel

Stowe, Vermont, USA
ABV: 5.7%

Go to von Trapp's beer hall in Stowe and you'll be surrounded by mountain views and hills alive with the sound of... brewing. The von Trapps are the same von Trapps from *The Sound of Music*. After a singing tour around the States in the 1940s, the family settled in Stowe, where the snow-capped mountains and bucolic countryside reminded them of Austria. They built a home that became a large lodge and over the years developed into a hotel complex. In 2010, they added a small brewery, then five years later they upgraded to a big brewery and opened their beer hall, and the whole place is still run by the von Trapp family today. They focus on lagers and they're very good at brewing them. The Dunkel is red-brown and pours with a creamy head. It's a little cocoa-like and a bit nutty, but mostly moreishly malty. The food in their beer hall is very good, with Austrian dishes made with local ingredients. As the brewery's tagline tells us: it's "a little of Austria, a lot of Vermont."

STRONG LAGER

The best-known strong lagers are Bock and Doppelbock. Bocks are typically around 6.0% ABV, while Doppelbocks are usually around 8.0%, with a color ranging from gold to almost black in either style. The history of Bock in Germany goes back to the early 1600s, when a brewer from Einbeck was headhunted to make beer in the Bavarian royal family-owned brewery. At that time in Bavaria beer couldn't be made between April 23 and September 29, so special beers were made in March (known as Märzen) and October, which were then lagered to be drunk in October and May (known as Maibock) respectively. Even today in Germany, these stronger lagers are not typically produced year-round—though there are some exceptions—and their release dates are important events in the beer calendar, giving a strong springtime lager for the beer-garden season, then another in October as they head back inside to the warm taverns. There's also a tradition for Weihnachtsbock (Christmas Bock). The other main German strong lager is Festbier, which is typically brewed to be slightly stronger, for serving at a festival. Oktoberfestbier is the best example. Today this is a golden lager similar to a Munich Helles but stronger (5.7–6.3% ABV). Oktoberfestbiers are commonly thought to be a rich amber color and malty in taste; that's no longer true in Munich, but elsewhere in the world, if you see an Oktoberfest-inspired lager, it'll usually be amber in color and in the Märzen style.

Chuckanut Fest Bier

Bellingham, Washington, USA
ABV: 5.5%

Chuckanut have been an important brewery for popularizing lagers in the Pacific Northwest, and a number of brewers who now make great lagers elsewhere learned how to brew them at Chuckanut. I could have picked a dozen different Chuckanut beers to go in this book: the Vienna, a Helles, Dunkel or Schwarzbier, a Bock or Doppelbock, a Mexican Lager or a Light Lager—you name a lager style and Chuckanut make a great and classic version of it. But I chose the Fest Bier because it's brewed like the kinds of beer you'd find in Munich, Germany. It's a bright, sparkling gold, and it has the best kind of toasty but not heavy malt richness. It has a load of hops in there and they make it nicely bitter and add some aromatic qualities that differ slightly from those you'd find in a Munich Oktoberfestbier—but that's a good thing. This is authentic Oktoberfestbier, brewed in Washington.

Bierbrouwerij De Roos Herfstbock

Hilvarenbeek, Netherlands
ABV: 8.3%

Bock arrived in the Netherlands from Germany and has since developed its own style and tradition there. Dutch Bokbiers taste somewhere between a German Bock and a Belgian Dubbel. They are typically dark red-brown, and have a tan foam, aromas and flavors of dried fruit, chocolate, and sweet malt, and a vibrant carbonation that most noticeably differentiates them from the German brews. Herfstbock is stronger than most at 8.3% ABV, though it drinks like a 6.0% ABV beer. There are some dark cherries, caramel, spices, almond and pear esters, and a long bitterness at the end. It's complex, interesting, and excellent and is released annually as the weather gets colder (*herfst* means "fall", which is exactly when you want to be drinking something like this.)

Klosterbräu Bamberger Bockbier

Bamberg, Germany
ABV: 7.0%

Klosterbräu, which was founded as a monastic brewery in 1533, is Bamberg's oldest remaining brewery. Their restaurant is small and cozy, especially in the fall with the heating turned up, and when—in mid-October—they release their Bockbier (a few other Bamberg brewers also have a Bock at this time, including Mahrs). Klosterbräu's Bamberger

Bockbier is 7.0% ABV, a deep golden color, and has all the structure, depth, and bitterness of a great IPA, just without the aromatic hops. It's a rich beer, but one that's balanced and deep with juicy malt flavor. It's also the kind of beer that'll get you in trouble pretty quickly, as you'll finish one, order another, then fall over. Klosterbräu make an unfiltered Pale Lager, an old-style Bamberger Braunbier, which is nicely nutty with Munich malts, and Schwärzla, an excellent Schwarzbier.

Brauerei Schloss Eggenberg Samichlaus Classic

Eggenberg, Austria
ABV: 14.0%

This is one of those classic beers that took me a long time to finally come around to drinking (or at least remember drinking...). For many years it was the strongest beer in the world, and it remains one of the strongest lagers in regular production. It's always made on December 6th, which is the Feast Day of St. Nicholas, hence the name—Samichlaus, or Santa Claus. After brewing, the beer is stored for 10 months in tank before being released, by which time it's evolved into a magnificently interesting beer. It's sherried, almond-like, nutty, and rich, with some dried cherry fruitiness and a deep complexity. It's a remarkable beer and one that's ideal with Christmas cakes or cookies.

Brauwastl Annafestbier

Forchheim, Germany
ABV: 6.0%

One of the best beer festivals in Germany is Annafest, held annually on St Anna's Feast Day in July, in Forchheim. It takes place in the town's *Kellerwald* (Forest of Cellars), which is literally in the forest up a hill. Dug into the hill are old cellars where brewers used to store their lager in the naturally cold spaces. They'd then transport the beer back into town to drink until someone realized it was actually nice to drink it in the forest, where the beer was perfectly cold and fresh, so they opened a beer garden. During Annafest, 23 beer gardens all open for the event and each has a different brewery's beer. One of the most popular is Brauwastl's, whose beer is made by a collective of local homebrewers. Annafestbier is amber-ish, malty-sweet, and low in carbonation (to help you drink more), with lots of herbal bitterness at the end.

Paulaner Salvator

Munich, Germany
ABV: 7.9%

Picture this: You're a monk in Munich in the early 17th century. Lent is approaching, which means 40 days of fasting, but liquids can be consumed, so the mischievous monks decide to brew an extra-strong beer to sip through the lean Lenten period, a double-strength Bock (or Doppelbock). It's a great story, but it's not true. Those monks did brew a sweeter and richer beer annually, but it wasn't for the Lent fast; in fact, they brewed it for a Feast Day, and they held a party which became so popular it was the Oktoberfest of its time. The special beer was called Sankt-Vaters Bier (Holy Father's Beer), which has since become Salvator. Bavaria loves a tradition and today, in March, the annual Salvatorfest sees people drinking liter mugs of Doppelbock, a lager that's strong, dark, and malty with flavors of dried fruit, toffee, and toast. Forget the story of hungry monks; this is a beer brewed for celebration.

HOPPY LAGER

This is where lager-brewing meets the modern thirst for hops and a taste for stronger beers. I think it's an exciting evolution, and we see how the subtle balance of great lager can be combined with the bold aromas of American, Australian, and New Zealand hops, creating beers that are somewhere between lager and IPA. The most popular style of Hoppy Lager is IPL, or India Pale Lager, which is pretty much an IPA brewed with lager yeast and a cold maturation. IPLs are often stronger than the Modern Pilsner category (see page 137) with base recipes closer to IPAs or DIPAs than a Pilsner, and where the intent is toward a bold hoppiness.

Most IPLs are brewed to around 6.0–7.0% ABV. Some are bright and crisp, while others are hazy and smooth, but the use of lager malts, clean lager fermentation, and an extended lagering time should give these beers a cleaner flavor profile than an IPA, and the best finish dry and bitter. Just as in the IPA category, we see session-strength versions and Imperial-strength DIPLs. I've also included some beers here which take lagers and hops in interesting directions and aren't just like lagered IPAs.

Wayfinder Relapse

Portland, Oregon, USA
ABV: 7.0%

Cold IPA is how Wayfinder describe this one. It's a combination of an American Pilsner base, meaning light malts plus 30 percent rice, and this gives a very pale lager that's crisp and lean, yet strong and bulked up to be 7.0% ABV (though you'd never tell its strength from tasting it—it's incredibly light), and it uses a mix of classic American hops that give grapefruit, melon, and lots of tasty citrus peel. It's lagered cold and filtered, so it ends really dry and crystal-clear (it's beautiful to look at), which goes to push forward all those aromatic hops and to enhance the beer's high bitterness and drinkability. It's the perfect combination of lager and hops, an anti-hazy IPA kind of beer, which shows how good clear beer can be.

Blackman's Brewery Juicy Banger

Torquay, Australia
ABV: 5.8%

Brewed by the beach in Torquay, Blackman's beers are some of the best in Australia, a fact recognized in 2019 when they won Champion Small Australian Brewery in the Australian International Beer Awards. Their full range is so well considered and well brewed, and everything has a rare brightness and clarity of flavor; their lager uses Citra hops to add some fresh fruity aromas, their Aussie-hopped Ernie Golden Ale is lush with tropical fruits, and this Juicy Banger IPL is all-American-hopped and a banging, juiced-up lager ripe with citrus fruit, sweet melon, passion fruit, and pine. You can drink in their brewery in Geelong, their beer and burger bar in Ocean Grove, or their original brewpub in Torquay, or just grab some cans and sit on the beach. The brewery is run by husband and wife Renn and Jess Blackman, and they are a brilliant team who have created something special.

Jack's Abby Hoponius Union

Framingham, Massachusetts, USA
ABV: 6.5%

Jack's Abby didn't start out with the intention of being a lager-only brewery. Instead, they had plans to brew a wide variety of styles, but a lack of cash in the beginning saw them start with just one yeast—a lager yeast—and they got hooked on the possibilities of brewing lagers. Yet, despite that, they wanted—*needed*—to have an IPA. Instead of introducing a new yeast into the brewery, they decided to make a lager version of an IPA. They won't say they invented the IPL, but they pretty much did, and Hoponius Union is still top of its class: resinous, citrusy, brightly orangey, and fresh, with a West-Coast character, a clean depth of lager fermentation, and a dry, bitter finish. It's brilliant. I love Jack's Abby for brewing a greater range of lagers than other breweries—just go to their taproom and you'll find at least 20 different lagers, from classic German Helles to barrel-aged Imperial Lagers, via the IPLs and some soured lagers. Jack's Abby are showing us just how varied lager-brewing can be.

Cloudwater Hoppy Little Lager

Manchester, England, UK
ABV: 3.9%

Celebrated for their excellent IPAs and DIPAs, it's often overlooked just how good Cloudwater are at brewing lagers. I once visited their brewery tasting room and they had seven different lagers on tap, including a Light Lager, Helles, Pilsner, Vienna, and some Hoppy Lagers, and all of them were very good. Hoppy Little Lager is their version of a lager-fermented Session Ale. It's pale and hazy yellow, with a characteristic lager base that's crisp and clean and definitely has malt flavor but isn't malty (Cloudwater really understand the importance of malt, and that's what makes them very good at brewing lager). The hops give the lager a zesty, floral, peachy, and lemony aroma that's restrained and enticing before a dry bitterness. Their Helles is also a very good—and reverential—British example of that style.

Donzoko Big Foam

Hartlepool, England, UK
ABV: 5.0%

Made by one-man-band brewer Reece Hugill, Big Foam is inspired by the traditions of Munich, Germany, inflected with the flavor of local spelt and zesty modern hops, and brewed in industrial Hartlepool in the north-east of England. It's a lightly hazy golden lager and the malt is bready and toasty with a zing of spicy spelt. The hops are lemony and peachy, really complementing the spelt, and they leave a lasting peppery bitterness—it's not intensely hopped, and not exactly a Hoppy Lager, but it has a very interesting hop character that defies any other categorization. Pour it hard into your glass to build up a big foam on the beer—it's a fun one to drink. Donzoko also brew Northern Helles, a lightly hoppy Helles-ish lager, and Garden Bier, a session-strength lager made with English hops.

Brasserie Artisanale Maltstrom IXPL Des Prairies

Lanaudière, Canada
ABV: 6.0%

IXPL is more on the modern IPA side of things, being unfiltered, hazy, and heavily hopped, but the lager base ensures it has a simple elegance underneath all the hops. Those hops—Citra, Mosaic, and Galaxy—are tropical, super-fruity, and resinous, just as you would expect from those varietals, and they give a juiciness that is great with the lager malts. Maltstrom also make IXXPL, a double IPL that's double dry-hopped, cloudy, and 8.6% ABV, and much closer to a hazy IPA than a typical lager—in fact, it's nothing like you'd ever expect a lager to be. They also produce a growing range of experimental lager hybrids, including a lager-gose and several hazy and hoppy lagers, while their core-range Pilsner and Dunkel are also more heavily hopped than classic examples.

EverBrew EverCrisp

São Paulo, Brazil
ABV: 6.6%

One of Brazil's top craft breweries and best known for their hazy IPAs like EverMont, EverMaine, and EverMass, plus Imperial Stouts and Fruit Sours, EverBrew's EverCrisp is a diversion toward something a little more delicate, though delicate here is used in relative terms because it's still a powerful beer, one that's heavily hopped and super-juicy with melon, citrus, and tropical fruit. The crisp part of the name arises from the fact that the beer has a drier depth and more noticeable fizz and bitterness than their hazy IPAs, and this reminds us that IPAs—whether made as a lager or not—can still be dry and bitter. It's the sort of beer that has the ability to shift the palate and expectation of drinkers back toward something more bitter, while also celebrating the diversity of lagers.

TRADITIONAL LAGER

So much of beer today is perpetually new and chasing trends, and we can bet that many of the hyped-up beers we find on the shelves today won't exist in a few years' time, having been replaced by new styles and tastes (or perhaps reversions to old classics). But there are some traditional beer styles and cultures that have remained for decades, or even centuries. Some of these are detailed elsewhere, like Amber Franconian Lagers, Munich Dunkels, and Belgian Lambic, but then there are some styles that are more traditional than others. Maybe it's truer to say that they are idiosyncratically traditional, or uniquely local, as they are specific to certain places and are the kinds of beer you have to travel for—they provide an insight into a location and its people as much as they show us a type of beer. What makes these beers important is that from afar some of them may seem unusual, but they are very normal to the local communities in which they're brewed and drunk.

Schafferhof Zoigl

Neuhaus, Germany
ABV: 5.0%

Zoigl is a beer that's unique to the Upper Palatinate of Germany, near the Czech border, and it's only made in five or six breweries. What makes those breweries interesting is that they are communally owned, and only certain citizens with brewing rights are allowed to use the brewhouses. If you have the historic rights, then you can source your own ingredients, brew your beer in the shared brewhouse, then transfer the unfermented beer into your own personal cellars where it ferments (as it would've been done a few hundred years ago), and then you can either drink it yourself or open up a "Zoiglstubn," which is basically a Zoigl living room or small restaurant, and sell the beer. Some 20 brewers have a Zoiglstubn in the region and they open to a pre-agreed schedule, typically on a three-to-four-week rotation (most have other jobs and only brew semi-professionally). All Zoiglbier is a bit different, but essentially similar in taste, as if the brewers are following the same passed-around recipe, but some just make it better than others. My favorite is Schafferhof in Neuhaus. It's amber-red in color, malty, a little sweet and toasty, bitter with German hops, and unfiltered. You can visit the family-run converted farmhouse with its large garden, where they serve the beer alongside snacks like bread, cheese, and cakes. Zoigl beer is maintaining a great and unusual tradition. Go to Neuhaus and neighboring towns to drink it, if you can (just check the schedule before you go so you know who's going to be open).

Schlenkerla Rauchbier Märzen

Bamberg, Germany
ABV: 5.1%

The original lagered beers came from somewhere around Franconia and north Bavaria, around 600 years ago. What made them lagers was a special yeast which favored cold conditions and the process of storing—lagering—the beer in cold cellars for many months. Those early lagers, known simply as "Braunbier," would have been dark, sweet, and probably smoky, because the malt used to make them was roasted over fire. Over time, as technology allowed malts to be dried over indirect heat, the taste of smoke disappeared, but two breweries in Bamberg—Schlenkerla and Spezial—maintained their own private maltings and continued to use beechwood to fire their kilns. They are keepers of the *Rauchbier*, or "smoked beer," tradition. Go to Schlenkerla's old tavern in Bamberg, as it's an essential world-beer experience. Their Rauchbier Märzen is served direct from a wooden barrel. It's a very dark brown that's red-ember-tinted at the edges. It immediately, impactfully smells smoky—think smoked sausages, smoked ham, bonfires, and ashes—and it tastes that way, too. It's richly smoked, sense-filling, overwhelming to begin with, but the more you drink, the more it becomes familiar and almost comforting, reminding you of a distant, innate liking of smokiness. Spezial's version is lighter in smoke, and more woody than meaty. Both are classic Lagers.

Ha Noi Bia Hoi

Hanoi, Vietnam
ABV: 4.0%

Drinking Bia Hoi in Hanoi is my favorite beer experience in the world. To me, nothing is more exciting than sitting at the side of the street, watching the fast-paced, real-world theater of Hanoi, and taking in the smells and sounds of the city while drinking light-tasting lager. *Bia hoi* means something like fresh draft beer. It originated during the American War (or what Westerners call the Vietnam War) as a way of bringing people together socially. Because of grain shortages, brewers used a proportion of rice, which lightened the beer, and they would brew, ferment, and then serve the beer in a short amount of time. The tradition was for beer deliveries to take place from 4am by cyclo pedal cart drivers, and each bar would get an allowance of kegs every day, with people going to the bars and drinking one or two beers, and when the kegs were empty, the bar closed. It started a unique beer culture in the city, which remains similar today: the kegs are still delivered daily; they have rudimentary storage and serving processes (a big icebox and a hosepipe); it's cheap, so everyone can afford a glass or two; it's low in alcohol; it's unpasteurized; and it's brewed relatively quickly (around two weeks). Bia Hoi is a special experience because of where you drink it, surrounded by locals and sitting on blue plastic stools in small corner bars beneath yellow and red awnings. Ha Noi Bia Hoi is the most popular beer, and it's made a few miles west of the old town in a brewery which was originally opened by the French (who introduced beer into Vietnam) in the late 19th century.

AMERICAN PILSNER AND LIGHT LAGER

The first lagers brewed in America were made by German émigrés in the 1840s, and they were directly influenced by German recipes and processes, albeit adjusted by necessity to suit American ingredients and equipment. Those beers, which were mostly drunk by Germans to begin with, were dark, malty, and moderate in alcohol, and quite different from the American spirits that were immoderate in alcohol and left a nation of drunkards. By the 1870s, as more Americans started to shift away from whiskey and toward beer, and as work shifted from farms to factories, drinkers came to want something lighter than what the Germans were drinking. At that time, the common brewing grain in America was six-row barley, which differed from European two-row barley in that it had a higher protein content and left a heavier, hazier lager. The German-American brewers started using rice or corn as a percentage of their grain bill, which produced a lighter, crisper beer, and a distinctive new kind of uniquely American lager.

By the 1980s, that lighter American lager had gone fully light, reduced in body, flavor, calories, carbohydrates, and alcohol, and it created a kind of monoculture for beer, which ultimately kick-started craft brewing. Jump forward another 40 years and American brewers are bringing back the old-style American Pilsners. These beers use corn or rice; they have some toasty malts in the body; they are low in both bitterness and hop aroma; and they're just good, beer-flavored beers like your great-grandfather used to drink. Alongside these, we're now seeing more craft versions of Light Lagers and Mexican Lagers, ostensibly riffing on Bud Lights and Coronas, and giving something very crisp, light, and unchallenging to drink.

Schell's Deer Brand

New Ulm, Minnesota, USA
ABV: 4.8%

August Schell left Germany in 1848 and arrived to start a new life in North America. That life eventually led him to Minnesota and to founding a brewery in 1860, and the brewery has been in the Schell family ever since. Deer Brand is a pre-Prohibition American Lager made with 70 percent barley and 30 percent corn, just like the old days—and given the brewery's history, they would know about "the old days." It's an easy-going, easy-drinking, unchallenging lager in the best possible sense in that it doesn't yell hops at you, it's not strong, it's not bitter or malty, and it's just damn good beer. The range features numerous other interesting lagers, including Cave-Aged Barrel-Aged Baltic Porter, which is matured in barrels in the brewery's old lagering cellars—not many breweries have cellars like that anymore, making it a rare treat.

Urban Chestnut Forest Park Pilsner

St. Louis, Missouri, USA
ABV: 5.2%

From the middle of the 19th century, St. Louis grew as a city with a significant population of Germans and a large number of breweries, where lagers were made with a German tradition and a new American approach. It still remains an important brewing city and still has an important German-American epicenter in Urban Chestnut. There, the beers are overseen by brewmaster and co-founder Florian Kuplent, a German brewer who's spent much of his career making lagers in America. Their Forest Park Pilsner is made with American six-row malt plus corn, like lagers from the late 19th century. It uses Cluster, the oldest American hop, plus some Hallertau Tradition, and those ingredients combine to give us something like the lagers people in St. Louis were drinking over 100 years ago. Urban Chestnut's beer hall combines a bit of Germany with a bit of America, and it's a great place to drink.

Little Harpeth Chicken Scratch

Nashville, Tennessee, USA
ABV: 5.25%

Nashville is a place for bar-crawling, listening to live music, and drinking cold lager with a bourbon on the side. There is a great local brewing scene, but when you're listening to the music, I feel like there's something incongruous about having an IPA. Not everyone wants a Bud, Miller, or Coors. Fortunately, Little Harpeth have provided a new American Pilsner for the city. This lager is a mix of Pilsner malt and white corn, with a big charge of American Cluster hops and some aromatic Czech Saaz to lift it all. It's dry and crisp, as it should be, and has a nice creaminess in the middle and plenty of malt to give it body. It's great with music, bourbon, or hot chicken, or just on its own, drunk by the mug in the brewery's taproom.

Night Shift Brewing Nite Lite

Everett, Massachusetts, USA
ABV: 4.3%

Night Shift's "craft light lager" was released in 2017 at the beginning of the trend for breweries to bet big on little lagers. With Nite Lite they've produced a beer to be bought by the case and it's unpasteurized, unfiltered, and gives some kudos to these previously scorned brews. Nite Lite is made with 20 percent corn, it's really light in color and body, and it's highly carbonated with little brisk bubbles. The foam laces down the glass and you'll get a nice fruitiness in the aroma. However, you don't drink this beer for hops or anything like that, but for refreshment and also for the pure, simple pleasure of just drinking a simple beer—that feels like a pleasure which has been forgotten in the search for rare Stouts and DIPAs. For those wanting more and not less, Night Shift make some excellent IPAs and sour beers, too.

HYBRID LAGERS AND ALES

Not every lager is exactly as it appears, and not every beer can be easily categorized. Here we're collecting together some beers that are somewhere between lager and ale, as a result of the brewing processes or just because of the taste. The most famous of the Hybrid Lagers are Kölsch and Altbier, two idiosyncratic German beer styles that are both fermented with *Saccharomyces cerevisiae*, which is an ale yeast, but cold-conditioned and with lager-like characteristics, especially the Kölsch. They come from the neighboring German cities of Cologne and Düsseldorf respectively. A great rivalry exists between the two cities based on their beer. Kölsch is bright yellow and light in taste, whereas Altbier (meaning "old-style beer," not aged old beer) is amber-brown and bitter.

The other well-known hybrid style is the California Common. Toward the end of the 19th century, almost all North American beer production was lager and it was made in increasingly large breweries that used modern technology such as artificial refrigeration to keep their beer cold during its long maturation. As the population spread West, brewers developed techniques to make lagers without the use of mechanical cooling. Brewers in San Francisco essentially copied the lagers of the Midwest and East Coast but had to ferment it at warmer ambient temperatures. To combat any potentially unusual flavors, the brewers made their beer, fermented it, then put it straight into wooden kegs and sent these to the taverns, where they were stored for a few days until needed, thus cutting out the cold-conditioning and dramatically speeding up the brewing process. A great amount of pressure built up in the barrels from further fermentation and this erupted as steam when the keg was tapped, so it became known as Steam Beer, although another story tells how the beer was cooled on San Francisco rooftops, which looked as though they were steaming. That name has since been trademarked by Anchor Brewing, so all other brewers call it California Common.

Päffgen Kölsch

Cologne, Germany
ABV: 4.8%

Päffgen is Cologne's oldest Kölsch brewery that's still running, and they have been making beer since 1883. Like all the traditional Cologne brewers, they follow the Kölsch Convention, a local rule which says that only breweries in Cologne can make a true Kölsch. The Convention states that the beer should be filtered, pale in color, notably bitter, and around 4.5% ABV. Go to Päffgen's traditional tavern and they serve the beer from wooden barrels into tall, thin, 7 fl oz (200ml) glasses. Their Kölsch is super-crisp, super-refreshing, deeply bitter, and very close to a lager in flavor. There are lots of other breweries in Cologne and it's fun to try a variety of them to see how their beers are similar or different: Früh, brewed by the Cathedral, is the most famous, very clean and nicely bitter, while I've always liked the fruity esters—think strawberries—in Mühlen's Kölsch.

Chuckanut Kölsch

Bellingham, Washington, USA
ABV: 4.5%

I was looking into American-brewed Kölsch and was surprised to see how many were unfiltered, dry-hopped, or made with fruit or coffee. That's *not* Kölsch, that's a light Pale Ale. I'm open to innovation and creativity, but I'm a purist when it comes to Kölsch because it's a very specific style and I want it bright, dry, bitter, and moderate in alcohol. Chuckanut's Kölsch is a true Kölsch, which is why I admire it so much: it's perfectly clear, yellow, and light in body, but not thin, bitter, or astringent; and it's lightly toasty and simple in the most delicious and refreshing of ways. It might be unfashionable to make beer that's this crisp, but I love it. They also make a great Altbier that's also true to style, giving lots of malt flavor and a deep, earthy bitterness. Some styles need to be done properly, and I think Kölsch and Alt are two of them.

Kürzer Altbier

Düsseldorf, Germany
ABV: 4.8%

Head 25 miles (40km) north of Cologne and you get to Düsseldorf. Those 25 miles might not be very far in terms of physical distance, but in beer miles it's a very long way. Here you'll find Altbier, a clear, bitter, brown ale that's reminiscent of a classic British Bitter but crisp and carbonated like a lager. Like Cologne, Düsseldorf has lots of breweries and taverns in the center, and you can try a wide range of Altbiers, from the very bitter Uerige to Füschschen's which has hints of cherry brandy. Last time I was there, I enjoyed Kürzer's the most. They have a modern brewery in a bar that feels like a Belgian beer café. The Altbier is poured into squat glasses (here it's 7 fl oz/200ml, but in other bars it's 8 fl oz/250ml). It's a little fudgy, chocolatey, and smooth, certainly giving more malt flavor than others in the city, and it has the dryness and peppery bitterness you expect in a traditional Altbier.

Uerige Sticke

Düsseldorf, Germany
ABV: 6.0%

Uerige's brewery and tavern occupy a large corner building right in the middle of Düsseldorf—you'll notice it because of all the people drinking small glasses of dark beer outside. Inside, the brewing happens over (at least) five floors, rising way above the ground and also going beneath the streets. On the first floor you can see the copper brewhouse, into which goes German malted barley and whole flower hops. The wort goes all the way up to the top floor and into a coolship, or "reefer" as they call it, then it works its way down, via a fermenter, to mature in tanks in the cold cellar for at least three weeks. Their regular Altbier is bitter, spicy, and peppery, while twice a year, on the third Tuesdays of January and October, they release Sticke, a special stronger Altbier that has a powerful herbal bitterness and a dried-fruit and cooked-apple sweetness. They also make an 8.0%-ABV Doppel Sticke once a year.

Anchor Steam Beer

San Francisco, California, USA
ABV: 4.9%

This is one of America's most important beers, both historically and in the craft-beer era. It's an original and indigenous American beer style, as described in the introduction to this section, and it's arguably the first proper American craft beer, modernized in the early 1970s. This beer gives us a glimpse of 19th-century West Coast lager: gold with a creamy foam, some bready malts, and a strong bitterness, alongside some spicy, peppery aromas. The beer is still made using traditional techniques like open fermentation, done at a warm temperature, and it's also kräusened, a process that involves adding some fermenting beer to finished beer to produce additional fizz. It's an American classic.

Capital Brewing Co. Coast Ale

Canberra, Australia
ABV: 4.3%

Capital's large warehouse brewery and taproom serves fresh beers and great food from local favorite Brodburger, and there's a big space outside that fills up quickly on warm afternoons—and being outside was part of the inspiration for this brewery, which is located not far from both the ocean and the trails. Coast Ale is an Aussie take on a California Common. It's brewed with Saaz, Hallertauer, and Superpride hops, giving a background of classic European bitterness to go with the Australian Superpride, a high-alpha Aussie hop, and it's the kind of beer that works for those hanging at the beach or hanging for a cold one after a long day hiking or running through the hills. It's got some chewy, toasty malts in the middle, but nothing overpowering, and those hops bring a zesty, pithy, piney kind of depth that's perfectly refreshing.

BiaCraft Artisan Ales Tram Phan Tram Crush Ale

Ho Chi Minh City, Vietnam
ABV: 4.4%

The Vietnamese are big-beer drinkers, the kind of drinkers who habitually meet with friends after work, go to a restaurant, order a case of cold beers, and drink the whole lot—then order another case. BiaCraft's Tram Phan Tram, a name that means "bottoms up" or "down your beer," is described as "refreshing and slammable for the discerning connoisseur"—the brewery is aiming to tap into the local way of drinking, while also linking in with the growing trend for drinkers looking to upgrade their beer to something better. This "Crush Ale" is lager-like and inspired by the local big brands and the way in which people drink them. It's light in body, easy-going, low in flavor in the best way, with a little citrusy hop at the end to make it a little different. BiaCraft have several great beer bars in Saigon and they can be credited with teaching the Vietnamese about the diversity of craft beer.

THE HISTORY OF LAGER

Lager is the world's most-drunk type of beer, and it has a simple, golden, refreshing ubiquity; wherever you go, if you ask for a beer, you'll probably be given a lager. But the flavor profile we associate with mainstream lagers is a recent taste, something that can be traced back to the middle of the 20th century; the origins of lager go back quite a few years further.

The foundations of lager

The simplest and earliest differentiation of lager over ale is that it was a beer fermented at a low temperature with a special yeast strain and then left in cool cellars for several months. Yeast, temperature, and time defined lager.

The first mention of something that we can reasonably link to lager came in the 14th century and this referenced a "lower-fermenting" beer. Until then, the world had only known "upper-fermenting" beer: that is, ale. When an ale fermented (and centuries ago it fermented in an open-topped wooden or clay vessel), yeast rose to the top of the vessel and brewers could collect that yeast and reuse it. Lager yeast fell to the bottom of the vessel, and once the fermented beer was moved into a storage and maturation barrel, the brewers collected the "lower-fermenting" yeast to re-use it.

Ale and lager yeasts are different species, though they are related; ale yeast is *Saccharomyces cerevisiae* and lager yeast is *Saccharomyces pastorianus*. *S. pastorianus* is a hybridization between *S. cerevisiae* and another *Saccharomyces* yeast called *S. eubayanus* (basically the yeasts bred). No one knows how, when, or where they hybridized (*S. eubayanus* has never been found in nature in Europe), but it's most likely that those yeasts met in the brewing environment, probably in a wooden barrel.

What we do know is that lagers were first brewed somewhere around what's now Franconia in Upper Bavaria, and out toward the Czech border, where it was common practice for brewers to make their beer above ground and then ferment and store it in cellars below ground, where the temperatures were naturally cold. Somehow the new yeast got into those beers and thrived in the cold, in a Darwinian survival of the fittest against the ambient-seeking ale yeast. Because the yeast was in the cold it worked more slowly and needed to be left for longer in the cellars. Lager was known as a "stored" beer, and its name is derived from the German verb *lagern*, meaning "to store."

The real beginning of lager

The first major development in the history of lager-brewing was the signing of what's now known as the Reinheitsgebot, or the German beer purity law, which was written into Bavaria's rule book in 1516. The law said that in Bavaria, and only in Bavaria, beer should be made with just barley, water, and hops (yeast was added later—brewers certainly knew yeast existed, but it's thought they just believed that the yeast didn't remain in the beer when it was drunk). How did this help lager? At that time there were two kinds of beer in Bavaria: Braunbier and Weissbier. Brown beer was brewed with malted barley and it was dark and stored in cold cellars—it was lager. White beer was paler because it was brewed with air-dried malts and some wheat, and it was brewed in ambient temperatures—it was ale. Banning the use of wheat in breweries effectively banned ales, making lager the natural beer of Bavaria.

In 1553, a new law came in which further confirmed lager's place in Bavarian breweries (and still only in Bavaria—lager was rarely brewed outside of Bavaria until the 1830s). This new law created brewing seasons and said that beer could only be made between September 29 and April 23 (for quality reasons—to ensure the beer could be kept cool enough—but also to alleviate fire hazards from brewing and malting in the summer). That created two types of Braunbier: Winterbier and Sommerbier. Winterbier was weaker, cheaper, made more quickly (two or three months), and drunk during the brewing season; Sommerbier was stronger, more expensive, cold-lagered for longer (taking four to nine months), and drunk outside of the brewing season, between May and October. This was the standard brewing process in Bavaria, and it continued in this way for several centuries, with the lagers mostly dark, sweet, probably a little smoky, and around 4.0% ABV. Back then, brewing was an empirical and local craft, which lacked any large scale. When scale, and then science, became important, lager changed dramatically.

Christian Staehlin's Phoenix Brewery was a large-scale industrialized brewery in St. Louis, Missouri.

The industrialization of lager

By the early 1800s, British breweries were significantly larger and more developed than any other breweries in the world. Those brewers had used all the advantages brought by industrialization to develop enormous beer factories. As the breweries got bigger, helped by the use of steam power, brewers employed new scientific instruments such as the thermometer and the saccharometer (which measures the sweetness in beer), and this enabled them to achieve more consistency. They also began using new malting techniques, which produced a better, paler malt. Most British ales were matured in barrels or vats for many months at ambient temperatures (not in cold cellars, as in Bavaria).

In the early 1830s, several German and Austrian brewers traveled to Britain and learned all about these new brewing techniques and technologies. They then returned home and started to gain a greater understanding of their lager beers. This led them to improve their process; they could now measure sweetness, temperature, and alcohol content, and they were controlling temperatures by harvesting ice to ensure their cellars stayed cold all year round (beers were fermented in one part of the cellars where it was usually 46°F/8°C, then matured deeper underground in the cooler areas—ice helped maintain the cold through the warmer months). Once they were making better and more consistent lagers, brewers started to increase the scale of their breweries. Then, once the breweries had increased in scale, it was finally possible for others outside of Bavaria to taste these lagered beers, and from the 1840s onward more and more brewers began using the Bavarian brewing techniques and their special yeast to produce their own lagers.

By the 1850s, there were three main types of lager: in Munich and Bavaria the lager was brown; in Vienna it was amber; and in Pilsen it was gold. Dark Munich lager and golden Pilsner lager would ultimately be the ones that traveled, and one of the first places they went to was North America, which would soon develop its own kind of lager.

The Americanization of lager

Lager was brewed in North America from the 1840s, which is very early in lager's relatively short history. In the middle decades of the 19th century, a wave of Germans emigrated to North America, settling in what became known as the German Triangle—Milwaukee, St. Louis, and Cincinnati—as well as in the big cities up the East Coast. A significant number of émigrés started brewing, mostly because they and their fellow countrymen missed the beers from home.

German brewers in America were making beer that was similar to Bavarian lagers, using old Bavarian techniques and digging underground cellars, and these beers were dark, low in alcohol, quite sweet, and mostly drunk by Germans—the Americans preferred whiskey. Over time, and through cultural and economic changes like workers shifting from rural farms to city factories, Americans began to drink more beer, but they didn't want dark, heavy beer. Instead, they wanted something more refreshing, which led the second generation of German-American brewers to develop new recipes that used corn or rice in the mash, so creating a paler, drier, crisper beer. The American Lager emerged in the 1870s.

By the end of the 19th century, a lot of significant scientific and industrial developments had facilitated bigger breweries and better brewing processes, and this meant

An early advertisement for Schlitz Lager, a typical German-style beer brewed in Milwaukee (far left). Blackman's Brewery Juicy Banger, a modern Hoppy Lager from Australia, part of the global spread of the lager beer style (left).

The globalization of lager

By the middle of the 20th century, lager was a worldwide drink and the next development saw it become engineered so it was more consistent, could be brewed more quickly, produced more cheaply, and made lighter in flavor. Meanwhile, marketing spend increased and big lager brands were able to become very large, so the world of beer was dominated by yellow, light-tasting, carbonated, refreshing, and cheap lagers (this isn't necessarily a negative: there's something important about always knowing what you're going to get when you order a beer and it also ensured that beer could be afforded by anyone).

By the early 1980s, as lagers became more prevalent and less interesting, and as more drinkers began to travel and taste other kinds of beer like Pale Ales, Wheat Beers, and Stouts, so began the first steps toward small breweries opening and giving drinkers a greater choice. Craft beer became the new and tastier alternative.

Back in Germany and the Czech Republic, the lagers maintained their traditions and qualities throughout all these changes (though Bavarian beer did shift in color from dark to light), and today that quality continues, while there's also a renaissance of great lager. People are reconsidering lager and its qualities, whether that's brewing a classic Central European style or innovating with new kinds of lager.

To a lot of people, lager is one type of fizzy yellow beer, but there's so much more to it than that, and it's got a much more interesting history than most drinkers are aware of. If you want to know even more, then you need to read my book, *A Brief History of Lager: 500 Years of the World's Favorite Beer*.

more people could drink lager. Pale malt production was now normal; scientists had discovered the secrets of yeast and fermentation, and worked out how to isolate single, healthy yeast cells, eliminating wild yeast and bacteria and making beer taste better; beer could be bottled on a large scale, pasteurization made those bottles bacteriologically stable, and they could now travel great distances by train, so lagers could be drunk by more people; wood was phased out of breweries and replaced by glass and steel; refrigeration ensured that lagers could be made in the cold all year round and, crucially, enabled fermenters and lagering tanks to come up above ground and into large chilled factories; and lagers could now be brewed in several weeks instead of many months. Now, lager could be made anywhere in the world, and if a new brewery was going to open in a new city, with very few exceptions they built a lager brewery and not one designed to make old English-style ales.

WEISSBIER

There's a long history of brewing with wheat in Germany, and for centuries it was a common ingredient in most beers in the north of the country. In the south, however, it was different owing to the Reinheitsgebot purity law, which stated that Bavarian beer could only be made with water, barley, hops, and yeast, meaning that wheat wasn't allowed. But there was one exception: the royal family had sole rights to brewing with wheat, which they monopolized, building dozens of Weissbier breweries. The first and most famous of the royal Weissbier breweries was based in what's now Munich's Hofbräuhaus. The royal family gave up their sole rights in the middle of the 19th century and others began to brew Weissbier. Today, it's one of Germany's major beer types.

Weissbier here collects together different types of German-style wheat beers, where a typical recipe will be roughly 50 percent wheat and 50 percent barley. The most common Weissbier or Hefeweizen is around 5.5% ABV and ranges from yellow to amber in color. Dunkelweizen is a dark wheat beer made with dark malts. Weizenbock is a stronger (6.5–8.5% ABV) wheat beer that can be pale or dark. Hopfenweisse takes a Weizenbock and adds lots of late hops for aroma. What connects all these beers is a distinctive Weissbier yeast with esters and aromas of banana, bubble gum, vanilla, stone fruit, pear, and sometimes clove-like peppery phenolics, plus they are usually unfiltered and cloudy in appearance, and have a low hop bitterness to emphasize the yeast character.

Weihenstephaner Hefeweissbier

Freising, Germany
ABV: 5.4%

Weihenstephaner Hefeweissbier is a hazy pale yellow and always comes with an ice-cream whip of white foam. The glass is beautiful: narrow in the middle, it curves up and out like a vase, then tulips at the top, catching all the foam and collecting all the fruity, banana-like aromas. It's a beer that plays tricks with you: it's full-bodied, yet light; perceptibly sweet, yet definitely dry; fizzy, but it won't fill you with bubbles. There's a pleasing creaminess to this beer, one that is enhanced by the banana aromas and a vanilla-cream quality, which makes it immensely satisfying to drink from a textural perspective and also for its refreshing qualities. It's a classic Weissbier and Weihenstephaner is an essential brewery to visit for many reasons: for this beer, for all their other beers, for the fact that the brewery is home to one of the world's foremost brewing schools, and, perhaps most of all, because it's the oldest brewery in the world and they are approaching their 1,000th birthday.

Schneider Weisse Tap 7

Kelheim, Germany
ABV: 5.4%

When the Bavarian royal family, who had sole rights to make Weissbier, decided that they'd rather just focus on brewing lager, they leased out the rights to other brewers. George Schneider was then the royal Weissbier brewmaster and held that job until 1872, when he opened his eponymous brewery a few blocks from the Hofbräuhaus, in a building that used to be home to Maderbräu, a popular working-class lager brewery in Munich. Schneider continued to brew Weissbier there before building a bigger new brewery in Kelheim, keeping the Munich location as a tavern, which remains popular today—especiallyso at breakfast time on the weekend, when you'll struggle to get a table unless you've booked. Schneider's Tap 7 is ostensibly a Weissbier from the late 19th century. It's amber in color, toffee-like,and toasty, with some banoffee and pepper aroma and a definite clove spiciness, and a full palate up front then a lightness to end.

Geipel Dunkelweizen

Gellioedd, Wales, UK
ABV: 5.2%

In the north-west of Wales, somewhere quite far away from the middle of nowhere, between Cwmtirmynach and Cefnddwysarn, there's an old Bavarian brewhouse in a barn that makes authentic and classic-tasting German-style lagers and ales. Geipel brew quietly, they don't shout loudly about what they do, and I rarely see their beers available anywhere—it's almost as though they're a mythical brewery, but then every now and then I see the beer, I drink it, and I love it. Their Dunkelweizen, a dark wheat beer, has the classic banana aroma along with some roasted nuts, cocoa, and cinnamon spice mixed in. It has the smooth body that makes a Hefeweizen great, then a classic and lightly citrusy and refreshing finish, all with a great complexity of darker malt and yeast in the middle of it. Dunkelweizen is a great choice with lots of different foods, especially Mexican tacos and Middle Eastern salads.

Stoup Brewing Dunkelweizen

Seattle, Washington, USA
ABV: 6.2%

Never did I ever expect that Dunkelweizen would become one of the styles I most enjoyed in 2019, yet somehow I kept seeing them, ordering them, and loving them. At Stoup's taproom, sitting in front of their brewery and faced with a range of hoppy ales, I ended up tasting the Dunkelweizen and liking it so much that I had a full pour of it. It's dark brown and immediately bready and toasty, with some banana-like esters, roasted banana, and vanilla—distantly reminiscent of a wholemeal bagel with banana on top—and I loved it. I was at the brewery soon after the hop harvest, which happens pretty close to Seattle, and their Citra Fresh Hop IPA was the best green-hopped beer I've had—intensely hoppy, bitter, and with a bright melon and orange hop profile that's often too delicate to be interesting in a fresh-hopped beer.

Spezial Weissbier

Bamberg, Germany
ABV: 5.3%

Spezial is one of the two breweries in the city of Bamberg that have their own wood-fired maltings, which they use to produce smoked malt for their smoked beers. Spezial also make a Weissbier and while it isn't impactfully smoky, there's certainly a depth of savory smoke in there, and with the wheat base and the fruity yeast, it brings a combination of roasted banana, piecrusts, clove, lemon, and toffee, with some umami savoriness at the end and lots of bubbles to keep it light. Spezial have a couple of locations in Bamberg: the brewery tavern (which has some nice guest rooms if you want to sleep) near the center of town, plus Spezial Keller, a short walk uphill out of town and a pretty beer garden with great views back over the city.

Brauerei Michael Plank Heller Weizenbock

Laaber, Germany
ABV: 7.8%

Most German-style wheat beers are around 5.5% ABV, a sweet spot of satisfaction and strength. A Weizenbock bulks that beer up and enrichens it with more grain and more alcohol, so that it's closer to 8.0% ABV. Brauerei Michael Plank are masters at making Weizenbock, routinely winning in big competitions, like the World Beer Cup. They brew a Dunkler and Heller Weizenbock—that is, a dark and a light. The Heller is a rich golden color and cloudy, as you'd expect. It smells like banana bread, vanilla sponge, and spiced honey, which is really appealing. The body is full and creamy, then the combination of carbonation, some cooked citrus, stewed stone fruit, and a lightly bitter finish keeps this strong beer from being heavy. Weissbier is typically a breakfast beer in Bavaria, but save this one for after dinner and have it with apricot or peach cake.

Live Oak Primus Weizenbock

Austin, Texas, USA
ABV: 8.0%

Primus is a dark Weizenbock that's full-bodied and richly smooth with wheat and malt which give it lots of caramel and chocolate. The typical Bavarian yeast is amplified, strained into giving out more aromas as it works to produce more alcohol, and that gives us barbecued banana, vanilla, some spicy phenols, and then a strength and warmth from the alcohol. It's a complex beer, a hearty one, a warming one, and, given that it's from Texas, it's a beer you should try next to brisket or ribs, or—perhaps even better—with coconut cake or banana pudding. If you want something lighter, then Live Oak are masters at making German-style beers, from their excellent Hefeweizen and snappy Pilz to the malty Big Bark Amber Lager. They also have a wonderful beer garden where you can sit in the warm Texas sun, drinking cold lagers. Just remember to grab some Primus to go and take it home for dessert.

Páramo Brauhaus Weissbier

Quito, Ecuador
ABV: 4.9%

Ecuadorian-German Uli Hahl's great-grandfather ran a brewery in Bavaria at the end of the 19th century, and something in that brewing ancestry convinced Uli that he should start his own brewery in Ecuador, a country without a huge amount of brewing heritage. Páramo maintain a tight range of styles including a Golden Ale, an Altbier, an Oatmeal Stout, and a West Coast-style Pale Ale, which is dark gold and hopped with Cascade. Their Weissbier is yellow and has the characteristic white foam. It has the banana aromas you'd expect, with the clove and spice being more prominent in this brew. The body is full and quite sweet, but the carbonation keeps it light. The brewery has a German-style beer hall and garden, serving up typical German dishes.

J Wakefield El Jefe

Miami, Florida, USA
ABV: 5.0%

Not quite a straight-up Hefeweizen, but then J Wakefield aren't quite a straight-up brew-'em-classic kinda brewer. Instead, they're better known for their big-flavored brews, thick Fruited Sours, and dense Imperial Stouts. El Jefe starts out as a classic Hefeweizen: it's that handsomely hazy golden orange with a fluffy white foam. It's got the usual yeast aromatics like banana, stone fruits, and some distant spiciness, and they combine with a smooth, soft body of wheat. The J Wakefield-ing comes when they add coconut, and that gives a creaminess, a tropical freshness, and almost a hint of savoriness, which is really nice with all the other elements in the beer. I'm a sucker for coconut in beer, although rarely am I really pleased with what I taste—but in El Jefe it's used perfectly. Enjoy by the beach in Miami with some spicy grilled seafood.

Microbrasserie Le Castor Citra Weisse

Rigaud, Canada
ABV: 5.0%

Imagine the fruitier aromas of a Weissbier—banana, bubble gum, pear—and then dose them with Citra hops. Not a massive charge of hops, but a balanced seasoning of them to give orange and lemon zest, peach, and coriander seed. In a beer like this, known as a Hopfen Weisse, you get the double fruitiness of yeast and hops, plus this one brings an underlying peppery spice and even a hint of pithy tartness, and they combine into a light, refreshing summery beer with a soft texture and that enticing aroma. Like most Weissbiers it's a great choice with food. Here I recommend Thai coconut-based curries or just a big bowl of guacamole and nachos.

WITBIER

Where German-style wheat beer is full, smooth, and has a banana-like fruitiness, the Belgian style of Witbier is generally lighter and drier with more citrus and spice than Bavarian banana, and it's typically brewed with actual citrus and spice—the classic combo is curaçao orange peel and dried coriander seed, which both bring a fruitiness (coriander seed is very high in linalool, which is also found in the fruitiest of hops). It's a regular, everyday kind of beer in Belgium and France, and one that's cloudy, refreshing, and light with low bitterness. Brewed with around 50 percent wheat and 50 percent pale malt, it is usually in the 5.0% ABV range.

Belgium has a long history of brewing with wheat and each town historically had its own specific style of wheat-based beer. At the end of the 19th century, we can reasonably say that these beers would've had an acidity to them or at best a rough tartness, but that was part of the expected character at the time—it's just what beer tasted like. As Belgian beers became less regional and more uniform they improved in quality and consistency, developing new styles like Pale Ale and Amber Ale, but, as a result, some of the old beer types and regionality were lost. One famous result of these developments was that a milkman from a town called Hoegaarden decided to brew a beer with the historic taste of his earlier drinking days, making it with wheat and spices to evoke the old tartness, but not making it sour. Hoegaarden became the classic Witbier and it rejuvenated the wheat-based brewing traditions of the Low Countries.

St. Bernardus Wit

Watou, Belgium
ABV: 5.5%

If you want to know what a true Belgian-brewed Witbier tastes like, then this is one of the must-try beers. It's the quintessential combination of soft wheat in the body and a distinctive floral and orangey aroma from the ground coriander. It has orange and peppery clove flavors, a frisky carbonation, and a dry, almost tart finish. The interaction of dryness, spice, and citrus defines a Belgian-style Witbier and gives a teasing complexity and a refreshing zing that makes Witbier one of the best all-round food beers—it's great with mussels and simple white fish, through spicy Southeast Asian salads and curries. St. Bernardus is an Abbey brewery and in 2018 they opened Bar Bernard, a bright rooftop restaurant next to the brewery that overlooks hop fields. This is deservedly a place for a beer pilgrimage where you'll work up to their superlative Quadrupel, Abt 12.

Allagash White

Portland, Maine, USA
ABV: 5.1%

Allagash White turned 25 in 2020, but it might've been a very different story if it wasn't for the determined belief that brewing a Belgian-style Witbier in north-east America was a good idea. It wasn't easy selling a beer like this in the early years. Beer to most people back then was a light, bright lager with limited flavor, not a hazy yellow wheat beer brewed with ground coriander and curaçao orange peel that was lemony, floral, creamy, smooth, and spicy. But Allagash's persistence and belief were based on knowing that they were making a damn good beer, and eventually everyone else realized it too—today it's one of America's most important craft beers, and one of the most loved among beer geeks. Go to Portland, Maine, if you can. Tour Allagash and spend some time in one of America's great beer cities, where a glass of White with a lobster roll is a perfect pairing.

Mad Scientist Tokyo Lemonade

Budapest, Hungary
ABV: 4.2%

Budapest is a brilliant beer destination. It has all the excitement of modern beer and brewing, plus its own drinking culture and spaces, especially the ruin bars. Built into derelict old buildings in the historic Jewish Quarter on the Buda side of the city, these are often large, simple spaces surrounded by bricks and literal ruin, and are packed with people and great beer. The daddy of all ruin bars is Szimpla Kert, and it's one of the world's great drinking destinations: a huge, rambling, multi-level, multi-space, multi-bar ruin pub. It's the sort of place you can work in during the day, go to for good beers in the evening, before partying there all night. One of the individual bars inside is run by Mad Scientists, a local brewer who makes a mad mix of different brews, including lots of Hazy IPAs and flavored Sours and Stouts. Tokyo Lemonade is a light, breezy, refreshing Witbier with yuzu, coriander seed, and orange zest. The yuzu is distinctive, zingy, zesty, and fragrant, and it makes this one almost like a citrus shandy.

Six° North Wanderlust Wheat

Laurencekirk, Scotland, UK
ABV: 4.6%

Inspired by Brussels and brewed six degrees north of there, in Aberdeenshire, this is one of the few British breweries to focus on the beers of its Belgian neighbors. Wanderlust Wheat is a straight-up Witbier. Nothing fancy or crafty, just a beer done in the Belgian tradition with orange peel and coriander seed, a simple light Pilsner malt and wheat base, and a couple of classic Noble hops. The coriander and some light, peppery phenols are strong in the aroma. The body is smooth and it's refreshingly carbonated, with a stronger-than-usual bitterness at the end. The brewery has bars in some of the main Scottish cities, and on tap you'll find a wide range of beers, from a crisp and bitter Pilsner to a German-hopped Pale Ale, a Dry Saison, and a spicy-citrusy Belgian IPA.

Brasserie du Mont Salève Blanche

Neydens, France
ABV: 5.0%

Mont Salève's Blanche is a familiar base brew to Witbier drinkers in that it's hazy yellow, light, spritzy with carbonation, refreshing, and fruity with yeast, then, instead of the typical spices and phenolic yeast, it's dry-hopped with American Citra hops. Those hops give a greater depth of hop flavor and an inviting aroma of orange, lychee, pineapple, and stone fruit. It's a really nice evolution of the classic white beer, as those hops—used delicately and not overdone—complement the fruitiness of their Witbier yeast and mirror flavors usually found in coriander seed and orange peel. Mont Salève also make Sorachi Ace Bitter, originally a 2.5%-ABV "small beer," but it's evolved into a low-alcohol and heavily hopped Witbier with aromas of coconut and lemongrass. And look out for their Mademoiselle Barberouge, a 6.0%-ABV Pale Ale brewed with French Barbe Rouge hops—it's floral and has a berry-like fruitiness.

Browar Kormoran Podróże Kormorana Witbier

Olsztyn, Poland
ABV: 4.6%

Brewed traditionally with barley, wheat, and oats, plus some spelt, then spiced with coriander seed, as well as bitter and sweet orange peel, Kormoran's Witbier is a great Polish example of this classic Belgian style. You get a beer with a full, sweet, and creamy body, almost more in the Bavarian style, but the orange and coriander come through prominently, while the fizz, the dryness, and a touch of grapefruit-y tartness help to keep it light and refreshing. The brewery is best known for its strong Baltic Porter, which also features in this book (see page 122), but they have a whole range of different beers. This Witbier is a good choice for cutting through some of the heavier or richer Polish food.

The Queer Brewing Project Flowers

London/Manchester, England, UK
ABV: 4.0%

Lily Waite founded the Queer Brewing Project in early 2019 to, in her own words, "provide visibility for LGBTQ+ people in and around beer, and to build community, advocate for LGBTQ+ rights, and raise money for vital LGBTQ+ charities." She has since brewed over 30 collaboration beers and raised thousands of pounds for charity, and in early 2021 Manchester's Cloudwater began brewing a range of core Queer Brewing beers, including a Pilsner, a Pale Ale, and this Witbier. Flowers is a classic Witbier, only lightened to 4.0% ABV, and it's brewed with the usual combo of curaçao orange peel and coriander seed, plus Saaz and Tettnang hops. It's elegant, balanced, refreshingly orangey, and noticeably floral from the coriander and the hops, plus there's a lovely creamy texture and a snappy dry finish. It's a really wonderful Witbier, and a little like a mini Allagash White.

SAISON AND FARMHOUSE ALES

In the early 1800s, most beer was brewed domestically. Some of that beer was made in the home, some in monasteries, some in castles, and some on farms. Saison is the most common of what's become the collected group of "Farmhouse Ales," which also includes lower-alcohol Grisette and maltier French Bière de Garde. Historically, most Saison—brewed seasonally and drunk by the seasonal workers, the *saisonnières*—was light in alcohol, probably sweet, probably tart, and it would've been funky from a wild and hard-to-control fermentation. By the middle of the 20th century, those old types of beer had become unfashionable, being replaced by clean Pale Lagers and Pale Ales, so they were reinvented as stronger, more robust beers to differentiate them from the ubiquitous Pilsners. When we talk about Saisons today, these are not beers from an old Belgian or French field, but beers from the interwar and post-war years when no one wanted to drink rough-edged, old-style ales. They are also, arguably, a beer style that emerged anew out of American craft breweries, creating a new family of beers, distinct from Belgian farmhouses.

To the modern brewer, Saison became a structure that could be interpreted in new ways, meaning it has become a kind of umbrella beer type with no strict definition, and all we can really expect (or at least hope for) is a distinctive yeast profile that gives some fruity, spicy aroma, while it's probably yellow to amber in color, with a very dry finish. Beyond that, it could be under 4.0% ABV or over 8.0% ABV; it could be clean or funky; brewed with one yeast or inoculated with many; barrel-aged or made in steel; dry-hopped, fruited, yeast-aromatic, or sour. The lack of definition has made Saison a style that's open to innovation, but concurrently it's a style which is returning to old local farmhouse traditions and being made in a rustic way with local ingredients.

Brasserie au Baron Cuvée des Jonquilles

Gussignies, France
ABV: 7.0%

Brewed right on the border between France and Belgium, Cuvée des Jonquilles is a great example of how the fluid borders in this region have produced a variety of different yet related beers. The brewery is in an old café-pub, which became a restaurant in 1973 with a brewery added in 1989, releasing their first batch of Cuvée des Jonquilles in the spring when their restaurant was surrounded by pretty yellow daffodils (or *jonquilles*, in French). The beer is effervescent and light; there are some biscuity malts; the yeast is delicate, while the hops are peppery, also adding some floral and stone-fruit aromas. Some bottle labels list this as a Bière de Garde, the traditional French style, though it has a Saison-like lightness. It's a great beer to drink with soft and funky French cheese.

Brasserie Dupont Saison Dupont

Tourpes, Belgium
ABV: 6.5%

Saison Dupont has become the style-defining Saison. Since the middle of the 19th century, the Dupont brewery made Saison beers on their farm to serve to seasonal workers. The beer is quite different today, though the brewery combines the old farmhouse with a modern brewhouse and still maintains some of the older brewing practices: the kettle is still direct-fired; the primary fermentation takes place in shallow square fermenters with the beer never rising above a few feet in depth; and the beer is bottled and then bottle-conditioned for months before being sold. To taste this beer at its best, buy a big bottle and age it for 6–12 months, as the flavors will continue to develop in the bottle. With Saison Dupont you should expect a beer that's deep gold with peppery yeast, a little stone fruit, almond, pear, and banana. The body is round and robust, with a caramelization from the kettle that gives it some richness, before the dry, bitter, and long-lasting finish. Today, if a brewer makes what they'd call an "authentic Saison," then it's probably modeled on Dupont.

Siphon Brewing Blinker

Damme, Belgium
ABV: 5.5%

Brewed with barley and wheat, hops from the Poperinge region of Belgium, and a yeast that attenuates down to an almost terminal dryness, Blinker seems to snap when you drink it, a snap of fizz and a spritz of lemon sparking together, with the bubbles improbably small and the flavor satisfyingly big. I think it's the combination of appetizing and almost savory grain and the spicy dryness that makes it taste so good. To counterpoint this summery Saison, every winter Siphon release a Quadrupel that's brewed with vanilla, orange, and dark candi sugar, which is deeply festive but with the brewery's characteristic dryness at the end.

Franschhoek Beer Co. La Saison

Franschhoek, South Africa
ABV: 8.4%

Set in wine country and surrounded by vineyards, their own organic garden, and a beautiful wrap-around view of the Franschhoek mountains, the Franschhoek tasting room looks and feels closer to a winery than a brewery tap, making this a smart place to stop for food, where they use much of their own produce in their cooking. La Saison is brewed using fresh mountain spring water, which gives the beer a very clean depth. The grain hangs out in the back and gives the beer that ideal combination of full structure without chewy sweetness. The yeast has ripped through the sugars, giving a very dry and crisp Saison and leaving behind a tiny tartness and some characteristic spicy, orchard-fruit, and peppery aromas. It's delicately dry-hopped, which adds some grapefruit, lemony, and lightly tropical hop flavors.

Blackberry Farm Brewery Classic

Maryville, Tennessee, USA
ABV: 6.3%

Blackberry Farm is a luxury hotel on a farmstead in the foothills of the Great Smoky Mountains, where the resort's restaurant uses their own-grown produce. They also have livestock producing cheese and meat. They added a brewery a few miles away, with the aim of supplying themselves and other food-focused locations with Old World-inspired beer. Their Classic is a Saison in the Dupont style. It's robust with alcohol and malt, with the simple, toasty grain base giving body and depth to the beer, and the yeast is prominent and gives a stone-fruit, pear, and pepper aroma. It's the body and the deep spicy bitterness that help it work so well with food, where its versatility makes it suitable to go with the lightest vegetables, the richest meat, or a selection of good farmhouse cheeses.

Brasserie Duyck Jenlain Ambrée

Jenlain, France
ABV: 7.5%

Bière de Garde originated as a keeping beer that was brewed after harvest time and stored until the following summer in the Farmhouse tradition. As brewing became more commercial and farmhouse breweries became less necessary, the brewing practices of northern France and Belgium diverged, with the French brews coming out fuller-bodied, sweeter, and stronger than those of their neighbors. These beers began to grow in popularity after the World Wars and became more defined, refined, and revitalized, giving France its own domestic beer style. Jenlain were partly responsible for Bière de Garde's evolution and their Ambrée should be seen as a classic example. It's amber-colored and has a malt sweetness of caramel and bread crusts, which even gives us a little bit of chewy bite, while the yeast provides a nutty and gently fruity aroma, lifted by some hops at the end.

Affinity Brew Co. Breeze

London, England, UK
ABV: 3.8%

You don't typically associate a pub cellar in south-east London with the beers of a Farmhouse tradition. But then Breeze isn't like many other Saisons in the very best of ways, and I think this is one of the most underrated beers in England. It's a lively little 3.8%-ABV Saison, brewed with lime zest and coriander seed. It's hazy blonde and beautifully dry; it has a savory element and a cracker-like malt depth, a spicy, peppery finish, and, when you're about halfway through your glass, the lime zest and the coriander pop out and then you get why it's called Breeze as somehow it lifts up with an exotic, exciting, enticing fragrance. It's a great and underrated London beer. As we go to print, the brewery have opened a location in the seaside town of Broadstairs.

Saint Mars of the Desert Jack D'Or

Sheffield, England, UK
ABV: 6.4%

Jack D'Or will be a familiar name to those of us who remember the remarkable beers of Pretty Things. Their Saison, which was first brewed in 2008, was a benchmark American-brewed Saison that modernized the style by using American hops, and it was surely partially responsible for the emerging thirst for Saisons Stateside. Pretty Things, who were based outside of Boston, stopped brewing in 2015, only to be reborn in 2019 in the suburbs of Sheffield as Saint Mars of the Desert. Now husband and wife Dann Paquette and Martha Simpson-Holley are brewing beers with a worldly inspiration, and they've brought back their old friend Jack D'Or, only this time he's a little different. A deep golden color with a lasting foam, the beer's hopped with Jester, Jarrylo, and Saaz; there's bready malt and a fullness of body, consistent with the old Pretty Things beers (I loved the body they always got in their brews); and there's some banana, citrus, pear, and spice from a combination of yeast and hops playing together. Welcome back, Jack D'Or, it's great to see you again.

Brasserie Auval Arrière-Pays Grisette

Val-d'Espoir, Canada
ABV: 4.5%

This beer is brewed on a farm surrounded by countryside, gardens, an apiary, and a farming space where they grow lots of different ingredients, fertilized by the poop of cows fed on their spent grain in a wholesome circle of production. They brew in the old farmhouse tradition, producing numerous Saison-style beers, which are wood-fermented in barrels or foudres, then matured, soured, and blended together, sometimes with their own honey and fruits added. The beers are very much of their place, accented with a house character and complexity from their yeast. I really like their Grisette, a low-alcohol style of Saison, which is barrel-aged and blended; it has a gentle and refreshing acidity and it's elegantly effervescent, with a light, white-wine character, some oaky tannin, a lemon and grape-like zing and fruitiness, and a bone-dry finish.

Hill Farmstead Anna

Greensboro, Vermont, USA
ABV: 6.5%

Hill Farmstead are renowned for their range of Farmhouse-style ales, which may originally have taken inspiration from Belgium but have since become archetypal of the American Saison, or the Farmstead Ale as Hill Farmstead have coined it. Anna is a foudre-aged ale and its brilliance lies in its ethereal lightness and stunning complexity. Anna pours a hazy blonde with loads of fluffy foam. The grain is very light, sweetened by an addition of honey, and you get some citrus to begin with, not the big, in-your-face American kind, but a gentle, fruit-peel kind, lemony and grapefruit-y, with some floral honey. There's white pepper, ripe stone fruit, and a tingling tartness. Every sip of the beer will reveal something different to you, which is a large part of its elusive charm. Shaun Hill is brewing on his ancestors' farmstead and many of his beers are tributes to the family, including Anna, celebrating old traditions in new ways.

INDIGENOUS BEERS

Here we gather together beers that are uniquely of a specific place. It may be a type of beer that is made only in a certain country or region, which has proved it has enough longevity—usually with traditional homebrewers—for craft beer makers to have learned about it; it could be an old beer type that's been resurrected by new brewers who are interested in bringing back a taste of what a local beer used to be like; or it could be beers that are brewed with ingredients gathered from a specific area, reflecting a season, a harvest, or a particular location.

Browar Grodzisk Piwo z Grodziska

Grodzisk Wielkopolski, Poland
ABV: 3.1%

Grodziskie, or Grätzer, is a curious old Polish style of light, tart, bitter, smoky wheat beer that almost became extinct. For many of you reading the words "light, tart, bitter, smoky wheat beer," it's perfectly understandable for your reaction to be "good, that sort of thing should be extinct," but it's seen a small local resurrection. Browar Grodzisk is in Grodzisk Wielkopolski, in west Poland, not too far from Berlin and the German region known for its sour beers. The style was once known as Polish Champagne (though I don't know if that was a compliment or not) and the modern version is served in tall flute glasses, which is supposedly how it used to be poured. The beer is made with 100 percent oak-smoked wheat and it's certainly unusual to begin with, with all its smoke, then gets more curious as a light acidity comes in, and then come the hops (Polish Lublin), which are persistent and very bitter. Yet, somehow, it's refreshing and easy to drink, and what is immediately unusual on the first sip tastes normal by the last. There aren't too many other breweries making this style, but Browar Grodzisk's is a very nice beer to try.

Upright Brewing Special Herbs

Portland, Oregon, USA
ABV: 6.0%

Hops became the primary bittering and flavoring ingredient in beer around the 16th century, helped by their antibacterial properties. Before hops, a combination of herbs, plants, and spices was used in a mix that was known as "gruit" in north Germany, the Netherlands, and Belgium. Some of the main herbs used were bog myrtle, wild rosemary, and yarrow, and the sale of gruit was centrally controlled as an early kind of taxation on brewing, as well as a way to try and make beer safe from the use of potentially harmful ingredients. For their annual release of Special Herbs, Upright make a hop-less brew and add different botanicals, fruits, and herbs, and it's then aged in old wine and gin casks. The resulting beer is hazy amber, certainly herbal, but also citrusy, botanic, and tannic, a little tart, and very complex—as the brewery explains, they are aiming for something between Saison, Gruit, kombucha, and herbal spirits. Upright is one of Portland's top brewers, known for their European styles, their barrel-aging, and their unique take on hoppy American styles.

Čižo Alus Keptinis

Dusetos, Lithuania
ABV: 5.0%

Knowledge of Lithuanian brewing has recently emerged thanks to the research and work of Lars Marius Garshol, a Norwegian brewing historian. He traveled to Lithuania, where he discovered a country of beers with no modern analogies and set about documenting them. Čižo Alus's Keptinis is a great example of a unique kind of beer that demonstrates some ancient brewing techniques. The brewing process begins with barley mixed with boiling water to the consistency of a thick porridge. This is then pressed into what look like large cake pans and baked in a very hot oven for several hours until it gets dark and caramelized on top. That's then mixed with hot water for a short time, extracting the sweetness from the grains, then the liquid wort is drawn off. Meanwhile, hops are boiled separately in water to extract their bitterness, and that "hop tea" is mixed into the wort—the actual wort itself isn't boiled, making it a raw ale.

These breweries typically have an old family yeast, which is uniquely theirs and adds a distinctive and different taste to every beer. Keptinis is dark brown and low in carbonation. It generally has an unusual aroma of banana, toffee, and spices, and sometimes some buttery diacetyl or other fermentation by-products. It's bready, molasses-like, rye-like, herbal, rough at the edges, and not like any beer you've ever drunk before. A visit to Vilnius should be on a beer traveler's list of places to go; just arrive there with an open mind and the expectation that you'll drink some unusual (and not always delicious) beers.

Tolokazi Sorghum Pilsner

Johannesburg, South Africa
5.5% ABV

In 2015, Apiwe Nxusani-Mawela became the first black woman to open a craft brewery in South Africa. She's a qualified brewmaster and spent years in the beer industry before starting her own venture, Brewsters Craft, where she predominantly employs other black women. She has the

ambition of developing African craft brewing and being at the forefront of education and training, for which she has her own lab and academy. An important part of the story is celebrating local ingredients. Sorghum is used in umqombothi, the traditional South African beer brewed by women, and that grain goes into this Pilsner along with some local hops. The result is a perfectly refreshing and balanced lager. In the Tolokazi range there is also an African Pale Ale, made using sorghum plus African Queen and Southern Passion hops, which add their lightly tropical fruitiness. This brewery is playing a very important part in the evolution of African beer.

Scratch Brewing Company Basil Ale

Ava, Illinois, USA
ABV: 6.7%

Of all the American breweries I've yet to visit, Scratch is one I most want to get to. I love their approach and their story: they brew an ever-changing mix of Farmhouse-styled beers, using homegrown and locally farmed and foraged ingredients, and serve them alongside house-baked breads and pizzas. The foraged ingredients they use include fig leaves, nettles, berries, dandelions, maple sap, paw paws, mushrooms, hickory leaves, lavender, and juniper. It's their Basil Ale that intrigues me the most. It's brewed using homegrown lemon basil, sweet basil, and tulsi basil, which gives the beer its aroma, while there's honey in the base brew and it's fermented with their house yeast culture. I'll make it to Scratch one day soon...

Eik & Tid Rå

Oslo, Norway
ABV: 5.0%

"Oak" and "time" is what the brewery's name means, and they make beers that combine old Nordic brewing traditions—which have quietly lived on in rural regions—with the modern production of sour beers. Eik & Tid's Rå is an unboiled beer that contains juniper, a classic taste of Norwegian Sahti beers. The juniper is spicy, fragrant, peppery, floral, herbal, and reminiscent of gin, then the beer is zingy and acidic at the end, with their heritage house Kveik yeast adding its own fruity, spicy character. They also brew Mosaikk, a wonderfully unique beer that combines the flavor of a hoppy Pale Ale with that of a raw, unboiled Norwegian sour beer, using a Kveik yeast. They mature it in large oak foudres, and always have a barrel which is topped up in a solera style. It's fruity and funky to begin with, then sweet in the middle, and tart at the end.

Dos Luces Brewery Pulque Metztli

Denver, Colorado, USA
ABV: 7.0%

Dos Luces make two types of specialty beer: Chicha and Pulque. Chicha is an old Incan type of beer brewed with corn, which was traditionally chewed to create the necessary enzyme activity to access the corn's starches (it was literally chewed in the mouth and spat out). Dos Luces buy malted Colorado-grown blue corn (so no chewing required), to which they add whole kernels of purple corn, clove, and a special yeast. It's a purplish beer, certainly strong with clove, and it's both sweet and tart, festive and spicy, and very interesting—you won't have tasted many drinks like this. Their Pulque is made using malted blue corn and the sap of the maguey (agave) plant, which is also used to make tequila. The brew includes cinnamon and uses several yeasts and bacteria, including some that are unique to the maguey plant. It begins tart, then ends sweet. It's spicy, aromatic with cinnamon, a little melon-like, and, despite the sweetness given to the beer by the sap, very dry. Make sure to visit their brewpub in Denver if you're in town, as these are special and unusual beers.

BELGIAN PALE AND AMBER ALE

In the middle decades of the 19th century, Belgian ales were low in alcohol, rough in taste, variable in quality, typically tart, and regional to their hometown. As Pilsners and Pale Ales began to spread through central Europe at the end of the century, the idiosyncratic and regional brews of Belgium started to change and the beers cleaned up, losing their edge of funk, though they remained low in alcohol, and this marked a shift to new European influence. The Pale Ales were inspired by the characteristics of British brews, but adapted to local tastes, with the fundamental differences becoming the use of a distinctive Belgian yeast and a higher carbonation.

Today we expect these Pale and Amber beers to be yellow through deep amber in color. They are 4.5–6.5% ABV; they have a light, bready to caramelly maltiness; and they are typically noticeably bitter, ending with some flourish from the Belgian yeast, which gives fruitiness (think banana, orchard, or stone fruit) and spice (think pepper, aniseed, and clove). They are briskly carbonated, bright, refreshing beers, which are more interesting than the Pale Lagers and not as strong as the Tripels and Golden Ales.

Orval

Villers-devant-Orval, Belgium
ABV: 6.2%

Orval is an outlier, an oddity, an idiosyncrasy, and a much-loved classic of a Belgian Pale Ale, which is perhaps the ultimate beer-geek beer. It starts its life as an Amber Ale brewed with pale malts, giving a toffee-ish depth. The hops, which are a mix of German, Slovenian, and French, give a firm bitterness and aromas of hay, grass, and hop sacks, a feature that is enhanced by the beer being dry-hopped with great bales of whole-flower hops. What creates the beer's distinctive and appealing taste is that each bottle is dosed with the wild yeast *Brettanomyces* and, as the beer ages, it gets drier and the hop aroma mellows while the yeast aroma develops. The *brett* yeast is lemony, leathery, and farm-like—the longer the beer ages, the more that flavor will evolve, meaning each bottle of Orval you open will be different. Orval is a Trappist beer brewed by Abbaye Notre Dame d'Orval, and you can visit and stop in the monastery's café, where they sell fresh and aged bottles of Orval, plus Orval Vert, a draft version that hasn't undergone a secondary fermentation with *Brettanomyces*. Now, here's a confession: I don't get why so many beer nerds love this beer so much. To me, it's overcomplicated and challenging, and I don't enjoy the *bretty* aroma. I like the beer fresh and I like Orval Vert, but not the aged bottles.

Spencer Trappist Ale

Spencer, Massachusetts, USA
ABV: 6.5%

The monks at Spencer Abbey originally produced conserves as a way of making a modest income to support themselves and their local community before one of the brothers developed an interest in brewing, which set them on a journey to becoming North America's first Trappist brewery. The monks traveled around the Trappist monasteries in Belgium, meeting other monks and learning about beer as they went, before returning home to start their new venture. Trappist Ale was their first beer, and it's reverential of classic Belgian ales while also being new and local to Spencer. The monks use American malts (they even grow their own barley) and hops and these combine to create a golden-amber beer that has a smooth bready depth, a snappy bitterness and fizz, an intriguingly fruity aroma—with their yeast adding some of its own fruitiness (think banana and vanilla)—and a little spice. Unlike their Belgian brewing brethren, the American monks make numerous modern beer styles, including Monks' IPA, which is all-American-hopped and sold in cans.

Brasserie de la Senne Taras Boulba

Brussels, Belgium
ABV: 4.5%

Taras Boulba is the modern Belgian Pale Ale. It's become a beer that is craved and chased by beer geeks, a beer that's an "extra-hoppy ale" but done with classic European hops, amplifying some lesser-tasted qualities like grapefruit, citrus pith, lemon, and hard herbs. Those hops come at you from all angles: in the aroma, where they grip to the foam; in the middle with a kind of slick citrus oil; then at the end with a long, deep, quinine-like bitterness. Brasserie de la Senne are masters of brewing hop-forward beers with exemplary balance, fragrance, bitterness, and character. If you like this, then you'll also like Zinnebir, a 5.5%-ABV Belgian Blonde, and Jambe de Bois, their Tripel, which is fuller in malt than others, but still superbly dry. They have a modern brewery in Brussels that you should visit.

Birrificio Baladin Nazionale

Piozzo, Italy
ABV: 6.5%

Baladin's Nazionale is influenced by the taste of Belgian Pale Ales and brewed with 100 percent Italian ingredients. Those ingredients include water from the Maritime Alps, barley grown in the south-east of Italy, hops from near the brewery, plus some orange peel, coriander seed, and the brewery's own selected yeast. The beer is a brilliant golden color with a fluffy white foam. The fruit, spice, hop, and yeast combination makes for an enticing mix of aromas, giving something evocatively Italian: spicy and herbal (like thyme, fennel, anise), honeyed, warming, orangey, and floral (like chamomile and orange blossom). The body of the beer has the ideal mix of weight for its strength, then dryness at the end, a dryness that meets the bitterness of the hops. It's totally Italian, yet it's also Belgian-esque, and it's a great beer for food: think grilled white fish, soft fresh cheeses with bitter salad leaves, white pizza, and much more.

Westvleteren Blonde

Vleteren, Belgium
ABV: 6.0%

Driving down winding country lanes, probably passing some cyclists or walkers, surrounded by silent, bucolic countryside, you'll eventually come to the Westvleteren monastery. This has long been a place of pilgrimage for beer geeks, ever since their Quadrupel, Westvleteren 12, was named the best beer in the world by Ratebeer.com in the early 2000s. It won it again and again and again, and was the original must-have hype beer. The 12 is a wonderful beer, but when I go to the monastery café, In de Vrede, it's the Blonde that always surpasses my expectations. Poured out of a plain unlabeled bottle with just the cap to differentiate the brewery's three brews (green for the Blonde, blue for the Westvleteren 8, their Dubbel, and yellow for the 12), the Blonde is bright gold and swirls around the gold-rimmed bowl glass, giving out fragrant hops that are peppery, peachy, honeysuckle-y, and reminiscent of hop sacks. There's some fruity yeast in there, too, and some toasty, almost almond sweetness, and a crisp bitterness. It's a beautiful beer.

Perennial Artisan Ales Hommel Bier

St. Louis, Missouri, USA
ABV: 5.9%

Hommel Bier is a classic-tasting Belgian Pale Ale, one that's turned spicy, stone-fruity, dry, and lively with a voracious, vivacious yeast. What makes it a little different and more enticing is how a delicate amount of American hops have been added to it. Those hops don't scream citrus and instead they add some pithy fruit, floral aromas, lemongrass, and lime, and something that becomes exotic with the interplay of hops and yeast, while that yeast also gives out its own fruitiness, notably orchard and stone fruits, leading the beer through to a peppery crack of dryness at the end. Perennial make a lot of Belgian-influenced beers and a large range of barrel-aged beers. St. Louis is an underrated city for craft beer and deserves more attention for the range and quality of beer brewed there, with Perennial being one of its premier attractions.

Brasserie Thiriez L'Ambrée d'Esquelbecq

Esquelbecq, France
ABV: 5.8%

Blonde, Amber, and Dark are three common beer types seen in French breweries, sharing similarities to the Belgian equivalents. Brasserie Thiriez L'Ambrée d'Esquelbecq is amber-red, and has some toffee sweetness, some red berries, and a deep hop character. It's the yeast that is important here and the brewery has their own strain, which it's believed became the source strain for one of the world's most used kinds of Saison yeast: even if you've never had a Thiriez beer, you've probably had a beer fermented with their yeast. That yeast presents itself differently depending on how the beer has been brewed, ranging from funky to fruity to phenolic. Thiriez have a wonderful, quirky, and quaint little tasting room that's a traditional beer café with colorful old beer towels, brewing memorabilia, posters, and interesting knickknacks hanging from the walls and rafters. There are a few taps poured from behind a beautiful old counter—it's hard to imagine a beer bar that's more classically and wonderfully French.

BELGIAN TRIPEL AND STRONG GOLDEN ALE

Tripel came from a monastic tradition and a pale beer that was stronger than the regular dark Dubbel—the first, Westmalle's Tripel, was brewed in the 1930s. Strong Golden Ale is a more modern development, with Duvel, brewed in 1970, considered an original. Flavorwise, you might expect a little more body in a Tripel, perhaps more malt sweetness and a richer color as well, less bitterness, and a yeast that is spicier instead of the fruitier yeast of a Strong Golden Ale. There is a surprising variety within these styles, especially among Tripels, and you could order several classic Belgian Tripels, pour them side by side, and get very different drinks: some more caramelly, others drier, some more spicy. The experienced Belgian beer-drinker knows their go-to Tripel.

These two classic Belgian-style beers are bright gold to light amber in color. They are robust in strength at 7.0–10.0% ABV. They have an aromatic and flavorsome yeast character, which might vary from fruity (like banana, citrus, or stone or orchard fruit) to spicy (like clove, anise, and pepper). The yeast's other contribution is to a pronounced dryness and a full, lively carbonation that gives the best of these strong ales an easy "digestibility," a word borrowed from the Belgian beer dictionary for strong beers of which you can have several without feeling ready to pop with bubbles or hefty malt sweetness. Sugar is often used in the brews to get them extra-dry and aid that digestibility.

Duvel

Breendonk, Belgium
ABV: 8.5%

This is my favorite beer. My desert island beer. The beer I drink more of than any other. It's the category-defining Belgian Strong Golden Ale, a beautiful, bright golden beer with the purest white foam. The fizz is electrifying, uplifting, energizing, elegant—I think it's the fizz that I like most about Duvel, and those bubbles pop with pears, stone fruit, and a little underlying citrus-oil fruitiness. It's snappily bitter with pithy European hops, and while the malt gives some toasty notes, it's not prominent. Despite this beer being 8.5% ABV, it's one of the leanest, driest beers you can buy. These characteristics come from its brewing process: primary fermentation takes a couple of weeks, where some sugar is used to get the beer as dry as it is, then it's matured in tank for a month or so. It's then bottled and undergoes a secondary fermentation where it's left for six weeks to develop all the bubbles and more yeast aroma, overall taking 90 days from brewing to drinking. I always have this beer in my fridge. I can drink this when I need refreshment or I can drink it when I want to contemplate a beer, and it brings me joy every single time I open a bottle.

De Garre Tripel

Ertvelde, Belgium
ABV: 11.0%

Those who know how to get to De Garre, a little brown café down a hidden alleyway just off Bruges's central square, delight in the difficulties that others have trying to find it. When you finally get there, you'll walk into a two-story bar that's cozy and filled with people, most of them drinking the house beer from a sturdy round-bellied glass that sits on a pretty lace doily next to a small bowl of cubed cheese—it's a specific and special presentation that adds to its excellence. De Garre's Tripel, brewed for them by Brouwerij Van Steenberge, is full of malts and a little cakey, but not sweet (think almond sponge soaked in nutty sherry), with a smooth, luscious depth of honey, apricots, and dried herbal spice. It's rich, the alcohol is prominent and powerful, and the beer is an intense experience, as most 11 percenters are, but it's a brilliant one. The first glass is a rewarding experience, a prize for finding the bar. The second one will leave you forgetting where you were and lost all over again.

Westmalle Tripel

Westmalle, Belgium
ABV: 9.5%

If Duvel defines the Strong Golden Ale, then Westmalle is the textbook Tripel. Brewed in one of Belgium's Trappist monasteries, Our Lady of the Sacred Heart (most people just call it Westmalle, though), this beer gives more malt backbone than Duvel, a sweeter malt flavor, some almond nuttiness, and even a little spirit heat of alcohol, then it dries right out into some spiciness and pepper. The aroma is fragrant with herbal hops, stone fruit, pear, white pepper, citrus peel, and bananas, but it's no exotic smoothie and all those aromatics are light and beguiling, and much like Duvel, the best of those aromas come from its secondary fermentation in the bottle. Westmalle's is my personal go-to Tripel. As a comparison, Tripel Karmeliet, another classic Tripel, is fuller in malts and sweeter. It's also darker and has a pronounced clove spice at the end, plus a hint of orangey ground coriander.

Nebraska Brewing Co. Mélange à Trois

Papillion, Nebraska, USA
ABV: 10.0%

The richness of malt and alcohol, and the presence of a lively yeast, makes Belgian Strong Golden Ale a great style to be barrel-aged. Nebraska's take on that puts the beer into oaky Chardonnay barrels for six months, and what emerges has taken on a remarkable new depth. It pours a hazy gold with lots of foam. The wood and the wine come out first, giving vanilla, oak, honey, grape, apricot, and citrus, with some of that fruitiness also coming from the American hops used in the brew. The body is slick and retains some sweetness, but it's cut by the oak tannin, the deep bitterness, and the playfulness of the yeast, which never intrudes but is definitely there, adding some extra fruitiness. The wood and wine never overpower this beer, meaning it keeps all the best qualities of a Strong Golden Ale, only with extra elegance and complexity.

East West Brewing Co. Modern Belgian Blonde

Ho Chi Minh City, Vietnam
ABV: 7.6%

East West is a hugely impressive brewpub in the middle of Ho Chi Minh City, and when you walk in you'll see the entire back wall dominated by the brewhouse and tanks. Their Modern Belgian Blonde is a deep gold in color, edging it somewhere between a Strong Golden Ale and a Belgian-style Amber. It's made using Vietnamese palm sugar, giving a local flavor, and that sugar adds some honeyed flavors while also letting the beer finish drier. It's aromatic with banana, sweet toasted bread, and some fragrant and floral spices. The body is relatively sweet and rich, reflecting the local taste for sweeter beers, with roast banana and honey flavors, and it's a rounded, smooth Strong Belgian Ale. If you get to the brewpub, then their East West Pale Ale is a great hoppy West Coast-style beer, which is defiantly bitter and a nice counter to the sweeter Belgian brew.

Bodebrown Tripel Montfort

Curitiba, Brazil
ABV: 10.0%

This is a punchy Tripel with a knockout 10.0% ABV. It's brewed with dried orange peel, pink peppercorn, and Grains of Paradise, and they hit your nose right away, making it reminiscent of a floral honey with fragrant pepper, sweet citrus peel, and some fruity banana and clove from the yeast. The base is muscular and toned, but definitely sweet, with some sponge-cake and candied-citrus flavor, and it leaves a strong, lasting finish. Alongside the Tripel, Bodebrown also brew three beers in their St. Arnould range of Strong Dark Belgian Ales, with the St. Arnould 10 being rich, plummy, and festively spiced.

Brewery Bhavana Bloom

Raleigh, North Carolina, USA
ABV: 8.1%

Brewery Bhavana is the slightly improbable combination of a dim sum restaurant, brewery, bookstore, and florist, yet the attention to detail throughout, plus a generally welcoming and communal feel, allows everything to weave together effortlessly. On the food side, the dim sum menu broadens further into and around China and Southeast Asia, with inspiration coming from the two Laotian cofounders, while the beer side has a Belgian inflection, with most recipes including a fragrant edible addition: they use figs in their Dubbel, mango and peppercorn in a Saison, and cardamom in their Tripel. Cardamom is a wonderfully fragrant ingredient in a beer like a Tripel, adding something that approximates a cozy creaminess, while also enhancing the dry spiciness in the back of the brew. Sharing a few small glasses of beer and a few plates of dim sum at Brewery Bhavana is a beautiful, refreshing, warming experience.

BELGIAN DUBBEL, QUADRUPEL, AND STRONG DARK ALE

Dubbels, Quadrupels, and Strong Dark Ales are beers of Belgian origin or inspiration and come from the monastic brewing tradition, where the Belgian breweries that make these kinds of beer typically have both a Dubbel and a Quadrupel, often with a lighter Blonde Beer and a Tripel in their range, too. These are styles prized for their depth and complexity in a beer world that's starting to forget what those things mean in its search for the immediate impact of an Imperial IPA. Returning to these classic brews, and taking the time to contemplate them, is a rewarding experience.

Dubbels range from 7.0–9.0% ABV and Quadrupels from 9.0–12.0% ABV, while Strong Dark Ale can be anywhere around those—there's no strict definition here. These beers are defined by their color, which ranges from red-brown to dark brown; flavors like sweet bread, dried fruits, dark berries, cocoa, vanilla, licorice, cinnamon, and clove; and they all have a dryness which is helped by the addition of sugar (historically dark candi sugar) during the brewing process. These are the kind of beers that can be aged in the bottle, as most of the classics are bottle-conditioned, so theoretically can continue to mature—the best examples get richer and softer, losing some of their fizz and phenols. A year or so is usually optimum for a Quadrupel.

Trappistes Rochefort 8

Rochefort, Belgium
ABV: 9.2%

Rochefort is a Belgian Trappist monastery, although unlike the others you can't actually visit this one. Not that that necessarily matters, as the other monastery cafés tend to lack atmosphere and feel like garden-center cafés when I'd much prefer to drink dark ales like this in a dark, old beer café, so drinking these at home is alright. Rochefort 8 is a classic Belgian Dubbel. It's like cocoa, licorice, and dried plums; it has more malt and sweetness than other Dubbels, being a little stronger and richer, which gives it more texture. There's also an element of stewed sweet tea, which is a comforting flavor. The end is characteristically brisk and carbonated, though that softens as the beer ages. The brewery has a weaker dark beer called Rochefort 6 and a stronger dark one called Rochefort 10, and in 2020 they added a Tripel. They are all excellent.

Juguetes Perdidos Jamaica Dubbel

Buenos Aires, Argentina
ABV: 7.0%

The "Lost Toys" is celebrated as one of Argentina's best craft breweries. Their Jamaica Dubbel is brewed with Jamaican allspice, which adds a complementary fruity spiciness alongside the flavors brought by the malt and the yeast—here a sweetness of teacake and caramel, some banana, dried plums, raisins, and clove. It ends with sweetness and the allspice, which lingers in a warming way. It doesn't have the complexity of a Belgian-brewed Dubbel, but it does have all the flavors you'd expect. They make several other Belgian-ish beers, including an IPA fermented with a Belgian yeast, which adds some fruity esters and peppery phenols to the hops, a passion-fruit-infused Saison, and a classic Tripel, which is rich with malts and bitter with Saaz hops.

Mount Saint Bernard Tynt Meadow

Coalville, England, UK
ABV: 7.4%

Mount Saint Bernard Abbey, in Leicestershire, is England's only Trappist monastery brewery and they started selling their beer in 2018, with all the work in the brewery done by the monks themselves, assisted from afar by the other Trappist brewers, especially Zundert. Their one beer is inspired by the classic Dubbels of their Belgian brewing brethren, only it's made using British ingredients and a traditional British yeast. Despite that, close your eyes, take away any knowledge of provenance, take a sip of this, and you'll think it's a Belgian brew. It pours a dark purple-brown and it's fruity and estery with dark berries, almond, banana, and allspice. The malt is like sweet tea, biscuity malts, chocolate, aniseed, and dried fruit, with a peppery hop finish and dryness. It's an impressively reverential Belgian-style Dubbel. Before brewing, the monks' main work was dairy farming, so, to pay homage, serve this with local aged Red Leicester cheese.

Oriel Dubbel

Bucharest, Romania
ABV: 8.0%

Oriel is a small Romanian brewery that focuses on brewing classic Belgian ales. Their range includes a Blonde, Saison, Dubbel, Tripel, and Quadrupel, with some versions also barrel-aged, and each naturally bottle-conditioned. The Dubbel is brewed with dark candi syrup and pours a ruby-brown color. You get all the expected dried cherries, plums, brown sugar, and some peppery spice, phenols, and banana from the yeast. The body is quite light, and it's not as rich as some Dubbels, but that's not a negative thing. Their Quadrupel bulks up the Dubbel, while there are barrel-aged versions that pull vanilla, toffee, cinnamon, and dried fruits from the wood, amplifying the depth in the beer. Papanasi is a traditional Romanian donut made with a ricotta-like cheese and served with cherries and cream, which is a great food match for a Dubbel or Quad.

Brasserie Dupont Moinette Brune

Tourpes, Belgium
ABV: 8.5%

Everyone knows Dupont's Saison, but not so many know that their best-selling beer in their local area is Moinette Blonde, their Strong Golden Ale. It's a wonderful beer that's got a sweet depth of bready malts, some soft toffee, lots of fruitiness and spice, and a bitter, dry finish—I actually prefer it to their Saison. In the Moinette range they also have an Amber and Brune; both are excellent. The Brune has a lovely malt sweetness, chocolate, raisins, sweet tea, roasted nuts, and a bit of festive spice and roasted apple at the end. The brewery also has a dairy which makes cheese. Serve the Moinette beers with the Moinette cheeses and some fresh bread, or I like this one with a big roast dinner.

Westvleteren 12, St. Bernardus 12, Rochefort 10

Belgium
ABV: 10.0–11.3%

What's the best Belgian Quadrupel? It's one of those much-argued-about topics among beer-lovers, and each has their favorite. The top three are widely regarded to be Westvleteren 12, St. Bernardus Abt 12, and Rochefort 10. Line them all up and they look a similar deep brown with red at the edges. They have a tan-colored foam. They smell like fruit cake, baked plums, figs, molasses (black treacle), sweet festive spices, rum raisin, and sometimes almond or banana, which I think we can all agree sounds delicious. Their yeasts come forward with stone fruit and almond and banana, but they also dry the beer right out and then give it a refreshing carbonation. My favorite? Normally Westvleteren for its figgy-pudding and sweet-tea richness, but sometimes it's Rochefort with its sweetly yeasty aroma of baking vanilla sponge, while other times I'll take the St. Bernardus and its spiced fruit cake, extra dryness and bitterness. Every time I think I know which one I prefer, I have one of the others and it changes my mind yet again.

Firestone Walker Stickee Monkee

Paso Robles, California, USA
ABV: 11.4%

The strong flavors of sweet malt, dried fruit, and heady spices in a Quad make it a naturally good beer to age in wooden barrels, which is what Firestone Walker have done with Stickee Monkee. This beer, brewed with Belgian candi sugar and Mexican brown sugar, and aged in bourbon barrels, has been dubbed a "Central Coast Quad" as an acknowledgment of their evolution of the style. The sugars give this beer a deep richness like molasses (black treacle) and toffee, the grain and yeast give sweet chocolate, toast, raisins, figs, dates, and cinnamon, all in a lusciously full body, while the barrel adds vanilla, oak, coconut, and bourbon to enhance everything. It's a dessert kind of beer— either on its own or with something like vanilla cheesecake or crème brûlée.

BELGIAN OUD RED AND OUD BRUIN

These soured and aged red and brown ales originate in the Flanders region of Belgium. They share similarities in color, and they are both (typically) fermented in steel tanks before undergoing a long maturation, hence the *Oud* ("old") part of their name. During the maturation time, wild yeast and bacteria present in the beer will develop a tartness that is typically acetic (think balsamic vinegar) compared to the acidic (think lemon) sourness in a Lambic or Gueuze. The main difference between Oud Red and Oud Bruin is that the reds mature in large oak barrels or foudres, while the browns spend all their maturation time in steel tanks, although this distinction is becoming blurred and unnecessary as red-brown becomes an amorphous style that's evolved through modern craft brewing. Similar to Lambic and Gueuze, reds and browns are blended before being drunk, mixing funkier, drier, and more acetic old beer with fruitier and sweeter young beer, where the greater proportion of aged beer in the bottle, the greater the complexity of the beer.

What you should expect is the beer equivalent of a Burgundy wine. They have a red-brown-purple color and are both sweet and sour, with a great complexity of oak, age, tannins, tartness, and fruitiness, ranging from fresh red stone fruits to vinous old dried fruits. Modern versions are often aged in old red-wine barrels, while brewers around the world often add fruits, such as plums, cherries, berries, and dried fruit, to give sweetness and depth.

Brouwerij Liefmans Goudenband

Oudenaarde, Belgium
ABV: 8.0%

Considered the hometown of Belgian Oud Bruin, Oudenaarde locals have been drinking Liefmans brewery beers for over 300 years. Since 2008 the brewery has been part of the Duvel-Morgaat family and now the wort is not brewed in Oudenaarde anymore, but instead made in other Duvel-Morgaat breweries and then trucked to be aged in the vessels in Oudenaarde (that's where the real character develops anyway, and not in the brewing vessels), with Liefmans now taking the name "Craft Blenders." *Goudenband* (or "Gold Band") is the classic Oud Bruin. It's matured for between 4 and 12 months, acidifying handsomely and gracefully, with caramelized malt flavors mixing with the sweet tartness of cherries and apples. There's dried fruits and plums, plus the mature flavors of nutty sherry and a light sourness. Liefmans's Kriek Brut is made with loads of cherries and is really good with a chocolate dessert, while they also make some less beery blends that are far too sweet for me but popular with others.

Rodenbach Grand Cru

Roeselare, Belgium
ABV: 6.0%

The cellar at Rodenbach is one of the best sights in any brewery, anywhere in the world. Under cobble-stoned streets, the cellars hold almost 300 wooden foudres, which range in size from 12,000 liters to 65,000 liters. The youngest of these barrels is around 60 years old, while there are some still in use that are well over 100 years old. They are neatly lined up, row after row, in the cool, dark cellars, which have a heady aroma of old wine, dried plums, and the sweet smell of fermentation. Rodenbach is the archetypal Oud Red. The base beer uses a decoction mash and is made with barley and some corn, plus a nominal amount of hops. The beer is fermented in steel and then either it's moved into wood, where it might age for up to four years, or it can be used young to blend with old beer. The standard Rodenbach is a 75/25 blend of young to old, but the Grand Cru is 66/33 old to young and it's more vinous and wine-like, with apples and balsamic, and a sweet sourness. You might also sometimes see Rodenbach Vintage, which will be from a single foudre (with perhaps a small amount of young beer to balance it).

Side Project Balaton

St. Louis, Missouri, USA
ABV: 5.0%

Balaton is described as a Wild Missouri Brown Ale, and it's fermented and aged in Missouri Chambourcin wine barrels on Michigan Balaton cherries. The brewery kept the ABV low on this one to let the complexity, wood, fruit, and funk all come through. The beer pours a deep brown with cherry-red edges. The cherries dominate the beer in a great way, adding loads of fruitiness in the beginning, hints of Bakewell tart or cherry pie, with a nuttiness, some vanilla and oak, then acidity at the end, which dries the beer right out. This beer mixes sweetness and sourness, plus the pure fruit flavor, really well, which is what makes it so good. Side Project also brew a Flanders-style sour that they age in wine barrels over blueberries. This is a bright purple brew with loads of tartness at the end and a plump blueberry flavor through it. Side Project are one of the most sought-after brewers for barrel-aged beers like these.

Birrificio del Ducato Oud Brunello

Soragna, Italy
ABV: 7.0%

This Oud Red-style beer is aged in Italian Brunello wine barrels, which neatly enhances the vinous character in this kind of beer. It pours a red-brown, and wine and wood are the first things you'll get, with a heady, dark fruitiness and some aged-sherry flavors in the background. It's pleasantly sweet to begin, with some berries and port wine, then it starts to reveal its layered complexity: balsamic, leather, oak, tannin, cherries, tart apple, something aged and savory, and, even though it has a sharp acetic edge, there's a softness in the middle. The brewery is based near Parma and not too far from Bologna, which helpfully gives us some great food pairings with Parma ham, Parmesan cheese, or alongside a bowl of ragu—the beer's umami-acidity is great with the richness of those foods.

LAMBIC AND GUEUZE

Just a generation ago, Lambic and Gueuze were oddities isolated to a small region around Brussels known as Pajottenland and the Senne Valley. Today, they are among the most prized and adored beers in the world. Lambic is made with barley and wheat, and a small amount of aged hops—hops that retain their antibacterial qualities, but don't provide much flavor, bitterness, or aroma. The wort that leaves the kettle is pumped into a coolship (see the image on page 22), a large, shallow pan, where it will cool overnight and become naturally inoculated by the wild yeast in the air all around the old brewery. From there, the wort moves into wooden barrels and is left to ferment then mature for as long as four years, evolving greatly as the different yeast and bacteria work through the sugars. If that beer is drunk "straight," typically between 12 and 18 months, it's known as Lambic. It's uncarbonated, tannic, and tart, and the flavor will depend on its age—the beer gets drier, more tart, and more complex as it ages. Fresh fruit can be added to barrels of Lambic and this will lead to a further fermentation as the yeast metabolizes the fruit sugars: cherries make Kriek, and raspberries make Framboise, while other fruits like apricots, peaches, grapes, and berries are also used. Lambic that's left to mature for longer will often be blended with a mix of old beer (three or four years old) and young beer, bottled with more yeast, corked, and then allowed a long secondary bottle fermentation to produce the bubbles. This blended Lambic is known as Gueuze. Purists (rightly) consider Lambic and Gueuze to be unique beers of the Pajottenland, so I've only included those here.

There are around 10 Lambic producers according to Lambic.info. In addition to these producers, there are several blenders, who buy wort from the brewers, then ferment and mature it themselves and blend it later: Oud Beersel, De Cam, Hanssens, and Tilquin are all blenders, whereas names like 3 Fonteinen, Boon, Cantillon, and Girardin are brewers and blenders.

Lambiek Fabriek Brett-Elle

Sint-Pieters-Leeuw, Belgium
ABV: 5.5%

Lambiek Fabriek is the youngest of the Belgian Lambic brewers, having only started out in 2016. It's the work of three friends—Jozef, Jo, and Stijn—who used to purchase Lambic and blend their own for fun before deciding to start brewing it themselves. They effectively taught themselves how to brew while building themselves a brewery south of Brussels and filling it with wooden barrels. Brett-Elle is their main Gueuze and, in the traditional way, it's a blend of their different Lambics. I think it's got a really nice elegance to it. There's a soft fruitiness, like biting into a tangy peach or apricot. There's a smooth texture and the underlying oakiness adds to that, while some citrus freshness lifts it up. It's a really nice and easy-going Gueuze.

Cantillon Lambic

Brussels, Belgium
ABV: 5.0%

Going to the Cantillon brewery is an essential beer experience. It's right in the center of Brussels, on a nondescript side street, but when you push through the door you pass through a time warp into an inner-city farmhouse. Do the self-guided tour and the brewery reveals itself as a marvel. There are the gnarly old brewing vessels that look nothing like any modern steel mash tun; climb some creaky wooden stairs and you'll see the copper-topped kettles; at the top of the building, in the pitched roof of the farmhouse, is the coolship; then you'll walk to where all the wooden barrels are lined up and stacked. The smell here is remarkable and intoxicating: wood, vanilla, berries, dried fruit, apple, sherry, and wine. Back in the bar you can get a sample of Lambic, poured from a stone pitcher. It's still, amber in color, cider-like, tart, but tempered by residual sweetness. It's almost too complex to be able to understand in one small glass, so get a second or a third. Or try a bottle of Grand Cru Bruocsella, an aged and bottled Lambic. You'll also want to drink the Gueuze while you're there, a Champagne-like beer that's alive with carbonation and a lemony, funky, acidic depth.

Gueuzerie Tilquin Oude Mûre Tilquin à l'Ancienne

Bierghes, Belgium
ABV: 6.4%

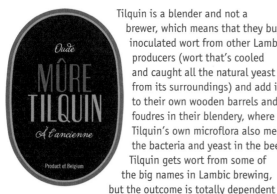

Tilquin is a blender and not a brewer, which means that they buy inoculated wort from other Lambic producers (wort that's cooled and caught all the natural yeast from its surroundings) and add it to their own wooden barrels and foudres in their blendery, where Tilquin's own microflora also meets the bacteria and yeast in the beer. Tilquin gets wort from some of the big names in Lambic brewing, but the outcome is totally dependent on the skill of the blending. Their Oude Mûre Tilquin à l'Ancienne adds blackberries to 18-month-old Lambic (350g per liter, which is a lot), which is then left to ferment and mature for a few more months before it's bottled and left again to carbonate naturally. It pours a red color and it's ripe and fruity, generally like berries, which leads into a dry, tannic, oaky, blackberry-pip finish. The Gueuze is also excellent, and they make a low-alcohol Draft version.

Boon Mariage Parfait

Lembeek, Belgium
ABV: 8.0%

Mariage Parfait is produced once a year and is a mix of different three-year-old Lambics, which is then bottled and left for another year until it's carbonated and ready to be opened. That additional time produces a beer with rarely rivaled depth and complexity. It's bright gold in color with a persistent white foam; there's lemon and grapefruit, sharp apples, apricot, oak, tannin, and tartness, but it's not aggressively sour or challenging—it's a glorious beer. There's a Kriek version of this that adds an enormous 14oz (400g) of cherries per liter of beer, giving a bright pink glass that's rich with a cherry aroma and a nutty, almond-like sweetness. Boon's Black Label is another favorite and it's a very dry, but still quite fruity, blend of one-, two-, and three-year-old Lambic. Boon make some spectacular Lambics and I favor them for their gentler acidity and naturally fruitier flavors.

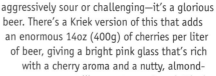

SPONTANEOUSLY FERMENTED BEER

There's an undeniable romance to the Lambic beers of Belgium. They come from the old traditions, and the combination of nature starting the fermentation with the nurturing control of the brewers who blend them. The lure of these beers has seen many brewers around the world install their own coolships and let their local microflora into the beer, creating something that's uniquely of the brewery in which it's made, and to which local fruits are often added. These long-matured beers speak of a time and place, and of the touch of the brewers and their blending abilities, and are in contrast to the current one-and-done approach of craft brewers always looking to make the next full-flavored beer. Spontaneously fermented beers take years to make; they are naturally risky, as brewers never quite know how the beer will mature, and this means that the blending is really key because even two barrels sat side by side and filled with the same base beer will not taste the same after a few years. Blending became the way to ensure a more consistent final beer, and that's still true today. The beers here are made like Lambics and fermented spontaneously (though not necessarily always in a coolship), and they reflect a long-term commitment for a craft brewer.

Herslev Bryghus Mark Hø

Herslev, Denmark
ABV: 4.9%

"Do you have anything local and unusual?" I asked against my desire to drink something local and *not* unusual. "Here, try this," the server said, passing me a glass of lightly pale and hazy beer. It was gently tart, the mouthfeel was soft and light, it was a tiny bit sweet right upfront, and then it eased back into something more... unusual... something reminiscent of the farm, but in a good way, like a barn, like wood, or like... "It's made with hay," the server said. I ordered a full glass and sat there, in a dark bar in Copenhagen, drinking this spontaneously fermented ale made with local organic ingredients from a farm 30 miles (50km) west of the city. Yeast cultures present on the hay contribute to the fermentation, while the hay also adds its own subtle savory flavor and is a substitute for hops, which are not used in this beer. The farmhouse brewery is focused on their location, their community, and being as sustainable and good for the environment as possible. Their hay beer was local and unusual and very good.

Jester King Spon Three Year Blend

Austin, Texas, USA
ABV: 6.0%

Lambic brewers don't make beer year-round, pausing over the warmer summer months when there's more risk of the brew turning into a bad sour than a good one. Given the year-round warm weather in Austin, Texas, it was never going to be easy for Jester King to make spontaneously fermented beer, limiting them to just a few short Lambic-brewing weeks each year. Their Spon range starts out as a classic Lambic, brewed with hops which the brewery age themselves (every Jester King beer includes some aged hops), and blended like a Gueuze. They also use many different fruits grown on their estate (the brewery is set on a large farm estate, surrounded by livestock and produce). Spon Three Year Blend has wonderful aromas of apricot, citrus, oak, and Champagne, and it's lightly acidic and deliciously complex. Jester King make a wide range of brews, each using their own house yeast culture that evolves through the year and with the seasons, meaning the same beer brewed in January and July will end up tasting different because of the yeast's natural variation.

Burning Sky Cuvée

Firle, England, UK
ABV: 6.7%

The plan was always for Burning Sky to make spontaneously fermented beers inspired by the great Lambics of Belgium. They demonstrated their patience early on by not rushing into it, and instead filled foudres and barrels with beer and let their brewery naturally settle into its farmhouse location in the Sussex countryside. When they were ready, they put a coolship in the barn next door, brewed a beer with barley, wheat, and heritage grains, left it to ferment spontaneously, then left it in barrels and big barriques, which used to hold wine, and repeated this the next year and the one after, before finally being ready to blend the best beers in the brewery for their annual Cuvée. It's a beer as good as any from Belgium: one that's light with the briskness of tiny bubbles, with a lemony, apple-like freshness, a gentle tartness which tantalizes, and oak all around it to give it structure and depth. It's exceptional.

Bokke Framboos Vanille

Hasselt, Belgium
ABV: 6.0%

Formerly known as Bokkereyder, then Methode Goat, and now (probably, I can't keep up) just Bokke, this is a Lambic blender based just outside of Brussels. Bokke is run by Raf Souvereyns, who buys wort from several Belgian Lambic brewers and takes a classic and traditional approach to his beers, but is unafraid to modernize them and introduce new processes and flavors, and that's seen Bokke beer become some of the most wanted in the world. His Framboos Vanille is a great example of old meeting new. It's a classic raspberry sour that also includes vanilla, which works like the perfect pinch of seasoning, lifting the fruitiness and the oak depth, and adding a hint of creamy sweetness to the raspberries, which somehow taste fresher in this than in any other fruited Lambics. There is a range of Bokke beers, all balanced, considered, and classic, yet modern, but good luck finding them—they are very rare and highly prized. Having tasted them, it's easy to see why.

Ca' del Brado Û Baccabianca

Pianoro, Italy
ABV: 7.9%

"Beer before wine and you'll be fine" is an old drinking adage that's irrelevant to the Italian Grape Ale style. IGAs have been brewed for many years in Italy and they are characterized by their combination of beer and wine—of barley and grapes. Wort is usually produced and then pressed grape must is added to it. The natural yeasts present on the grape skins start a spontaneous co-fermentation, and malt sugars and grape sugars both ferment at the same time, before the beers are long-matured in wine barrels. That's how Û Baccabianca is made (the Û part means "grape" in the local dialect). It uses white Grechetto Gentile grapes and also adds *Brettanomyces* yeasts, with the beer maturing for more than six months on the grape skins. The beer at the end is amber, leathery, complex, and woody with some underlying grape sweetness, which all makes it close to a natural wine in flavor. They also make a version using red-wine grapes.

Lindheim Ølkompani Coolship Cherry

Gvarv, Norway
ABV: 7.0%

Lindheim is a 100-acre (40-hectare) fruit farm in a region of Norway famous for its fruit, and especially known for apples. To supplement the farming, and to make additional use of their produce, Lindheim renovated an old barn in 2013 and added a brewery. Today, that barn has a coolship on the top floor and a cellar filled with barrels of aging beer. Lindheim's Farmer's Reserve series of beers are all made with wild yeast, whether from the coolship, from the skins of fruit, or by having *Brettanomyces* added. Their spontaneously fermented Coolship Cherry pours a cherry-red with a thin lace of foam. The cherries give their tart sweetness and a hint of cherry brandy; the local microflora is rich thanks to the orchards; and the beer has an apple- and plum-like tang. It also has a great texture and fullness, which is sometimes missing in beers like this, while the wood-aging gives subtlety and elegance, not a brash, overwhelming sourness. You can visit the farm and brewery, just check ahead for opening times (and take a big bag to fill with fresh, delicious fruit).

Mills Brewing Running Beer

Berkeley, England, UK
ABV: 5.0%

Running Beer is one of Mills's few regular releases, though you can expect it to change from batch to batch—they list on their bottle when the beer was made and the blend's specific details. It always begins in a similar way, with a base brew of barley, rye, oats, and wheat. That'll naturally ferment with their house yeast culture and then mature in numerous barrels before a blend is made and then bottled. Running Beer has the soft and gentle sweetness of young Gueuze with the deeper, more complex funk of aged Gueuze, plus a floral and earthy quality to it and a sherbet-like lift. The carbonation is really nice in this, lifting the palate and enhancing the tartness. Mills brew a variety of aged beers, often adding fruit to them, but they are made on a very small scale so aren't easy to find.

Wild Creatures Tears of Saint Laurent

Mikulov, Czech Republic
ABV: 6.2%

Mikulov, in the south-east of the Czech Republic and near the Austrian border, is in the middle of Czech wine country, and the beers of Wild Creatures take some inspiration from their surroundings—they also take the benefits of the wild yeast from all those vineyards to assist their fermentation. Tears of Saint Laurent is spontaneously fermented then matured in old Czech red-wine barrels for around 18 months until the following wine harvest. Freshly picked Saint Laurent grapes are then added and the beer is left to co-ferment and mature some more. The beer takes on a blush-red color. It's wine-like, plummy, sherried with age, beautifully structured in the body, then dry and tart at the end, with a very clean finish. It's a uniquely Czech beer.

Funk Factory Geuzeria Meerts

Madison, Wisconsin, USA
ABV: 4.0%

Meerts is a low-alcohol, quicker-to-produce, Lambic-styled beer, which Funk Factory base on an old Belgian style of young sweet Lambic that was historically made with a weaker second running of wort out of the mash tun. It's 4.0% ABV and gets just three months of fermentation and aging in wooden foudres before it's ready. The lighter body and relatively quicker time on wood result in a beer that's gently tart, crisp like a ripe apple, and a little floral, with a finish that balances youthful sweetness and some emerging funk, making it super-refreshing. They make stronger fruited versions of Meerts and some more typical, stronger (6.0% ABV), longer-aged (a couple of years) Lambics, usually aged on berries—the Frampaars, aged on purple raspberries, is especially good, giving lots of jammy fruit and a zingy acidity.

The Ale Apothecary Sahalie

Bend, Oregon, USA
ABV: 9.8%

Brewed with well water and local malt and barley, the Ale Apothecary's beers are made on a very small scale. They center their production around wood, including wooden mash tuns and then barrels to ferment and mature the beer, taking yeast from the air and barrels all around. It's generally a slow process, involving leaving the mash overnight, and then boiling and leaving that over the following night. Like the best Wild Ales, these are distinctly of their place and the peculiarity of the processes used to make them. Sahalie is an amber color and gets around a year in wooden ex-brandy barrels, plus it includes a dry-hop addition. It's then bottle-conditioned with an addition of Oregon wildflower honey—there's also honey in the brew for this beer. The result is strong, wild, and wonderful, with a rich texture, a beguiling mix of fruitiness, some tannins, sweet alcohol, and yeast funkiness.

SLOW SOURS AND AMERICAN WILD ALE

Slow Sours are beers that are typically matured in wooden vessels for an extended period of time, as their flavor evolves—time is really important because it's the extended maturation which properly develops the beer's profile. They usually contain a pitched culture of wild yeast, rather than being spontaneously fermented (though some are fermented that way), while they may also rely on yeast and bacteria that are residual in the old wooden barrel to inoculate the beer further. Most of these beers are mixed fermentation, meaning a variety of yeasts and bacteria will be present, though some will just rely on *Brettanomyces*. Those *brett*-only beers might come into the American Wild Ale category, which are beers that use wild yeast and are long-matured but don't have a strong acidity. These categories often contain fruits for additional fermentable sugars, or use a distinctive barrel to draw specific qualities from it. Slow Sours are a varied, interesting, and (literally) ever-evolving category of beers, and the base brews can vary greatly, as can the final beers once they are ready for drinking.

Sante Adairius Rustic Ales
West Ashley

Capitola, California, USA
ABV: 7.3%

This starts as a Saison and then moves into Pinot Noir barrels with apricots and the brewery's house yeast and bacteria culture, where it's all left until it turns into a beer that's rich with apricots and super-fruity for something so long-matured. It's unfiltered and hazy, giving a juicy kind of fullness to the body, which enhances the stone-fruit and grape character, with some tartness, spice, and funk all weaving through it. It's really good, but then most of this brewery's beers are really good, especially Saison Bernice, a straight-up Saison that's brightly carbonated, zingy, a little tart, and peppery. The beers are rustic, yet refined, and they are funky but don't taste like the farm, giving a Californian accent and substance to these Belgian-ish brews.

Holy Mountain The Goat

Seattle, Washington, USA
ABV: 4.7%

From the bar in Holy Mountain's bright, cool taproom you can peek into the production side of things and see the steel tanks, but what you can't quite see are all the wooden vessels they have—from barrels to puncheons to foudres—as Holy Mountain was built around the desire to influence their beers with time in wood. When I visited there were numerous Saison-styled beers, all of which had been in wooden barrels and emerged out the other side as crisp, zingy, elegant brews, low on acid. The Goat is a foudre-aged *brett* Saison, the kind of American Wild Ale you swirl around your glass for 20 minutes, loving every sip and sniff. There's subtle *brett*, smooth coconut, lemon, brisk bubbles, and a light, soft, pleasing, and refreshing finish that is only gently tart. I also really liked their Gethsemane Pale Ale, which is fermented in oak with *brett*, then dry-hopped, giving a funky, fermented fruit flavor.

Mikkeller Spontandoubleblueberry

Copenhagen, Denmark
ABV: 8.4%

This is a bonkers beer: a strong ale with a ridiculous quantity of blueberries added as it ages in oak and slowly sours. It pours a deep purple-red and it's juicy with berries, with the fruit's tartness meeting the beer's, and some boozy sweetness running through the middle. There's a lot of fruit in it, but it keeps its sour beer qualities, which isn't quite true of the other lines of this beer that Mikkeller make: this is the double version; there's also a triple one and a quadruple one, which uses an astonishing 5½ lb/2.5kg(!) of blueberries per liter, while it's also usually stronger in alcohol, making it something like a blueberry port wine. It's terribly expensive but worth a try if you see it (and can justify the expense).

The Kernel Bière de Saison

London, England, UK
ABV: 5.0%

The Kernel started brewing in September 2009, which makes them one of the oldest craft breweries in London. They are known for their ever-changing range of hoppy ales, which come with the comfort of knowing that whatever it is, it's going to be good. Alongside the hoppy beers, and tucked deep beneath the railway arch where they brew in Bermondsey, they have an area dedicated to wood-aged beers, some of them in small, old wine barrels and others in larger foudres. Bière de Saison is matured in the barrels, tasted, then typically mixed with either fruit or hops, and left to age for even longer. The Damson and Sour Cherry versions of Bière de Saison have been particularly good, while the hopped versions give a zesty, floral aroma above a base brew that's lean, oaky, dry, and tart. This is the kind of beer to share and to drink alongside some really good cheeses and a loaf of fresh sourdough bread.

Little Earth Project Organic Harvest Saison

Mill Green, England, UK
ABV: 6.7%

Little Earth Project are closely connected to the world around them: they harvest their own organically grown hops and barley, they forage for local ingredients, and they have their own house yeast culture, which they isolate from local apples, all of which they use to brew farmhouse-style Sours. The Organic Harvest Saison is brewed with fresh green hops at harvest time. It gets a primary fermentation in steel with a Saison yeast, then it's transferred to wooden barrels with the brewery's house strain of wild yeast and left until it's ready. The finished beer is gold in color, cider-like in the aroma, floral and woody, with those green hops leaving behind a complex oiliness, and it finishes with a funky farmhouse cider-like acidity.

Casey Brewing & Blending Casey Family Preserves

Glenwood Springs, Colorado, USA
ABV: 6.0%

Using almost exclusively Colorado ingredients, Casey Brewing ferment and mature all their beers in old oak barrels with a mixed culture of *Saccharomyces*, *Brettanomyces*, and *Lactobacillus*, then leave it for time to have its natural way with the beers. Time is the key extra ingredient here and, once ready, the beers are hand-bottled and left to secondary-ferment and bottle-condition for several more months, creating a standout lightness and brisk bubbles. Everything Casey makes is worth trying, and you can go to their taproom (where they also have clean, non-soured beer) and their barrel house to see the brewery. Casey Family Preserves is an oaked Saison brewed with a large addition of Colorado fruits (blackberries, apricots, cherries—they vary), which gives a jammy, rich fruit flavor that leads to a tart and elegant acidity at the end. The beers are intriguingly excellent and rightly highly sought after.

Burning Sky Saison à la Provision

Firle, England, UK
ABV: 6.5%

Burning Sky's beers come from a deep love and appreciation of Belgian brewing. These beers are not modern adaptations from a craft-beer style guide; they are brewed with reverence and a deep understanding of process, ingredients, taste, and, crucially, time. Saison à la Provision is 6.5% ABV and brewed with barley, wheat, and spelt. It has a primary fermentation with a Saison yeast, then it spends several months maturing in large wooden foudres with a house culture of wild yeast and bacteria, turning lightly tart and becoming very dry. It's elegant, and has a little pepper from the Saison yeast, some funk from the *brett*, and an orchard fruitiness and tartness from the bacteria, while the wood gives structure and tannin.

Molly Rose Brewing Sour Tom

Melbourne, Australia
ABV: 5.5%

Sour Tom is a Saison-ish beer aged in wine barrels with strawberries. The fruit and wine come together to give a creaminess and smoothness to the body, the strawberries are delicate, but you know they're there, and there's a cherry sweetness, which is a little like a crisp rosé wine. It ends with a nice, gentle tartness, making this a beer you could equally gulp by the schooner, or share a big bottle of with a few friends and have with dinner. If you want one of Molly Rose's clean beers, then Kuro is a Black Lager that's brewed with smoked malt and konbu to give a really nice umami depth. They have their brewery and bar in Collingwood (as well as brewing on a vineyard 100 miles/160km north of Melbourne), and sell toasties and great wine alongside their excellent and interesting beers.

Wildflower Brewing and Blending Amber

Sydney, Australia
ABV: 6.0%

Brewing what they call "Australian Wild Ales," Wildflower Brewing and Blending use mostly local ingredients and their own foraged house yeast culture, which was propagated from local plants, making their beer a unique taste of where it's from. The brewery is pretty much a barrel warehouse housed inside a 19th-century barn. They brew their beer in other breweries before fermenting it in the barn, often in oak barrels, until the brewers make judicious blends from the barrel stock and put them into bottles, which are then left for several months to develop a lively carbonation. Amber is created using an extended boil that gives the beer a caramelized depth, rich color, and malt flavor. After a long oak-aging process, the beer emerges a deep amber-red, with a root beer-like flavor profile that mixes with spice, cherries, red grapes, and a vinous dark-chocolate richness. Wildflower Brewing and Blending is a fascinating brewery making wonderful beers.

de Garde Brewing Hose

Tillamook, Oregon, USA
ABV: 5.0%

Hose is a Gose-ish beer that's spontaneously fermented and then matured in oak barrels for a year, along with coriander seed, sea salt, and orange zest and juice; it's also dry-hopped. It has a big fruity aroma, with red grapefruit juice and tart gooseberries; there's a lot of bitter orange, and the floral coriander comes through. It's juicy and has a complex tartness and funk, some lemon and white wine, and a bracing, deep bitterness alongside some spiciness. All de Garde's beers are spontaneously fermented and aged, often with different fruits.

FAST SOURS

Lambics, Spontaneously Fermented beers, Slow Sours, and American Wild Ales all take a long time to develop their complex maturity, but craft beer is often impatient and wanting the next new beer as quickly as possible. This has created a widespread development of sour beers that are brewed fast and drunk even faster. In Fast Sours it'll be bacteria that acidify the beer in a short amount of time (instead of wild yeast in a Slow Sour), giving the beer its tartness and a crisply refreshing flavor. Two old German styles informed the interest in this kind of beer: Berliner Weisse and Gose. They both come from a simple barley and wheat base. They are usually light in alcohol and body (which helps with the acidification) and also light in bitterness, with Gose classically seasoned with salt and coriander seeds. They are typically soured with *Lactobacillus*, a type of bacteria that metabolizes sugars and produces lactic acid—it's the same bacteria in kimchi and yogurt. *Lactobacillus* doesn't tend to add much complexity and it's just a way to get a clean tart depth.

In a Slow Sour beer's production, the *lacto* is usually inoculated into the beer in the mash or the kettle (you'll often see "Kettle Sour" as a description). To do this, brewers produce their wort, then cool it. They then add either a *lacto* culture to it or some malts, which naturally have *Lactobacillus* on them. The wort can be held in the tank for as long as is needed to create the desired acidity, then it's boiled to stop further sourness. It is then made with a regular yeast and conditioned as normal (it can also be soured after the boil if the beer is very low in bitterness). Another way to get acidity into a beer is simply to add lactic acid until the beer is as sour as you want. To some, this is seen as cheating; to others, it's a more convenient and controllable process—traditional Gose is made with lactic acid added in this way, while some heavily fruited and stronger beers (which feature in another chapter) also use this method because it gives greater control over the acidity. Overall, Fast Sours typically produce a clean acidity in a low-alcohol beer without much depth. This means that brewers will typically add other ingredients to Slow Sours, which might be fruit or a dry-hop for aroma.

The idea of a Berliner Weisse and Gose today comes from an ostensible inspiration, but the reality is that the modern Fast Sours have nothing to do with Berlin or Leipzig, in the same way that modern IPA has nothing to do with India. The new brews came from looking back at old recipes and turning them into something that beer-drinkers want today; from taking a flavor profile and some processes which brewers knew worked, in order to create something new.

Siren Calypso

Finchampstead, England, UK
ABV: 4.0%

Calypso is a dry-hopped sour and it's a briskly refreshing light beer with a gentle kind of tartness—it isn't like sucking a lemon, and you get the impression of tasting something that's fresh, juicy, and fruity, like scooping out the middle of a ripe passion fruit. Calypso is the kind of beer that you can crush straight from the can on a hot day, while it's also a good match with spicy foods like Thai curry and salt-and-pepper squid, or tofu. For those who prefer their hoppy beers unsoured, Siren's Soundwave is a very good and reliable IPA, while their Suspended In series showcases rotating hop varieties in a hazy, juicy Pale Ale.

Bayerischer Bahnhof Original Leipziger Gose

Leipzig, Germany
ABV: 4.5%

Today, Gose is a surging craft-beer style, inspired by an odd old German brew. This sour wheat ale was a local idiosyncrasy, which kept going through a sense of tradition, but was certainly not hugely popular as a beer type beyond its locale. When craft beer discovered Gose, it didn't necessarily go straight to the classics, but instead took the *idea* of it and made it into something new that has since been blown up into supersized versions, made way stronger and packed with fruit. If you want to know what that classic beer tastes like, then you need to have a Bayerischer Bahnhof Gose, brewed in the style's second home of Leipzig (it has some earlier history in Goslar, from where it got its name). It's a pale yellow wheat beer that's made tart with lactic acid. The big surprise on tasting this might be the floral and orange aroma from the coriander seeds, plus how the salinity of the salt adds a savory taste (but doesn't taste salty), which is moreish and pleasing. Their brewpub is in an old train station in Leipzig, and it's a good place to go and drink. Their Schwarzbier is also very good and they brew a Berliner Weisse, too.

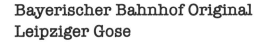

Schneeeule Marlene

Berlin, Germany
ABV: 3.0%

Berliner Weisse almost disappeared from Berlin—or was at best an old curiosity of a beer served with a syrup to sweeten it—and even as craft brewers around the world began to brew beers inspired by the old style, the local brewers were slower to react. But that's changing and more Berlin brewers are making the style that bears their city's name—and many are brewing them like the historic beers. Schneeeule's Marlene, named after Marlene Dietrich, is only 3.0% ABV and is fermented with a yeast strain taken from a 50-year-old bottle of Berliner Weisse. It's a very pale yellow. It's very aromatic and fruity, like lemon and elderberry. There's *Brettanomyces* in there and it's light, the body is also light, and it has a refreshing dryness, with the *brett* and some *Lactobacillus* giving it a ping of funk and acidity. This beer has been brewed to be like the old-style Berliner Weisses, which were once described by Napoleon as the "Champagne of the North." The brewery makes several other Berliner Weisses, including one with jasmine, some with fruits, and Kennedy, an American dry-hopped version.

Wild Wave Yuja Surleim

Busan, South Korea
ABV: 5.3%

South Korea might seem like an unexpected craft beer location, but there's a wonderful breadth and depth of beer there, with a generally high quality of brews. In Busan, Wild Wave established with a focus on making sour beers, though they do brew a few non-soured styles, like Pale Ales and Porters. Surleim is their flagship sour, which is lemony and fresh, while this Yuja variation adds Korean yuzu—I'm a sucker for yuzu and love it in a tart beer like this where it adds a distinctive orange, lime, and grapefruit funkiness. Wild Wave have a cool brewpub in Busan, where you'll find them using lots of local fruits and other ingredients in their ever-changing beer line-up.

Stomping Ground Watermelon Smash

Melbourne, Australia
ABV: 4.2%

The founders of Stomping Ground were responsible for opening Melbourne's Local Taphouse, one of Australia's top beer bars, and for starting GABS, the country's number-one beer festival, so you expect good things heading into the brewery and beer hall. It's housed in a converted warehouse in Collingwood, with the brewery on show, surrounded by iron, brick, steel, and wood, making it an impressive space that's unsurprisingly popular. Their Watermelon Smash is a Gose-style sour that's easy on the acidity and big on the juicy fruitiness, with the crisply refreshing finish reminiscent of biting into an ice-cold slice of melon. Smash is a series of sours, and they also make one with guava and one with passion fruit. If fruity sours aren't quite your thing, they also make great Pale Ales and IPAs.

Brassneck Quenchmeister

Vancouver, Canada
ABV: 4.0%

A Gose with black limes, lemon, and salt, Quenchmeister is an appropriately named beer. It's a hazy, smooth kind of Gose. The combination of lime, lemon, and salt gives a suggestion of a cold margarita, where the acidity is gentle and gives the beer an amazing amount of quench and refreshment. I thought this was a perfect beer in many ways: the balance, the depth of flavor, the way the body was full for 4.0% ABV and held the lime flavor really well. Its perfection was confirmed when I drank it alongside a plate of tacos because I've never had a more excellent beer with tacos (and I've had a lot of beers alongside a lot of tacos). Everything I drank from Brassneck was incredibly impressive—very few breweries can master every style from a pre-Prohibition Lager to a Mild to Sours to IPAs, but everything was exceptional. And while I don't know if they brew this beer often, I'm including it because it was just too good to leave out.

8 Wired Palate Trip

Warkworth, New Zealand
ABV: 6.5%

Palate Trip is brewed like a regular IPA, with some toasty malts for backbone and sweetness, and just a light bitter addition of hops, then it's soured to give the beer a cut of acidity instead of the bite of bitterness. It's an intense and juicy beer that's big on hop aroma, assertively sour, and definitely a trip for the palate, with all the hops coming to taste like the ripest tropical fruit on the tree. 8 Wired also brew Hippy Berliner, a 4.0%-ABV, dry-hopped Sour Pale Ale, which is light and juicy, plus a Cucumber Hippy, which adds fresh cucumber.

Cervejaria Dogma Sourmind

São Paulo, Brazil
ABV: 4.4%

Just looking at the can art gives you an idea of what to expect with this Brazilian Berliner-style sour with added mango and guava juice. It's a hazy orange, almost the color of mango flesh. You get fruit in the aroma right away, as you'd expect, and it's a surprisingly gentle and invitingly fresh aroma, one that is enhanced by a light dry-hop to amplify the fruitiness. They brew this one with some rye and that adds some peppery fruitiness of its own, as well as enriching the body a touch, which helps to push forward the fruitiness. I like that the fruit never overpowers the beer and you still get that tart, light, refreshing base beer coming through, with that tongue-sticking-out acidity right at the end.

Bellwoods Brewery Jelly King

Toronto, Canada
ABV: 5.6%

Bellwoods are one of Toronto's top beer attractions and a brewery that's evolved and grown since they first opened in 2012. They now have a brewpub as well as a larger brewery with their wild and barrel-aged program. You can—and should—visit both. Jelly King is the brewery's excellent sour, which is dry-hopped with Citra, Amarillo, and Cascade. It's really juicy, like sweetly tart tropical fruits and stone fruit, and it's fun and fresh and refreshing, with a great light texture. They also make a few variants with fruit added to them. They brew some wood-aged sours, too, including the unusual Donkey Venom, a strong, dark sour ale which tastes like those soft strawberry candies covered in dark chocolate and cacao—very intriguing and cleverly balanced.

FRUIT SOURS

I'm not sure where this kind of super-fruit smoothie came from, or where it might go, or whether this will even be a thing in another few years, but, as I write this, heavily-fruited Sours are an increasingly popular beer type all around the world, with brewers seemingly challenging themselves to pack as much fruit and other flavorings into a beer as possible. I think that part of the appeal is how they look to the Instagram generation, with the beer coming in an illuminated palette of bright colors, and they also have a palate of even brighter flavors.

One of the main proponents of this kind of fruit-forward brew is the Florida Weisse, a light sour wheat beer that became Florida's local style and uses fresh seasonal fruit. Some of these are light in body and freshly fruity, while some go to the smoothie extreme. Brazil has also seen its own Fruited Sour emerge with the Catharina Sour and a beer that uses local fruits in a subtle way. These beers are fast-soured, and most are made to be as fruity as possible, so I suspect the tartness comes from lactic acid and the fruit, rather than kettle-souring. We're also seeing Imperial-strength versions of these beers and, increasingly, there are heavily fruited beers containing lactose (milk sugar) and vanilla to make them even sweeter and more full-bodied.

Cerveja Blumenau Catharina Sour Son of a Peach

Blumenau, Brazil
ABV: 4.1%

Brazilian craft brewers have created a new kind of beer style that has been recognized by the Beer Judge Certification Program (BJCP) as deserving of its own category. The Catharina Sour is a Berliner Weisse-style beer, only brewed a little stronger, and it includes fresh fruit like guava, peach, and mango. That fruit dominates the flavors, although it doesn't go as far as some of the Florida Weisses or the modern trend for smoothie-style sours, and it's named after the region of Catharina in Brazil, from which the style emerged. Blumenau's Catharina Sour is one of the originators of this style and Son of a Peach is hazy yellow, lightly tart, and abundantly peachy and fruity, making it a fun and refreshing beer.

The Answer Triple 3 Scoops

Richmond, Virginia, USA
ABV: 9.0%

3 Scoops is The Answer's much-loved, 3.5%-ABV, triple-fruited sour, which is flavored with passion fruit, lemonade, and mango (no, I don't know what "lemonade" flavor is). It's basically a breakfast drink. The Answer also make Imperial 3 Scoops, which is extra-juiced, has peach instead of lemonade, and is plumped up to 7.5% ABV. That's still pretty much a breakfast drink. Triple 3 Scoops, however, is a serious beer while simultaneously being the least serious beer you might ever drink. It's 9.0% ABV and tastes like a smoothie with a slug of vodka in it. They also make heavily fruited beers with names like Triple Toothsicle, Triple Puffsicle, and Triple Swirlsicle, and in their brewpub they serve some beers as slushies. People go crazy for this stuff. I'm not necessarily one of those people, but I think these kinds of brews are part of the zeitgeist of beer right now.

North Brewing Co. Triple Fruited Gose

Leeds, England, UK
ABV: 4.5%

North Brewing Co.'s Triple Fruited Gose is a beer that is always available, but always with a different combo of fruits. These beers pour thick and smooth; they are almost chewy with the fruit and the fruit's natural sugars; they are lightly tart at the end and it's the kind of fruity, creamy tartness you get in a bowl of fresh berries, under-ripe tropical fruit, and natural yogurt. This flavor and fullness are indicative of a contemporary taste in non-beery beers, but it's easy to see why they're popular when you taste them and get all that juicy, tangy fruit. North Brewing Co. was set up by the team who started one of the early British craft beer bars, North Bar. You can drink there, in the brewery, or they have a taproom, all in the center of Leeds.

J Wakefield Miami Madness

Miami, Florida, USA
ABV: 7.0%

Miami Madness is a Florida Weisse, a sunshine-state style that's emerged as a result of the brewers adding abundant tropical fruits to their stronger-than-usual sour beers. They tend to be full-bodied, literally juicy, and tart but not puckering. Miami Madness is a beer that tastes like you've sucked the seeds and flesh out of a passion fruit, while drinking a boozy guava and mango shake. It's super-juicy with the combination of a lush body, sweetness, fruit, and the tartness at the end, which matches what you'd naturally find in the fruit. The brewery has created controlled scarcity by making this beer an annual release at the end of September, meaning hype and anticipation grow as the beer's fruit plumps up and ripens. Alongside Miami Madness they usually release DFPF, a sour made with dragon fruit and passion fruit, plus Cuvee de Wakefield, which is a combination of Miami Madness and DFPF.

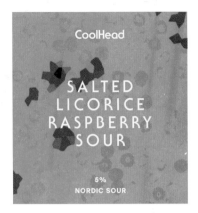

CoolHead Salted Licorice Raspberry Sour

Tuusula, Finland
ABV: 5.0%

CoolHead started in 2016 with the deliberate intention of making sour beers that clash together exotic flavors with Nordic ones. That might sound weird, and many of their beers are quite unusual, but they have successfully been able to combine some crazy flavors in unique ways, and this Nordic Sour is a great example. It's got local raspberries which give the beer its red color and a tangy, sweet, raspberry-pip bite, while salted licorice, which is a flavor loved by many Scandinavians, gives the beer a sweet, umami, aniseed depth that is unexpected but somehow works really well with the raspberries, softening their tartness and making it reminiscent of a candy.

Garage Beer Co. Whale Mist

Barcelona, Spain
ABV: 8.5%

Garage are the best known of Spain's emerging craft beer scene. They started out with a brewpub in the center of Barcelona in 2015 and expanded into a larger facility two years later. Both now run side by side and the central brewpub is open every day (the main brewery is open for events only). They frequently collaborate with other brewers and have an ever-changing line-up of beers, mainly either hazy and hoppy or sour and fruited. Whale Mist is a strong Fruit Sour made with blueberry, blackberry, and blackcurrant, plus some lactose. It's thick, both tart and fruitily sweet, with a creamy-smooth texture that's very juicy. Their Soup IPA is a really good IPA made with Citra and Mosaic. Make sure to go and visit Garage Beer Co. if you're in Barcelona.

Great Notion Brewing Blueberry Muffin

Portland, Oregon, USA
ABV: 6.0%

"Culinary-inspired" is how Great Notion describe their Sours and Stouts. By "culinary" they aren't thinking fine dining here; they're thinking ice cream parlors and breakfast buffets. It's pancakes and maple syrup, peanut butter and chocolate, coffee and smores, and fudge sundaes. Their Blueberry Muffin contains actual blueberry muffins as well as fresh blueberries. It pours a light purple-orange color, but you'll soon forget that once you smell the beer because it's exactly like a blueberry muffin. It's a sweet beer upfront that carries the doughy, bready, muffin-like flavor, some sugar and vanilla, and then the blueberries come in with their fruitiness and a bracing tartness at the end—it really is unnervingly like you're eating a muffin while drinking sour fruit juice. Great Notion sometimes make a version that contains cinnamon and lactose, and they call it Cobbler. They are fun beers.

FRUIT AND SPICE BEER

Here we've got beers that use an unlimited shopping list of different ingredients in a full variety of beer styles. Brewers can add anything and everything to their beers, from an entire basket of fruits to items from the spice rack. They can brew beers that replicate desserts or snacks, or they can make beers which are a little more subtle and try to tell a story of local ingredients, tastes, or processes. There are no rules here.

Pasteur Street Brewing Passionfruit Wheat Ale

Ho Chi Minh City, Vietnam
ABV: 4.0%

I've never tried to write a list of my ten favorite beers. It might be a pointless endeavor because the list would be constantly changing, but one thing I can guarantee is that Pasteur Street's Passionfruit Wheat Ale would be on that list. Just thinking about it while sitting in the library on a gray London afternoon makes me feel an exotic breeze and a deep, deep thirst. What makes Pasteur Street interesting to me is how they utilize local ingredients in almost all their beers: jasmine or pomelo in IPAs, coffee in their Porter, pepper and spices in Saisons. The Passionfruit Wheat is light blonde, hazy, a tiny bit tart, deliciously fruity, and just about the most refreshing thing you can drink in the whole of Southeast Asia. Vietnam is a country that doesn't have access to local barley or hops, but they do have endless baskets of exotic local ingredients to use in their brews, which gives them a distinctly Vietnamese accent. The only thing that hasn't worked in a Pasteur Street beer? Durian.

Garage Project DFA

Wellington, New Zealand
ABV: 7.5%

Imagine an IPA that's bursting with Citra, Centennial, and Amarillo hops, being all orangey and tropical. Then pulp some mango into it, squeeze in some lime, chop up some chilis, and tear in some aniseed-y Vietnamese mint, and that's what you get in DFA, or *Demus Favorem Amori* ("We Stand for Love"). It's an amber-colored IPA with a chewy malt middle that holds on to the hops and adds some sweetness to enhance the fruits and temper the chili. It's a complex beer, one that sways between bitter hops, juicy hops, exotic fruit, and the fragrance of the mint and chili. Garage Project's taproom is a must-visit spot in Wellington, and you'll find a varied and exciting range of beers, many using unusual ingredients—one to look out for is Cereal Milk Stout made with cornflakes, oats, dark wheat, and lactose (milk sugar).

Neon Raptor Total Eclipse

Nottingham, England, UK
ABV: 7.4%

Most of Neon Raptor's beers have dinosaurs on the can. Of course a fluoro-colored can with a dinosaur on is going to sell well. We're all Gen-X adults who grew up with *Jurassic Park* and can't fail to be roused when the theme tune starts up. Combine that with a pop-culture reference to a popular teatime treat (which might be lost on non-Brits), and this is a beer that sells out quickly. To explain: in Britain, say the words "Total Eclipse" and people will often think of Jaffa Cakes, a small, sponge-based cookie with a ring of orange gel topped with chocolate. There was a long-running commercial that showed a teacher explaining the phases of the moon by eating Jaffa Cakes, and the "full moon, half moon, total eclipse" phrase has stuck in the nation's collective slogan memory. The beer is a slick, lush Stout made with cacao and mandarin orange. The chocolate is rich with a sweet fullness, then around the edges and at the end comes just a hint of orange. Good with Jaffa Cakes and *Jurassic Park*.

Mussel Inn Captain Cooker Manuka Beer

Onekaka, New Zealand
ABV: 5.0%

Mussel Inn, in the middle of nowhere, somewhere in the north of New Zealand's South Island, is the sort of place that should have heritage status. Jane and Andrew Dixon built this bar and brewery by hand in 1992 (having previously built their house, which is behind the bar). It's a single-room pub with a large garden wrapping around it, and also has a hopyard and orchard. They grow their own produce for the kitchen and brewery. The kitchen produces simple fare—quiche, pie, salads, mussels, and fresh fish. They have live music on most nights. The brewery makes a small range of beers—including a Pale Ale, an English IPA, a Pale Lager, and a Dark Ale—but it's the Captain Cooker that's their hero beer. It's a hard beer to classify, being a bit like an English Bitter or Red Ale, with a berry-like sweetness in the middle, a herbal, piney flavor from the addition of manuka tips, and a gentle carbonation like a cask ale. It's a beer of its place, and this is the only place you should want to drink it. The Mussel Inn is in my top ten of must-visit places.

Furbrew Bia Pho

Hanoi, Vietnam
ABV: 4.4%

One day, Danish man Thomas Bilgram decided to quit his job, pack up a limited amount of stuff, put it in a container, and ship it to Hanoi, in Vietnam, to start a new life as a craft beer brewer in a country that didn't have any craft beer. Inspired by fellow Danish brewery Mikkeller, the aim for Furbrew was to be known for making a large variety of different styles, from the straight-up Chinook IPA to those using local inspirations, like Lime Leaf Wheat, which is brewed with the zingy, zesty herb in a light ale that gives Hanoians an evocative taste reminiscent of a popular and nostalgia-inspiring chicken dish. Bia Pho is brewed with the six essential aromatic ingredients in Vietnam's famous noodle soup—cardamom, cinnamon, star anise, coriander seed, ginger, and chili—and every drinker picks out the aromatics differently (I mostly got the star anise). The beer is quite sweet, like Hanoian pho, and it has an umami depth. It's a curious and interesting beer, which you can drink in the brewery's taprooms.

Funky Buddha Last Snow

Oakland Park, Florida, USA
ABV: 6.4%

In America they have Mounds bars, while in other places around the world there are Bounty bars. They are similar: a soft, shredded-coconut filling covered in chocolate. Last Snow, a Porter brewed with coconut and coffee, is the beer version of those bars. It's dark brown with a tan foam, but you'll barely notice that because you'll be too busy smelling all the delicious coconutty aromas (you have to really like coconut to like this beer, by the way). That toasty coconut flavor combines with sweet coffee, caramel, and vanilla all the way through the brew. Funky Buddha are known for their flavored Floridian beers, such as a pineapple Blonde, a Brown Ale with apple-pie flavors, a key-lime-pie Sour, and a range of barrel-aged beers inspired by cocktails. I'm the guy who picks the Bounty out of the Christmas chocolate selection box, so Last Snow is my kind of beer.

Jing-A Koji Red Ale

Beijing, China
ABV: 5.5%

This Beijing-brewed beer is made with red koji rice, which is more typically used in sake or in *huangjiu*, a Chinese rice wine (Shaoxing wine is the most famous of these). That rice turns the brew a pinkish red and gives a subtle nutty, woody, whiskey-like flavor. To go with the rice, this beer also contains wasabi root and ginger, which give an earthy, spicy warmth. Jing-A are a superb Beijing brewery who are known for great local beers and for making many collaboration brews around the world. If you're in Beijing, then you'll be aware of the smog—if it's particularly bad, head to Jing-A's taproom because their excellent Airpocalypse Double IPA gets cheaper as the Air Quality Index gets higher, encouraging you to stay inside and drink.

Taihu Brewing Bright Ale

Taipei, Taiwan
ABV: 4.5%

One of Taiwan's top craft breweries, Taihu make a full range of beer styles to a high standard, adding a local flavor to many, and serving them all in different taprooms and bars, including one in a retro-fitted Airstream. Their best-seller is a very good IPA, which is the bitter, resinous, sticky malt-and-hop IPA instead of the juicy-fruits kind of IPA. They have a popular Kölsch brewed with local calamansi, a kind of kumquat, and Bright Ale, which is made with local roasted barley tea. This tea is nutty and sweetly malty, and in the beer that adds to the profile of the golden malts, giving more depth and a fuller flavor, while a light hopping lifts it all.

Cigar City Good Gourd

Tampa, Florida, USA
ABV: 8.8%

I couldn't omit pumpkin ales, no matter how much I wanted to. It's a fall seasonal for many American breweries, timed to go with Halloween and Thanksgiving. Some use loads of pumpkin in the brews, others use pumpkin-pie spices, some use both. Some are subtle, others are not. Good Gourd is not one of the subtle ones. It's an 8.8% ABV dark amber beer that's sweet, rich, and spicy. It's brewed with cinnamon, allspice, cloves, nutmeg, and vanilla to emulate a pie, and it does that almost too well, meaning you should really like pumpkin pie before opening a bottle of this. It has a creaminess from the pumpkin, which is spiked with the clove and warmed by the nutmeg, all while a piecrust malt flavor hangs in the background. They've also previously made a 13.8%-ABV Good Gourd Almighty, an intense beer aged in bourbon barrels.

Black Hops Brewery Eggnog Stout

Burleigh Heads, Australia
ABV: 5.8%

This story starts with three mates sitting in the pub talking about beer. That led to them homebrewing an eggnog-inspired Stout (for some strange reason) and in the following weeks, while waiting for the beer to mature, they came up with the whole idea for what would, eventually, become Black Hops. They borrowed a brewery at the end of 2014 to make a commercial batch of Eggnog Stout and friends drank the first keg in just over two hours. They knew they were

onto a winner, and by 2016 they'd built their own brewery and made the Eggnog Stout commercially. It's a classic Dry Stout which is infused with cinnamon, nutmeg, and vanilla, and it's pleasingly subtle and balanced with all those aromatics adding a spicy warmth. The story that started with three mates in the pub continues with the same mates now drinking in their own taprooms. It's a great success, all built on great beer.

Cebu Brewing Co. Mangga-J

Cebu, Philippines
ABV: 5.1%

What's the food that brings you most pleasure? For me, it's perfectly ripe fruit, whether that's a crisp apple, a juicy fresh cherry, or just a really great banana out of the fruit bowl. I've never had better fruit than when I've traveled through Southeast Asia: mangosteens, rambutans, longan, fat and squat bananas, passion fruit, but it's always the mangoes I love the most. Tangy and sweet, soft yet with just enough bite, buttery, creamy, heady, honeyed, and exotic. Cebu Brewing was one of the Philippines's first craft breweries and they add local ingredients to all their main beers, like coconut sugar in PIPA, their Philippine Pale Ale, or Cebu mangoes in Mangga-J, a particularly juicy mango from the island which infuses a tropical sweetness into the beer.

Vault City Marshmallow Smoothie Sour

Edinburgh, Scotland, UK
ABV: 11.5%

This is a crazy beer. It's so voluptuous, so sweet and fruity, and joyful to drink. There's vanilla and a thick body which makes it smoothie-like, there's something softly sweet and pillowy like marshmallow, and then just enough tartness to cut through it at the end. It's not like any beer you'll have had before, being somewhere between a fruit wine and a cocktail. It's remarkable, as are most of Vault City's beers. They focus on fruit-forward and flavored soured beers, the sorts of sours that are refreshing, tart, and opulent with fruitiness. They make dry-hopped tart Session IPAs, sours inspired by desserts—including some with vanilla and lactose which are creamy and delicious—and sours that showcase fresh local fruit. These beers are really good, and really good fun.

LOW-NO ALCOHOL AND LO-CAL BEER

I always want to drink beer, but the trouble is that I can't always be chugging cans of DIPA—I value a little life balance and a few days off the booze every week. Those dry days don't stop me craving a cold one, though. Thankfully, there's now a delicious range of alcohol-free and low-alcohol beers available, beers that taste like beer and have all the characteristics we want from a beer, just without the alcohol.

Non-alcoholic beer can range from 0.0–0.5% ABV, but that 0.5% ABV is so small that your body can metabolize it without effect—you get the same level of alcohol in kombucha, a glass of orange juice, or even an over-ripe banana. In this category I've also included Radler, a low-alcohol mix of beer and fruit soda that has become a popular beer type in recent years, as well as beers aimed at the active beer-drinker. As I'm writing this, the latest trend in North America is Hard Seltzer, which is essentially flavored fizzy water with an ABV of around 5.0%. This is a trend specific to a certain kind of American drinker who values calorie content over flavor. Note: vegans might need to check the labels on alcohol-free beers as they often contain lactose, or milk sugar, which gives the beer a fuller texture.

Lucky Saint Unfiltered Lager

Germany or England, UK
ABV: 0.5%

Lucky Saint is brewed in Germany and sold in Britain. It's hazy amber and has a malty middle that's reminiscent of chewing grains, which gives a full body before it dries right out and ends really refreshing with a light citrusy quench. This is my go-to alcohol-free beer—and I've drunk almost all of the boozeless beers out there. I like how beers such as Lucky Saint have put beer back on the lunch table or given us something really good to drink when we choose not to have alcohol. Personally, I drink it while cooking dinner, or I'll have one soon after finishing a long run, and it's a beer that is always in my refrigerator.

Browar Pinta Mini Maxi IPA

Żywiec, Poland
ABV: 0.5%

A mini beer with maximum flavor, Browar Pinta's Mini Maxi IPA is hopped with Citra and Mosaic. It pours an almost bright golden yellow and those hops immediately burst out of the glass as tangy citrus and pine. It's very hoppy, which leads to a strong, tea-like bitterness. The body is light, as you'd expect, and that makes this a little like a hop soda—no bad thing. They also brew Mini Maxi Mango, which is made with puréed mango and passion fruit, giving a beer that's fruity, light, and refreshing, and a great alternative to alcohol. Pinta are better known for their high-alcohol, high-impact beers, like their barrel-aged Imperial Stouts and punchy IPAs, but it's nice to get a little balance sometimes, especially when it still brings a whole load of flavor.

Stiegl Radler Grapefruit

Salzburg, Austria
ABV: 2.0%

You know how drinking some beers has the ability to immediately make you smile? That's what Stiegl's Radler does to me. It mixes Stiegl's Goldbräu lager in a 40 to 60 ratio with an organic homemade grapefruit, orange, and lemon soda. It pours a pale, hazy yellow (if you choose to

pour it, that is—I usually just drink it from the can) and immediately just zings with fresh, sweet grapefruit. It drinks like grapefruit soda, too, but it's not sweet and the lager gives it some refreshing balance. If you want to try a slightly harder version, then add a little Campari to your glass or can—I love that flavor combination. Stiegl is a 400-year-old independent brewery and if you're in Salzburg, then you should go to the brewery, or Stiegl Keller, to drink their lagers. If you're lucky, you might also see their rare, vintage, barrel-aged beers, which are extraordinary.

Two Roots New West

San Diego, California, USA
ABV: 0.5%

A new category of beer has become available to drinkers based in American states where marijuana has been legalized. These beers are alcohol-free, but contain tetrahydrocannabinol, or THC, the principal psychoactive chemical in cannabis (you might also see beers with CBD, or cannabidiol, a non-psychoactive part of the cannabis plant). Different beers contain different levels of THC, often 5mg and 10mg doses, and the aim is to give a similar experience and buzz to drinking beer, but without the drunkenness or the hangover. New West is Two Roots's San Diego-styled IPA, which is citrusy, but not overpowering, and has a nice bitterness at the end. They also make a Lager, Blonde, and Dark Beer, plus seasonals, all with THC, and they brew a full range of alcohol-free "near beer" without the THC.

Big Drop Brewing Co. Stout

Ipswich, England, UK
ABV: 0.5%

Big Drop started in 2016 with an exclusive focus on making beers of 0.5% ABV. They brew a wide range of styles, including a Pale Ale, IPA, Sour, and Lager, plus this Stout. For a beer without alcohol, it is decadent and has a chocolate depth that's enhanced by the use of lactose (milk sugar) and cocoa nibs, which also bring hints of vanilla and coffee. The Big Drop beers are also available on draft, which is a significant and important development in the alcohol-free category, meaning I can sit with mates and still drink a pint; it's just not a pint of alcoholic beer.

Rothaus Weizen Zäpfle

Grafenhausen, Germany
ABV: 0.5%

The best culture for alcohol-free beer is in Germany, and everywhere you drink they'll have at least one on offer—even in bars that only serve three or four beers, one will be without alcohol, and that's because going to the pub to socialize is such an important part of German culture: people want to meet with friends and enjoy a beer, and it doesn't matter if that beer has alcohol in it or not, because it's the experience that counts. You often see Pale Lagers and Weissbiers that are alcohol-free. Rothaus make both, and both are exemplary. The Pale Lager is only a little sweet and has a great bitterness, while the Weissbier has a really smooth and pleasingly malty texture, and a nice refreshing finish.

BrewDog Punk AF

Ellon, Scotland
ABV: 0.5%

It's no exaggeration to say that I wouldn't be writing this book now if it wasn't for BrewDog. Back in 2008 I liked beer, but I'd drunk almost everything in the grocery store and was wondering if there was more to beer than just bottled real ales. Then I had a Punk IPA (the original version) and a beer called Chaos Theory. Both were intense with hop aroma and bitterness, and made me want to know and drink more. BrewDog have since become a global beer phenomenon. They have over 100 bars around the world. They have numerous breweries and brewpubs. They're sold on every main street and in every grocery store in the UK, and they are easily the most accessible craft beer available. The BrewDog beer that I drink most nowadays is Punk AF, their alcohol-free beer, and I think it's superb. Great citrus aroma, a cut of bitterness, and all the IPA flavor, but no booze (just a warning for vegans: it contains some lactose/milk sugar).

GLUTEN-FREE AND ALTERNATIVE GRAINS

Barley might be the main brewing grain, but there are increasing numbers of drinkers who either can't consume gluten or choose not to, which has led to a large category of gluten-free beers. There are two ways to make a beer gluten-free: use grains that don't contain gluten, which means replacing the barley and wheat with other cereals and alternative starch sources like oats, sorghum, millet, corn, rice, buckwheat, sugar, and more; or brew with grains that contain low amounts of gluten and then use a processing aid that can remove almost all the gluten, reducing it to below 20ppm—in Europe these can be called "gluten-free," while in the US, Australia, and New Zealand they are "gluten-removed" or "gluten-reduced." Those who are celiac should use their own judgment when ordering a gluten-removed beer.

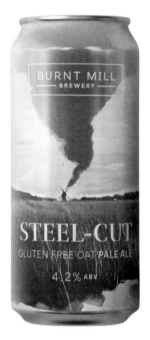

Burnt Mill Brewery Steel-Cut

Badley, England, UK
ABV: 4.2%

Burnt Mill's brewer, Sophie de Ronde, is gluten intolerant (something she ironically discovered while working for a malt company), and so has created her own gluten-free Pale Ale to go alongside the hoppy brews for which Burnt Mill have gained a strong reputation. Steel-Cut is brewed with 80 percent oats, plus buckwheat, maize, and sorghum. The oats give a lot of texture and body, while the other grains lighten it and add some nutty complexity. But this isn't a beer in which you taste the grain base, because it's heavily hopped with modern varieties, which change with each brew, to give a lot of citrus, melon, and tropical fruits. This isn't one of those "it's good for a gluten-free beer" kind of beers; this is good beer, which is made more impressive by being barley-free.

Glutenberg Gose

Montreal, Canada
ABV: 3.5%

Glutenberg has a fully gluten-free brewery and they make the full range of craft beers, from a Witbier to an IPA to a Stout, and even an alcohol-free beer without gluten. Their Gose uses millet, buckwheat, and quinoa as the fermentable grains (as do most of their beers), while they also use corn, rice, and sugar as starch sources. It's a classic-tasting Gose that's light and refreshingly tart. It uses Mandarina Bavaria hops, which add their own orangey fruitiness to the lime, lemon, and grapefruit used in the brew. Gose's usual pinch of salt fills the body with some satiating salinity to balance the gentle acidity. Their Stout uses coffee and cocoa nibs, and that gives a great roasty depth to the beer.

Ground Breaker Dark Ale

Portland, Oregon, USA
ABV: 5.5%

Portland's Ground Breaker is a 100-percent gluten-free brewery and gastropub. Their base brewing ingredients include sorghum syrup, organic lentils, tapioca, cane sugar, Belgian candi sugar, and Oregon-grown chestnuts, which the brewery roasts as if they were malt. They also source their hops from the nearby Willamette Valley. They make a wide variety of beers, unrestricted by style, and core-range brews include a Pale Ale, IPAs, a fruit beer with raspberry and rose hips, plus this Dark Ale. It's in this beer that you get the best taste of the roasted chestnuts, which give chocolatey, nutty flavors to a beer that's quite light of body and reminiscent of an English Mild. The food they serve is local, seasonal, and typical of a gastropub: burgers, tacos, sandwiches, and snacks, just with no gluten.

CR/AK New Zealand IPA

Campodarsego, Italy
ABV: 7.0%

New Zealand IPA is a gluten-removed beer, meaning they make this just like a regular IPA, one that's super-hoppy with lots of tropical fruit, gooseberries, mango, and grapes, then add an enzyme that is able to pull all the gluten out of the beer, but with zero detriment to the beer itself. The base of this IPA remains light for its strength, and it's made as a brighter and more bitter kind of IPA. Crak are based 25 miles (40km) west of Venice. They have a cool bar and beer garden with 24 taps, and they serve Roman-ish slabs of baked bread dough (not so good for celiacs, unfortunately) with various toppings—they are a great beer snack. The rest of their beers contain gluten and you'll find a good session IPA called Mundaka, plus lots of interesting experimental brews.

THE BEER BUCKET LIST

In my book *The Beer Bucket List*, I gathered together some of the world's essential beer experiences, including the most important old breweries and the industry-changing new brewers, the greatest world beer bars and pubs, and the must-visit cities to go drinking. Here's some inspiration for your own Beer Bucket List.

Drink in the Pilsner Urquell brewery cellars

The birthplace of golden lager, this is a must-visit beer destination. Go on the brewery tour and you'll get to see both the large modern brewery and the historic old one, including an original copper pan used in 1842. The best part of the tour takes you deep underground into the old brewery cellars (which used to be cut for 6 miles/9km beneath the city) where they still mature lager in large wooden barrels—and you'll get to taste it. It's astonishing.

Drink all the Belgian Trappist beers

You could go and visit all the Belgian Trappist monasteries, if you like, but I actually prefer the experience of sitting in small beer cafés in cities like Bruges, Brussels, Antwerp, and Ghent, and ordering bottles. Work your way through all the Trappist beers and you'll get a great understanding of Dubbels, Tripels, and Quadrupels, plus some of the variety within those styles, as you get beers from Chimay, Orval, Rochefort, Westmalle, and Westvleteren. Can't find the rare Westvleteren? Then go to their brewery café to drink it.

Go to Cantillon and drink Belgian Lambic

One of the most remarkable breweries in the world, Cantillon is a working museum of Belgian beer tradition. Go on the self-guided tour through the inner-city farmhouse and you won't believe that they still make beer there. You'll go up, down, and all around the old wooden building before passing hundreds of barrels of slowly maturing beer—it's one of the best-smelling buildings in all of the beer world. Back in the bar you can drink Cantillon's Lambic and Gueuze, plus you can buy big bottles to share.

Go to Oktoberfest, the Hofbräuhaus, and Augustiner-Keller

Oktoberfest is unbelievably big, it's loud, it's busy, it's brilliant fun, and you've got to do it at least once. Walk around the huge tents, find one you like, and order a liter of Oktoberfestbier, a strong golden lager. Sit back and enjoy the live music and the happy madness inside the tent. While you're in Munich, go to the Hofbräuhaus, a huge old beer hall with a lot of history. Drink a liter of Dunkel. And then (or before—choose your own adventure), go to Augustiner-Keller, a 5,000-seat beer garden where they serve Augustiner Hell from big wooden barrels. Think you know what a Bavarian beer garden is like? You don't until you've been there.

Left to right: The exterior of the Pilsner Urquell brewery; Westvleteren Trappist beer from Belgium; the Oktoberfest parade in Munich.